Oceans of Time

The Musical Autobiography of Billy Hart

As Told to Ethan Iverson

Cymbal Press

Oceans of Time: The Musical Autobiography of Billy Hart
© 2025 Billy Hart. All rights reserved.

Published by Cymbal Press, Torrance, CA USA
cymbalpress.com

This and other Cymbal Press books may be purchased at cymbalpress.com. Volume and education discounts are available.

ISBN
Paperback: 978-1-955604-24-6
Hardcover: 978-1-955604-25-3

BIO004000	BIOGRAPHY & AUTOBIOGRAPHY / Music
MUS050000	MUSIC / Individual Composer & Musician
MUS025000	MUSIC / Genres & Styles / Jazz

All marks are the property of their respective owners.
Photos are from the private collection of Billy Hart unless otherwise noted.

Publisher: Gary S. Stager
Editor: Sylvia Martinez
Cover design: Gillian MacLeod
Cover photo: John Abbott

While every precaution has been taken, the publisher and author assume no responsibility for errors, omissions, changed information or URLs, or for damages resulting from the use of the information herein.

Praise for Oceans of Time

A wonderful book. Reading it, you're sitting there listening to Billy Hart talk effortlessly and incisively about music and the remarkable people who make it. And you don't want him to stop.
  —Lawrence Block, author of *When The Sacred Ginmill Closes*

Billy Hart has been an inspiration, mentor and friend for almost 30 years. I previously heard many of the anecdotes in this memoir but was amazed at the thoroughness and the spirit captured in these pages. This addition to America's music history is a must have for drummers, music enthusiasts and the casual fan's library.
  —Jason Brown, drummer

I love this.
What a story. What a storyteller.
Billy Hart has brought so much light into the world.
Anyone reading this book will see his beautiful spirit and magic.
His sense of humor, humility, generosity, curiosity, honesty. The history.
There is a treasure trove here.
I'm so thankful for this.
  —Bill Frisell, guitarist

Billy Hart reigns over the drums with the arch profundity of an artist who misses nothing and has more stored up than he ever needs to show. His playing indicates wisdom—a wisdom that stirs every page of this extraordinary book. From his first sentence, collating swing and religion, *Oceans of Time* is a non-stop gift. As edited by Ethan Iverson, it is a genuine "as told to" rather than a ghosted story. Billy's companionable, no-bull narrative will gladden the heart of every jazz lover.
  —Gary Giddins, author of *Visions of Jazz*

Ethan Iverson brings his ever-curious musical intelligence to document the amazing life and legacy of Billy Hart, one of the true living legends in jazz. Fast-paced and insightful, Billy's vast musical universe shines brightly. Immensely readable and a must-have for any jazz fan.
  —Fred Hersch, pianist

There are far too few autobiographies/biographies of our jazz greats, both ancestral and living. And now along comes Ethan Iverson's as-told-to treatment of the great Billy Hart's modern jazz drumming odyssey. This exceptional volume quite cannily explores more than a few great drum techniques, but also goes deep into the dynamics of that most essential vehicle of jazz expression…the *band*. Hart provides fascinating commentary on great bands for which he has played an integral role: from the subtleties of the Shirley Horn Trio, to Wes Montgomery, to Jimmy Smith's B-3 band, his contributions to Herbie Hancock's explosive 1970s Mwandishi unit, McCoy Tyner, Pharoah Sanders, and Miles Davis *On The Corner* session, Billy Hart proves to be an enormously insightful tour guide. What is intended as a purely "musical autobiography" certainly delivers on that tip, and although some may label this a "musician-to-musician" exploration, there is much to be learned & derived here for the general jazz and modern music enthusiast as Hart compels readers to seek out the recorded evidence of his mastery and the bands he indelibly enhanced.

—Willard Jenkins, co-author of *African Rhythms: The Autobiography of Randy Weston*

Jabali Billy Hart has such a great story to tell, and he tells it generously, looking back on a path of making music, of building and balancing a career, of being a spiritually rooted African American representing a proud legacy. The details of his life are remembered in detail and sharp definition. The music worlds of the '50s, '60s and '70s come alive. He examines his motives as deeply as his musical progress. He weaves his own, straight-forward voice and invites in those of others—like Shirley Horn, desiring more assertive support, telling Hart "Don't tickle me…" Like his first wife guiding him, for musical reasons, to tour with Jimmy Smith, rather than James Brown. Like Herbie Hancock's manager stepping on his toes, calling him "a real rock and roll drummer." Like Miles Davis putting his nose to Hart's, saying: "The next time I need a drummer I'm going to call you." Hart himself declaring, "As far as I'm concerned, clavé is another name for God." His book is deep, resonant, and historically rich, filled with life lessons that have not stopped being relevant.

—Ashley Kahn, author of *A Love Supreme: The Story of John Coltrane's Signature Album*

Billy Hart, one of the most versatile and maybe *the* most prolific of all jazz drummers, has penned a memoir that's flush with as much passion, joy, erudition, and intensity as his music. He paints colorful portraits of the many men and women who shaped his style and paved his career—a cast that includes most of the great figures in post-1960 jazz, some famous, some lamentably unsung—and also makes a compelling case for the drums as the soul of music and music as the heartbeat of life.
  —Fred Kaplan, author of *1959: The Year Everything Changed*

Billy Hart's *Oceans of Time* (as told to Ethan Iverson) is a rich testament to his perpetual artistic innovation. As a contemporary African Griot, Hart disseminates the inner recesses of the culture, history, and practice of America's classical music in a revelatory way. This book is not just a must-have but a wellspring of inspiration and motivation for any practitioner, educator, or passionate advocate of the art form.
  —James Newton, composer and flutist

Oceans of Time: The Musical Autobiography of Billy Hart is an instant classic of the genre. Co-author Ethan Iverson captures the voice of the still-going-strong octogenarian NEA Jazz Master, who describes his experiences with a who's-who of jazz expression during his 65-year career with the same multi-dimensional perspective that marks his drumming, simultaneously factoring historical context, psychological perspicacity, impeccable craft, and transparent emotion into the flow.
  —Ted Panken, co-author of *Life in E Flat: The Autobiography of Phil Woods*

Billy Hart is rightly well-loved not only as a musician but also as a person. Here he recounts his experiences as a Black musician in the U.S.A., working with Herbie Hancock, Stan Getz, McCoy Tyner and many others. Hart speaks with candor, humor and insight. Iverson stays completely in the background, but he is surely the right person for this task. The details will be of interest to everybody, not only jazz fans.
  —Lewis Porter, author of "Playback" on Substack and the Coltrane biography

Despite the fact that I've known Billy for many, many years, I've learned so much more about him from his autobiography. Written from a distinctly drummer's point of view, it's a fascinating picture of the jazz world he's a part of and helped develop. He chronicles the music he continues to excel at after so much time. Read this book! I couldn't put it down.
   —John Scofield, guitarist

I had the privilege of meeting the great, Billy Hart when I was a teenager and have enjoyed being in his presence as his student, fan, drum tech, and colleague. Recently, I got to observe Mr. Hart in a recording session—watching and listening to him "get levels" with the engineer was life-changing. I remember thinking he sounded like a whole choir of drummers, with the perfect balance, dynamics, and touch. Thank you, Mr. Hart, and all who helped share this treasure trove. I look forward to referencing this memoir for years to come.
   —Evan Sherman, drummer

There is a hidden history of jazz that has eluded the grasp of even the most diligent scholars and critics. Billy Hart's *Oceans of Time* feels like a crucial corrective to that oversight. While it contains a wealth of vivid—and at times inspiring or scathing—behind-the-scenes anecdotes of the jazz life, perhaps more importantly, it reads like a long-form unpacking of the mysteries of what we know as 'swing.' Hart has seemingly made it his life's mission to register, internalize and process the innumerable subtleties of the American vernacular rhythmic tradition, and as the book goes on, his recounting of his on-the-job research begins to feel like a Rosetta stone. This book is instantly indispensable for anyone—musicians, historians, fans—who would seek to understand jazz on a molecular level. It's the next best thing to hearing Billy Hart play the drums, and I foresee going back to it for the rest of my life.
   —Hank Shteamer, jazz journalist

When Ethan initially told me about this book project, I thought to myself that Mark Turner had probably already heard most of what he would get, because Billy doesn't always say much on the road. Boy was I wrong!!! This book fills in so many gaps, and it is fascinating from beginning to end. Thank you, Billy and Ethan, for something I will treasure for years to come.
   —Ben Street, bassist

Billy Hart's *Oceans of Time* is an extraordinary gift. The most majestic and soulful living drummer in jazz, Hart is also a philosopher and autodidact of profound depth. He has given us the rare jazz memoir that digs into the marrow of the music, dropping wisdom on nearly every page that unlocks the mysteries and magic of the bandstand. From the indivisible – but overlooked -- connection between swing rhythm and the clavé, to nuanced discussions of drummers both famous (Tony Williams) and unheralded (Donald Bailey), Hart guides readers through the complex dance of art, folklore, tradition, and exploration that define the best in jazz, including himself.
—Mark Stryker, author of *Jazz from Detroit*

I can't remember how or when I first met Billy Hart (Jabali), suffice to say that since that time we have been involved in many projects together—tours, recordings, gigs, etc. If I knew that Billy was going to be on any of the above, I always let out a sigh of relief because I knew that the rhythm section would be "tight as the nuts on a bridge."
—Mickey Tucker, pianist

I always tease Billy, "You've got more gigs than you can handle." But Billy is also so dependable, he always gives himself completely to the music. His beat is entrancing, passionate, exuberant, emotional, full, and complete—and it all comes out in this book.
—Buster Williams, bassist

The way Billy Hart tells his story takes you *inside*—inside the band room, inside the band, inside the music and the way it evolves, handed on through the generations. For the reader, the access is priceless. I read it in a single sitting and learned something on just about every page.
—Richard Williams, author of *The Blue Moment: Miles Davis's Kind of Blue*

A unique feature of the book is a collection of 22 living drummers discussing Billy Hart in the first appendix, including Terri Lyne Carrington, *"I think of Billy Hart for the answers"* and Peter Erskine, *"Billy Hart turned the key for me."*

Table of Contents

Preface by Ethan Iverson	i
Introduction: The Meaning of Swing	1
My First Drum Set	7
The D.C. Beat	19
Deep in the Blues	27
Lessons from Wes	37
New York, New York	45
Miles Davis, the Teacher	61
Mwandishi	71
In the '70s with McCoy Tyner	85
We All Have a Stan Getz Story	95
Striking up the Band	107
Dramatis Personae	125
Professor Hart	143
The Big Picture	157
Appendix 1. Other Drummers Discuss Billy Hart	163

Kush Abadey, Nasar Abadey, Barry Altschul, Jeff Ballard, Johnathan Blake, Obed Calvaire, Terri Lyne Carrington, Billy Drummond, Peter Erskine, Bill Goodwin, Hyland Harris, Eric McPherson, Allison Miller, Lewis Nash, Adam Nussbaum, Bobby Previte, Jorge Rossy, Damion Reid, Vinnie Sperrazza, Nasheet Waits, Lenny White, & Jeff Williams

Appendix 2. Partial Discography as a Sideman	179
Appendix 3. Jabali's Drum Set	195
Acknowledgments	197
About the Authors	199
Also from Cymbal Press	201

Preface by Ethan Iverson

Billy Hart connects the glory years of jazz to the latest contemporary concerns. He does this primarily through his peerless drumming, but he is also a wonderful talker. Nothing escapes his notice, and he has a discourse ready for any topic.

While I enjoy a career as a player in this music, I did not come up within the tradition. From the minute I first shared the bandstand with Billy over 25 years ago, I *knew* that carrying his bag was what I needed to do. Along the way, I asked him questions, questions, and more questions. While I may have initially doubted certain assertions, everything he told me has been proven right.

For this memoir we did many hours of new interviews; I also consulted older sources, including previous interviews I had done with Billy. My job was to supply transitions and shape the narrative, but in terms of the actual intellectual content, the ideas remain all Hart. (The footnotes, all written in third person, were supplied mainly by our researcher Scott Douglass with a few assists from me. George Korval did additional fact-checking and supplied several valuable historical details.)

At first, *Oceans of Time* recounts his early years and road time with bona fide legends Shirley Horn, Jimmy Smith, Wes Montgomery, Eddie Harris, Pharoah Sanders, Herbie Hancock, Miles Davis, McCoy Tyner, and Stan Getz. The narrative then resists strict chronology, so the last four chapters roam freely, offering an overview of Billy's own bands and recordings as a leader, a collection of diverse anecdotes about other important people, a peek under the hood of what Billy teaches, and a final summation of his philosophy.

The first appendix collects words of other drummers about Billy Hart, the second appendix lists a partial discography, and the final page reveals the tuning and treatment of Billy's drum set.

Introduction: The Meaning of Swing

The first time someone asked me to define swing, it was a Japanese interviewer in Nagoya. I was dumbfounded—how *do* you explain it? Can you explain a religion in a word or two? A person of African descent would never have asked that question, especially if they had grown up in the Black American church. Finally, I said, "'Swing' is a musical system that causes joy, euphoria, and optimism."

When I was a high school student in Washington, D.C., I only got 35 cents a day for lunch money. If I saved up all week, it was just enough to go to see the great singer and pianist Shirley Horn play at the Brass Rail on the weekend. Her drummer was the top drummer in town, Harry "Stump" Saunders, who also played a lot with the local saxophone legend Buck Hill. Stump was tight with Jimmy Cobb, and they had a similar approach, with this serious Washington, D.C. beat.[1]

Wow, this cat could play! Stump had a head on his bass drum that wasn't just cowhide, it still had the cow hair on it. When he hit that bass drum it was like somebody punched you in the chest. Man, you can't imagine that groove. The groove was so deep and they were swinging so hard and Shirley was singing. Wow!

Listening to Shirley Horn and Stump Saunders certainly taught me something about euphoria. Stump was in the line of Kenny Clarke, Max Roach, Roy Haynes, Art Blakey, Philly Joe Jones, Louis Hayes, Art Taylor and the other magnificent midcentury masters of American classical music. I still try to play like Stump to this day.

There's not a lot to write about whatever "swing" is that looks absolutely correct. Those with African heritage value the oral tradition over the printed page. Still, there are a few things one can explain about the four limbs at the drums in the matter of a Stump Saunders.

---

[1] Jimmy Cobb is the drummer on the Miles Davis album *Kind of Blue*.

The meter is in 4/4. Not too long ago I worked with Archie Shepp in Paris. John Coltrane was like an uncle to Archie, so I asked Archie if he had talked to John about odd meters like 5/4 and 7/4. According to Archie, Coltrane said, "You know, I've tried *everything*, but nothing swings as hard as 4/4."

"Swing" also means that the beat fluctuates a bit. You need accurate time, of course, but if you play as accurately as a metronome that ends up sounding stiff.

On the ride cymbal, the right hand plays a blues shuffle with a couple of the middle notes left out: "spang, spang-a lang, spang-a-lang." Apparently, that beat is the invention of Kenny Clarke. A great drummer can play the hell out of that cymbal beat—I modeled my own ride cymbal style on Max Roach and Art Blakey.

But the cymbal is not quite enough on its own to generate euphoria; it needs to be related to the other limbs.

The wonderful drummer Eddie Moore started his students not with straight 4/4, but with what is sometimes called "The Universal Rhythm," a basic syncopation heard in almost all the cultures of the world. In Brazil it is in the baião; in Cuba, the tumbao; it's in Indian and Japanese music; the second-line; James P. Johnson's "The Charleston;" and so many other places. Of course, the true antecedent is Africa. You can notate this rhythm as 3-3-2, or as dotted quarter note, dotted quarter note, and quarter note.

In jazz drumming, the left hand can play fragments of the Universal Rhythm as well as other kinds of commentary. I sometimes think that the most swinging left-hand accent is the "and" of beat three. Billy Higgins could really play that accent with *drama*.

When discussing the rhythmic properties of jazz, I'm afraid my young D.C. jazz crowd regularly made fun of white people as the stiffest and most un-swinging people around. Yeah. We'd do high comedy, always with the implication that the Caucasian community had *no idea* what the emotion of "swinging" was, unless they got ahold of the wrong end of that basic idea and displayed it in an over-dramatic fashion. There was nothing better than joking about European people clapping on beats one and three for a polka or a hoedown. The way a jazz drummer plays beats two and four on the hi-hat emulates an Afro-American dance party, where people are clapping their hands. Whatever we did, we made sure not to do it "white."

Introduction: The Meaning of Swing

The right foot on the bass drum keeps the 4/4 going with "feathering," a soft hum of quarter notes. The early New Orleans music swung hard, no doubt, but the music settled into an even deeper groove in Kansas City and the Southwest a decade or two later—they called some of the important groups from that era "Territory Bands." It's possible that feathering the bass drum comes directly from the low tom-toms of the Native Americans. You can't hear the feathering on the records as clearly as the other limbs, someone has to show you how to do it. Buck Hill was the first person to tell me about feathering.

Occasionally, I describe jazz as "America's classical music," and one person who taught me that was Buck Hill.[2] Buck played so good, everything was correct, and everything around him on the bandstand also had to be correct.

All cultures start with music for dance, ceremony, and communication, and develop folkways and mores concerning this local music. But after mastering those folkways and mores, some musicians are curious about other possibilities and seek to combine their indigenous culture with sounds from other places. The United States is the one country that had all these cultures rubbing right up next to each other. You don't even need to go around the block to find something different, it's right across the street.

As the music evolves, it transitions from folk music for dancing to classical music for listening. When we say "classical music" we often think of Europe. But within Europe, all the classical music is different: the French, the English, the German, the Italian, the Spanish. The Russians are a whole 'nother thing. They all have a different nationalistic folk base. Unlike all those European classical musics, in America, our classical music was deeply informed by the classical musics of India, South America, and especially Africa.

Human nature is the same anywhere. We all get happy or sad, we all violate the Ten Commandments in our own little ways. Folk music reflects this basic human understanding. It's important for me to keep a folk perspective in my own approach. I've noticed that those who go

---

2 Billy Taylor's 1975 doctoral dissertation "The History and Development of Jazz Piano: A New Perspective for Educators" (University of Massachusetts) begins: "Jazz, a unique American phenomenon, may now be considered America's classical music." Critic Grover Sales published *Jazz: America's Classical Music* in 1984. In 1952, Lionel Hampton told *DownBeat*, "In my opinion, two of Ellington's compositions, *Sophisticated Lady* and *Black, Brown and Beige* will be classical music in the next century, just as Beethoven and Brahms are today."

strictly in an academic direction start criticizing all sorts of music. If you can stay connected to folk music, you have more love for variety. Apparently, both Charlie Parker and John Coltrane never had a bad word for any serious musician.

Nobody played more complex music than John Coltrane, but he always had that folk perspective in play. Black gospel is one of our American folk musics, absolutely crucial to American classical music, and Coltrane always remained a church musician, no matter the intellectual density of his sound. Any classical music has its rules and regulations too, of course. Some people think "jazz" means, "play whatever you want," but that is simply not the truth.

Dave Liebman says I am a devil's advocate—that whenever someone offers a strong opinion, I say the opposite. Dave has yelled at me more than once: "Jabali! Take a stand! Right or wrong, take a stand!"

Buster Williams has said something similar. After I won the NEA Jazz Master award in 2021, Buster called me and said, "Well, enough of this bullshit act you've been pulling for all these years. I hope you're finally ready to tell it like it is."

I tried to gain time by telling him, "But, man, Buster, *you* should have gotten the award, not me!"

"That's *exactly* what I'm talking about!" Buster countered. "No more of that bullshit!"

My short acceptance speech at the NEA awards included one equivocal word:

> John Coltrane said that he wanted his music to be a force for good. Coltrane's comment has inspired my own path of purpose. This path started many years ago in Washington, D.C., before sending me on to play with so many friends, heroes, mentors, and students. Getting this recognition tonight from my government apparently validates this path—this path of purpose. Thanks to the National Endowment of the Arts, SFJazz, and everyone else who has helped me all these years. I am happy to have walked this path!

The equivocal word, of course, was "apparently," and it got a big laugh.

Introduction: The Meaning of Swing

Three of the 2022 NEA Jazz Masters:
Billy Hart, Stanley Clarke, and Donald Harrison.
(Photo by Ethan Iverson.)

1

My First Drum Set

My parents met at Howard University. Ira Loretta Diggs, born 1920, was from Washington, D.C. and William Alfred Hart, born 1915, was from Philadelphia. I was born on November 29, 1940, and we lived in an apartment at 5024 Jay Street in Suburban Gardens, a black neighborhood of D.C. My brother, Ronald Alfred Hart, was born four years after me.

My parents' social circle was a fairly sophisticated, middle-class scene. Everyone had graduated from college. An informal "club" met once a week to play cards and discuss current events; one of those friends was Minnie Shumate Woodson, who wrote a couple of important books about black history.[1] Musically, my parents were *hip*. Jimmie Lunceford was my mother's favorite band, while my father's favorite was Duke Ellington. Later on, they both liked Louis Jordan.

My mother worked for the IRS, and my father drove a cab. Being a cabbie was something of a political statement. My father had a degree in mathematics, and for a time worked in the government, training incoming workers. However, since he was black, he couldn't advance past a certain station. That didn't stop the white people—some of whom he had trained himself—from being promoted and making more money. When his politically advanced family back home in Philadelphia heard about the racism in the government pay scales, they told my father he'd be better off being his own man and driving a cab.

My father's mother, Viola, was a concert pianist with associations to several pioneering Afro-American musicians including the legendary contralto Marian Anderson, whom Viola accompanied on several early recitals. Anderson sent my grandmother a signed copy of her

---

[1] A novel, *The Sable Curtain*, and a family history, *The Woodson Source Book*. Some historians believe one of the family's ancestors, Thomas Woodson, was the son of Thomas Jefferson and Sally Hemings. Minnie Shumate Woodson later became D.C. school board president.

Billy Hart's parents, Ira and William

autobiography *My Lord, What a Morning*; I liked to take that volume off the shelf and look at that famous signature.[2] Viola also knew Paul Robeson and conductor James DePreist, another black musician from that powerful Philadelphia circle. My father investigated communism because of Robeson's influence. Later, Viola moved in with my family and was an influence on me musically. She would tell me these names like Bach, Beethoven, Liszt, Wagner, and Verdi, and would play me her opera and symphonic collection on a self-contained turntable; a particular favorite was "Scheherazade" by Rimsky-Korsakov.

My first grade school was Burrville on Division Avenue; then I moved over to Merritt, where I graduated from sixth grade. In those years I loved baseball, especially the Brooklyn Dodgers, because of Jackie Robinson

---

2 Anderson recounts in her memoir how the junior choir director at her church, Alexander Robinson, "entrusted" her and her neighbor Viola Johnson to sing the hymn "Dear to the Heart of the Shepherd" one Sunday as a duet. Johnson sang the upper part. Anderson calls it "my first public appearance."

My First Drum Set

and Roy Campanella. Later I also liked the New York Giants and Willie Mays. I didn't pay any attention to the Washington Senators, because their owner Clark Griffith was a flagrant racist. It was only after I started at Kelly Miller Junior High School that I began to explore music. First I tried out for the choir. When they turned me down, I tried out for the drum and bugle corps—and they turned me down too!

It was Othello Savoy, the printing teacher, who was in charge of the drum and bugle corps and was even a tenor saxophone player with whom I eventually played a few gigs. When Mr. Savoy told me I didn't make it, I started to cry. He took pity on me and said, "You have to understand, you don't play as good as these other students. It would be unfair of me to allot a drum for you when we only have so many drums. But ... if you *buy* your own drum, I'll let you play."

I asked my mother to buy me a drum and she said no, absolutely not. So I went over her head to her mother, Alberta Diggs, whom my father called "The Duchess." The Duchess liked to spoil me as a boy; she also danced and drank cocktails. Later on, she gave me an LP with Buck Clayton, Sir Charles Thompson, and Jo Jones, and tried to set me up on dates with girls she liked. We went to a pawn shop together, and

Brothers Ronald and Billy

the Duchess bought me a marching drum that you could strap across your chest.

The corps included eight snare drummers, two bass drummers, two tenor drummers, and eight or nine bugle players. The uniform was maroon pants, maroon jacket, and a maroon cap with a plume. We rehearsed over and over for the big day, when various drum and bugle corps from all over the country came to Washington, D.C. to march in the National School Patrol Parade. We marched down Independence Avenue and Constitution Avenue past the White House.

When our part of the march was over, my mother tried to find me in the huge crowd. Sadly, before she could get to me, I ran into a store to buy a soda. The man behind the counter told me, "I'm really sorry son, but I can't serve you." D.C. was still segregated, and I wasn't allowed in this store.[3]

After I got home, I put my drum in a corner and didn't play it again for a few years.

Our next house was in Brookland, 3115 13th Street NE, and the Afro-American school was Langley. The year after integration in 1954, my class moved to the next building over, McKinley Technical, which had previously been all white. That was the first time I had ever been in a school with white kids. It was weird, and it didn't go very well. Generally, the black kids sat on one side of the room and the white

---

[3] *The Evening Star* (Washington, D.C.), May 12, 1951: "Bands which won prolonged applause along the parade route included one from St. Paul's Academy and another from the Kelly-Miller Junior High School. The latter organization was led by 12 young drum majorettes." And on the front page: "The largest contingent from a distance came up from Georgia, 3,250 strong. Many of the young Southerners waved Confederate flags and treated the judges and reviewers to a high-pitched chorus of rebel yells."

kids on the other. Previously, I had teachers that taught black history and black heritage, but now, these white teachers never alluded to that perspective. In time, I would conclude that students are intentionally kept from knowing how wealth was created in this country. Racism is part of the larger design.

My brother went to school with Howard Chichester, who lived down the block and had a set of green sparkle Gretsch drums. When I would sit and try to play Howard's kit I felt something inside, like real interest in the drums. I asked my mother for a drum set for Christmas, and—after giving me trouble about giving up on that snare drum before—she found the absolute cheapest drum set ever made in the history of this planet. It had a tiny ride cymbal, a snare drum, and a bass drum that was sort of blue and gray. No hi-hat and no tom-tom. After a while I dug up my drum and bugle corps snare and used that as a floor tom; there was no stand, so I'd place this "tom" on a suitcase.

At first, the drums were in the living room, but after a few weeks my mother said, "I can't stand this anymore," and ran a wire from the radio and 78 player in the living room down to a speaker in the basement, where I could play with the radio and even some records. After starting a 78 upstairs, I'd run downstairs and start playing along.

Pretty soon I was in the Scholars, a doo-wop group at another school, Spingarn. It was a bunch of kid vocalists, a piano player, and me with my sad drum set. When performing, we all wore a white sweater with a green "S" on the front.

There was also a drum corps in Northwest, the Police Boys Club. When we practiced we'd all learn the cadence from the lead drummer, the best drummer of the corps. During my time, that was Aubrey G. Saxon, but just before that, the lead drummer in the Police Boys Club was Lloyd McNeill, who later started the jazz program at Rutgers University.

The Duchess was living on Division Avenue across the hall from Buck Hill and his wife Helen. I didn't know who Buck was yet. (If this story happened again today, I'd have a better chance of knowing who Buck was, since there is a huge mural of Buck at 14th and U Streets NW.)[4]

Helen saw me hanging in the hallway waiting for my grandmother and invited me inside the Hill apartment. When Buck got home he noticed that I had drumsticks in my back pocket. "You're a drummer, huh?"

---

4 "The Wailin' Mailman: A Portrait of Buck Hill" by muralist Joe Pagac. At the time of creation in 2019 it was the tallest mural in Washington, D.C.

Buck had a new hi-fi for LPs, so he gave me two older Charlie Parker 78s. *Charlie Parker with Strings* had "Just Friends" and "If I Should Lose You." The other 78 was "Au Privave" and "Star Eyes" with Max Roach.

It was something I had never heard before.

I mostly liked doo-wop records, and other kinds of pop and rhythm and blues: The Sparrows, The Drifters, The Clovers, and many others. My favorite group was Frankie Lymon and the Teenagers.[5] (Later, Tony Williams told me that his favorite group was also Frankie Lymon and the Teenagers.) But when I heard these Charlie Parker records, I fell in love and couldn't stop listening. There was no contest, no argument, nothing. This was *it*. I just looked up and checked the time, and here I am writing this memoir 65 years later.

According to my father, whoever got the better grades didn't have to do so many chores, a contest that was perfect for my brother: Ronald would work hard for the grades and I'd do the dishes. That's how I started listening to jazz music on the radio, while everybody else was upstairs watching television. As I did the dishes, I heard programs from Willis Conover and Felix Grant. On Grant's radio show they would advertise where people were playing, and that's how I figured out there was a black section of town and a white section of town.

The Spotlite Room was just five blocks up from my house in Brookland. That's where I first saw Ahmad Jamal, Miles Davis, Buddy Rich, and so many others.[6] I couldn't get in, I was too young, but—since clubs didn't have air conditioners yet—there were big fans in the window. In the winter, they didn't use the fans, so there was some space between the fan blades. I could go down to the club and look through the blades and see the bandstand while freezing to death outside. Miles's band in those days included John Coltrane, Cannonball Adderley, Bill Evans, Paul Chambers, and Jimmy Cobb.

There was a used record vendor on the street right in front of the club, where I bought a 45 of Elvis Presley singing "Heartbreak Hotel."

Guitarist Quentin Warren was two years ahead of me in school and later recommended me to Jimmy Smith. It was only years later that I

---

5 Their 1956 hit "Why Do Fools Fall in Love" landed at No. 6 on *The Billboard*'s R&B charts behind Bill Doggett, Fats Domino, Little Richard, Little Willie John, and The Platters.

6 Jamal recorded a live album at the Spotlite for Argo in September of 1958, *The Ahmad Jamal Trio, Volume IV*. A Spotlite broadcast of Miles Davis Sextet in August 1958 was released on the CD compilation *Miles Davis All-Stars Featuring John Coltrane – Live in 1958-1959*.

My First Drum Set

learned Quentin had been coming by my house and looking in the basement window, watching me play with the records.

Quentin wasn't the only Warren family member important to the Washington D.C. jazz scene: Eddie Warren was a good piano player and the father of Butch. Eddie used to have jam sessions at his house with serious visiting New York players like Jackie McLean and Junior Cook. When Quentin decided I was good enough, he took me over to Eddie's house for a few of those jam sessions. Quentin's decision to bring me to that community marked the true beginning of my life in this music.

I even got to sit in with the great swing-era violin player Stuff Smith at Eddie Warren's house. That was the first time I ever heard any talk that related music to romance. Stuff Smith told the bass player, "Play the beat like you are sweet-talking a woman."

I had no idea what Stuff Smith was talking about—I was still shooting marbles. But I filed that comment away as valuable information.

While Butch Warren was barely older than me, he was already accepted on the scene. Butch could actually get into the clubs and hang out. For one matinee, Butch took me along to see Ahmad Jamal, Israel Crosby, and Vernel Fournier at the Spotlite Room. I'll never forget seeing Vernel play his famous "Poinciana" beat, which is a version of the second line parade beat orchestrated for drum set. Vernel played the cymbal with his left hand. Only New Orleans drummers do that, because the original marching band musicians played the cymbal with their left hand mounted on the bass drum strapped to their chest while the right beat the drum.

Art Blakey brought his Jazz Messengers to the Spotlite, with Johnny Griffin and Bill Hardman. From then on, Blakey was one of my great influences. When I hear him now, I can appreciate that he was also a piano player, someone who heard the music from a harmonic perspective, whether he was playing with Clifford Brown or Wayne Shorter. But when I was young I simply responded to all the love and passion in Art Blakey's beat.

On another occasion I got to spend a few afternoons watching Horace Silver's band rehearse in the afternoons at the Spotlite Club. I really loved his drummer, Louis Hayes, not just because he was great, but because he was close to my age.

Another drummer close to me in age was Tootie Heath. When Tootie had a gig in town he would stay with Roland Wilson, who was an architect. (Roland helped with my college entrance exam and eventually moved to New York and made a few records as a bass player.)[7] If I was walking down to the club, I would knock on Roland's window and see if Tootie was there.

Tootie was a bad boy, and we really hit it off. He was charismatic and hilarious, and he played his ass off with the Jazztet, a wonderful group that included Art Farmer, Benny Golson, Curtis Fuller, Cedar Walton, and Tommy Williams. A couple of times, Tootie would come to my high school and make some kind of face or something in the window. I'd have to excuse myself, come out of the class, and then just be gone for the rest of the day. Tootie told me about the new sounds of Ornette Coleman and even made up lascivious lyrics to some of Ornette's tunes. We would need to go to Kitt's Music Store in Northwest to buy drumsticks. In those days, you had to test the sticks because a lot of the sticks would be bent. That's when I noticed Tootie's facility, that kind of academic knowledge and control of the sticks.

Louis Hayes and Tootie Heath were people just a few years older than me that I could emulate or at least take inspiration from. There's one more from that period I could mention, Clifford Jarvis. Jarvis isn't so well known today but he appears on a few classic records with Freddie Hubbard, Barry Harris, Jackie McLean, and Sun Ra. I didn't know Jarvis as well as I knew Tootie Heath or Louis Hayes, but I saw him the first time I went to New York. The Duchess had a job in Manhattan, and for my high school graduation present I stayed with her for a week. Jarvis was playing with Randy Weston at the Five Spot, and that's the first time I had ever seen a drummer my age who could play that good. I remember his attitude. I remember how he was dressed. He wore a trench coat with his collar up. I *thought* I was hip until I saw him—just the way he was dressed was so different, let alone the drumming. Jarvis was super hip and I was this country bumpkin.[8]

Being hip was important. In D.C., we all rode the bus, and one time I saw a cat sitting on the other side of the aisle with a trumpet, but in a paper bag. There were only two things it could be: either he was down and out—a crook or homeless or something like that—or he was just

---

7   Roland Wilson can be heard on Donald Byrd's *Fancy Free* (Blue Note, 1969), Archie Shepp's *Attica Blues* (Impulse!, 1972), and James Moody's *Never Again!* (Muse, 1972).

8   Like Tony Williams, Clifford Jarvis was a Boston prodigy who studied with Alan Dawson. Jarvis was born in August 1941, 9 months after Billy Hart, which means that Jarvis would have not yet been 17 when playing with Randy Weston in the summer of 1958.

hip. I took the romantic position and thought he was really *hip*.

His name was Freddie Michaels, but because he wore a certain kind of cap, everybody called him "Brim." I started a conversation, and after he realized that I knew who Horace Silver and Art Blakey were, he encouraged me to stay on the bus, taking me all the way to a rehearsal with pianist Lawrence Wheatley. Everyone called Wheatley "Fox." Fox had a long beard and tried to play like Thelonious Monk. He tried to act like Monk, too: When Brim took me into the apartment, Fox shook my hand, but he wouldn't let go, just kept staring at me.

Brim and Fox ended up getting a gig playing five nights a week at the club Seventh and T. I couldn't take those sad drums anymore, so I went to the Duchess again, and she lent me the money to buy a black set of Gretsch drums. It was a quartet or a quintet; Buddy Wrench played tenor sax, and if we had a bassist—which, many times, we didn't—it was Butch Warren or Teddy Smith, who later worked with Horace Silver. Brim and Fox would play a lot of Thelonious Monk and Miles Davis repertoire. When we did "Dr. Jackle" really fast, my right hand would freeze. Brim would turn around and yell at me, trying to be mean. "What's wrong with you?"

"My hand is frozen," I'd yell at Brim. I can't hold the stick!"

"Man, get it together!" Brim would yell back.

Seventh and T was around the corner from the Howard Theatre, which was the big venue for Afro-American music, like the Regal Theatre in Chicago and the Apollo Theatre in Harlem. In fact, all three of those major venues looked identical both outside and inside.[9] A lot of the Howard Theatre concerts were pop music, but there was the occasional jazz night. A good set would feature instrumentalists like Miles Davis, Horace Silver, or James Moody, vocalists like Sarah Vaughan or Ella Fitzgerald, and close with Count Basie's big band. There'd be a comedian and other non-music events to mix it up, and over the weekend they might do three or four shows a day. On their breaks, great musicians would come by and hang out at Seventh and T. One night Oscar Peterson and Ray Brown came in, because they were playing next door at the Howard.[10]

---

9   The Howard opened in 1910 and is the oldest of this circuit.

10 The Oscar Peterson Trio with Ray Brown and Ed Thigpen opened at the Howard for one week in September 1959, headlining on a program that included Jimmy Smith, Betty Carter, the Bennie Green Quintet, and comedian/MC Dave Friedman.

I was still so young! Brim and Fox were acting really cool, sometimes *not even showing up to the gig*, that level of cool. There was some booze and pot around I guess, but they kept that away from me. I was just totally inexperienced. I was in a dream world, not even drinking beer.

We would all talk about music, but nothing was said of a notably academic nature. To this day I regard myself as essentially self-taught, because I never had a proper drum teacher or took any piano lessons.

The most important part of studying was simply listening. At home, I was playing with my records and singing the melodies and solos. An early favorite was *Presenting the Gerry Mulligan Sextet*. I listened to that daily when it first came out—I was 15 or so. Soon after, I learned the Clifford Brown/Max Roach records backwards and forwards, along with the Miles Davis records featuring Philly Joe Jones or Jimmy Cobb. To this day, I can sing along with all the solos on Art Blakey's Messenger albums at the Cafe Bohemia with Kenny Dorham, Hank Mobley, Horace Silver, and Doug Watkins. Young Louis Hayes tore it up on Horace Silver's *6 Pieces of Silver*, but I also loved *Further Explorations*. That's an occasion where Horace Silver is going especially deep into composition. (Later on, another great composer, Cedar Walton, told me he called Silver "Horatio.")

It was about time for me to meet some other people. From Felix Grant's radio show, I learned where the other gigs and the jam sessions were. When I went to see these guys play live, I thought, "Well, I can do that."

So then I started asking if I could play, and nobody would let me play. *Nobody!* Nobody even thought I was cute or something. This was *serious*, and they kept me off the bandstand.

I went back and called poor Buck Hill. Buck and I weren't tight yet; he was just this cat that knew my grandmother. At this point, I certainly didn't realize he was the top saxophone player in town. But I called him, and said, "Man, I been trying to sit in and play with the cats." Today, of course, I can see him thinking, "Aw, man…what'd I get myself into with this little motherfucker?"

Buck hesitated a bit but finally said, "Okay. I got a matinee on Saturdays at Abart's. You can come down and I'll let you play one with us."

Abart's Jazz Mecca was an important club owned by the brothers Abram and Arthur Spencer. Occasionally a major act from New York would play Abart's on the weekend, but during the week, local musicians held down the gig.

My First Drum Set

The 4 to 7 matinee jam session was *packed*. Buck called me up to sit in with these older cats who sounded really good. They started, and I immediately relaxed, because it was a tune that Fox had taught me, "Nutty" by Thelonious Monk. I played that, and the other cats on the bandstand showed their approval. But then they called "Donna Lee," which I didn't know and was much faster, and I fucked up the tempo and lost my place in the tune.

What a loss! Everything that was bright is now dark and rainy. And I don't know anybody, I'm just there by myself, the cats are back to ignoring me. Buck isn't around. So, I'm trying to find a place where I can keep from crying, and somebody grabs me by my belt and says, "You know, it wasn't all your fault. It takes three of us to make a rhythm section."

And when I turned around, it was Shirley Horn. I was so into myself, I didn't even realize she was the piano player up there with me!

That's how I met Shirley Horn.

2

The D.C. Beat

Shirley Horn meant the world to me, both personally and musically. She was somewhere between my first love and my grandmother. At first I didn't know that she could sing; she was simply a great piano player, someone who could play like Ahmad Jamal and Oscar Peterson. And then I found out she had her own gigs at the Brass Rail.

When I first started showing up to her gigs, Shirley thought I was cute like a young kid. She would ask Stump, "Man, Stump, let him play one." Stump would reply, "Naw, man. This little motherfucker, he can't play."

So, in all that time I was saving up my lunch money for the door charge and not eating at school, I never got a chance to play with her. I started getting better and better, and I learned a lot of her repertoire from listening to her gigs, but I wasn't good enough to play with Shirley yet.

Charlie Hampton was an alto player connected to the Howard Theatre and Abart's Jazz Mecca. When I started to play more around town, Hampton was one of the most important people to call me and get me work. The strict chronology of the next five years, 1958-1963, is not so clear in my mind: I graduated high school and went to a little bit of college while playing both jazz and pop gigs with a whole slew of people. [1]

Some of the good pop gigs Hampton hired me for at the Howard or around town included Jackie Wilson, Sam Cooke, Joe Tex, The Isley Brothers, Sam and Dave, Patti Labelle, Otis Redding, and Smokey Robinson and the Miracles.[2] I did a whole week at Abart's with Aretha Franklin, when she was still singing a lot of jazz—one of her hit records from her early years was a beautiful rendition of the standard "Skylark."

---

[1] In 1961, Billy Hart made his first record date, *The Buck Clarke Sound*. Hart doesn't remember much about the occasion, but it is an impressive and soulful platter with strong Washington D.C. players. The arrangements are by Charles Hampton.

[2] The career of The Isley Brothers took off when Howard Bloom of RCA caught their act at the Howard Theatre in 1959. That July they recorded "Shout" for the label.

Aretha could play good jazz piano at that point.[3]

Hampton was in charge of the resident big band at the Howard Theatre, a kind of shifting group of musicians that backed up the pop acts. I almost became the regular drummer for that pop big band, but I kept going back to jazz. There was a rambunctious little running crew there with cute nicknames: Dog, Little Dog, and Booty. I don't think I ever saw any sheet music—for me or any other drummer—for those kinds of transient pop gigs. We just needed to know the songs from the radio. One time I saw a pop person ask Dog (whose real name was Hirschel McGinnis, and who was a great doubler on all the reeds) to make a big band arrangement of one of the current radio hits. Dog wanted the lead sheet, which surprised the other guy, who asked if Dog hadn't heard the record. "Are you kidding me?" Dog replied. "I don't listen to any of that shit."[4]

More importantly, I played jazz with Charlie Hampton at Abart's for a short time before Buck Hill took Hampton's place. The rhythm section was completed by Lewis Powers, a good bassist who played with Shirley and Stump, and a piano player I soon became close friends with, Reuben Brown. After three months or so Butch Warren returned from New York and took over from Lewis. The trio would play during the week and Buck would join us on weekends. That was a crucial learning experience for me: The year of working with Buck, Reuben, and Butch at Abart's was definitely a step up from the group with Fox and Brim.

Reuben Brown was my favorite piano player after Shirley; he was advanced harmonically and knew all the tunes. As Reuben got established, he became the top-call cat in D.C.—a position he held for decades, working with players at the level of Benny Golson or Milt Jackson when they came to town. Reuben never really got out of D.C. too much, but eventually in 1994 we did record *Ice Scape* for Steeplechase, a nice trio album with Rufus Reid that shows Reuben's musical conception fairly well. In those early days, Reuben was rather philosophical in outlook; we would talk about religion and life and read Krishnamurti, Carl Jung, and *Autobiography of a Yogi*.

---

3   Aretha Franklin's recording of "Skylark" is on *Laughing on the Outside* (Columbia, 1963).

4   McGinnis was born in Chicago, but graduated high school in Washington, D.C. and attended Howard University. He served in the Army Band and taught music and English for 23 years, including at Hart's alma mater McKinley Technical High School. As a saxophonist, composer, and arranger, he worked with Wild Bill Davis, Lloyd Price, Pearl Bailey, Cab Calloway, Harry Belafonte, and the Supremes.

Butch Warren was a prodigy, really into Ray Brown and Paul Chambers, and very mature for his age. He had played with Kenny Dorham, Charles Davis, and Steve Kuhn on his long trip to New York, and then returned to D.C. like a conquering hero. A few years later, after another excursion to New York, Butch reported back that Ron Carter was going to be the next cat after Paul Chambers, and that a young kid named Tony Williams had a lot of potential.

That year with Buck Hill at Abart's was a phenomenal learning experience. At times it was challenging emotionally, because I could tell Buck Hill wasn't always pleased with the rhythm section. We weren't quite up to snuff, especially when someone at the level of Sonny Stitt or Gene Ammons would sit in. Buck wasn't mean or nasty, but I could tell he wasn't always happy. When he got drug with the rhythm section, he would call the tune, "Everything Happens to Me."

As with Reuben Brown, I eventually helped Buck Hill get a record date for Steeplechase, *This is Buck Hill* from 1978, with Kenny Barron and Buster Williams. When I listen back to that album now, after so many more years of experience, I am freshly impressed with his consummate artistry. Buck Hill could *really* play—especially considering he worked at the post office his whole life!

Buck Hill, Buster Williams, and Billy Hart, early '80s at Sweet Basil in NYC

There was something about the larger world of having a music career that didn't suit Buck's personality. When we were hanging out at Abart's one night, I told Buck, "I want to get out there!"

Buck looked at me and said, "You will." But the way he said it was like a warning. During some of the harder moments of my life on the road, I've remembered that warning.

In the early '80s, after his Steeplechase album came out, Buck and I played not just in New York, at Sweet Basil with Kenny Barron and Buster Williams, but even at the North Sea Festival in the Netherlands, with Reuben Brown and Wilbur Little. That was the completion of a cycle, when all of us hometown cats played one of Europe's biggest festivals over 20 years later.[5]

Buck didn't try to capitalize on that attention. He simply went back home, kept working at the post office, and swung everyone to death on the weekends.

Our Abart's gig didn't pay much—10 dollars a night at most—but when it ended I felt it as a tragic loss. The next steady gig I had was completely different, playing in a band for dancing at The Spa.

We worked 8 p.m. to 2 a.m., 40 minutes on, 20 minutes off. It was really strict like that, because people were there to dance. While nobody was coming in to see how creative you were—mainly we played songs off the radio—everyone knew if you were truly dealing or not. You had to *hit*.

Now and then, some of the cats I knew from the jazz situation would come in. Their attitude was, "Aw, man, Billy Hart is a *jazz* cat. I mean, he's not *that* great as a jazz cat, but he's *really* not a funk cat. What is he doin' up there?"

I didn't really have the guts, the thing; maybe I was too academic or too slick to be a real funk cat. Washington, D.C. is still the funk capital from Virginia to Philadelphia, but back then, the scene was even more raw than it is now. The leaders of the pop acts couldn't always afford to bring a whole band on tour. A lot of bandleaders and musical directors would look for musicians from D.C., halfway between the North and the South—especially drummers. If you were a drummer out of D.C., people knew you could *groove*.

At that time, the most popular D.C. drummer was Thomas Tribble Jr.,

---

5   Four sets of Washington, D.C. music were recorded at North Sea in 1981 and released on Steeplechase. Buck Hill's *Easy to Love* and *Impressions* feature Reuben Brown, Wilbur Little, and Billy Hart; Shirley Horn's *All Night Long* and *Violets for Your Furs* feature Charles Ables and Billy Hart.

who we called "TNT Tribble." You can hear TNT's incredible drumming on the 1961 Bobby Parker hit "Watch Your Step."[6]

There were a bunch of us around then. If we had a jazz gig, we were in the Jimmy Cobb line, and if we were doing pop, we were like TNT Tribble.

In addition to Stump Saunders, there was Dude Brown, Bertell Knox, Hugh Walker ("Little Dog," who also went by "Hamza"), and Bernard Sweetney (who replaced me on more than a few gigs). I won't be able to remember everybody, but Mickey Newman was the first person to demonstrate a few Max Roach licks in front of me, while Jerome Monroe (also called "Stump," or sometimes "Little Stump" to differentiate him from Saunders) told me about James Brown's great drummer, Clayton Fillyau, and showed me some of those beats.

At The Spa, I was playing in the manner of Tribble or Fillyau. A couple of the guys in that band actually ended up playing with James Brown, so it was a pretty serious group. There was sawdust on the floor and dancing and partying all night. I had finally started drinking—I guess that pop beat did that to me—and my beverage of choice was "Purple Passion," a mixture of wine and gin. Onstage, the bass player would occasionally take the bass and spin it around his head, and the only time I could hear what the singer was doing was when he turned around and faced me, yelling, "Louder!"

One night, Shirley Horn walked into the Spa. When I saw her there, I wanted to protect her, thinking something like, "Oh no! My angel has walked into this den of iniquity!" I didn't realize until after I started working with her that she probably could drink anybody in that club under the table. Shirley told me that night, "I think it's time for you to come and play with me."

Shirley and Stump would fall out all the time—there was a lot of drama, and Stump was always playing with other top people in town. So Shirley gave me a chance.

I was in heaven playing with Shirley Horn and Lewis Powers. She had elaborate arrangements derived from Miles Davis, Oscar Peterson, and Ahmad Jamal, but her smoky voice took it to another level. She liked me because I knew all of those Ahmad Jamal and Miles Davis beginnings

---

6 In *The Beatles Anthology*, John Lennon talks about Bobby Parker with TNT Tribble. "'Watch Your Step' is one of my favorite records. The Beatles have used the lick in various forms. The Allman Brothers used the lick straight as it was."

and endings, the way they played cut time and then swung the bridge, little secrets like that. The Miles Davis records with John Coltrane, Red Garland, Paul Chambers, and Philly Joe Jones seemed to be the bible, the way it was supposed to be done, but there weren't too many other young cats in town who were trying to play that kind of music.[7]

I sort of thought Shirley was influenced by Bill Evans, but she told me she never listened to him. According to Shirley, a lot of her harmonic ideas came from French and Russian composers like Debussy, Ravel, Rachmaninoff, and Scriabin. She accompanied herself like the soundtrack of a movie, building drama and then releasing the tension.

As with Reuben Brown and Buck Hill, I eventually got Shirley a record date with Steeplechase: *Lazy Afternoon*, with Buster Williams, recorded a few months after *This is Buck Hill* in 1978. I feel especially good about *Lazy Afternoon* because that was truly the beginning of something big. In a few more years, everyone in jazz was raving about Shirley Horn, she signed to Verve, and she finished out her career at the very top of the heap. On that opening swinger from *Lazy Afternoon*, "I'm Old Fashioned," I was trying to play the way I was taught by Shirley and Stump Saunders, with that deep Washington, D.C. groove.

In addition to swinging hard, Shirley had something outstandingly personal on a ballad. I think she might have gotten the way to really lay back on the time at a slow tempo from Ray Charles. I heard Charles play his hit "Drown in My Own Tears" while really delaying certain beats at the piano. Musicians, especially drummers, can complain about trying to play with this kind of thing—you are simply forced into following the pianist around—but Ray and Shirley delayed those beats for good dramatic reasons. Part of it is to emphasize the triplet: In a slow 12/8 rhythm and blues situation, the backbeat can be severely delayed. Of course, Ray Charles is the number one teacher for the whole school of rhythm and blues. Eventually, Shirley Horn recorded a beautiful tribute to Charles, *Light Out of Darkness*.

In later years, Shirley had her steady trio with Charles Ables and Steve Williams. Charles was a very quiet kind of cat, while Steve was outgoing. Ables was a great guitar player who really understood harmony and seemed destined to be the George Benson of Washington, D.C.;

---

7   Miles Davis, John Coltrane, Red Garland, Paul Chambers, and Philly Joe Jones recorded six studio albums in 1955 and '56: *Miles: The New Miles Davis Quintet*, *Round About Midnight*, *Cookin'*, *Relaxin'*, *Workin'*, and *Steamin'*.

he stayed on electric bass guitar when he moved to the lower register. Williams followed Stump Saunders and me in Shirley's drum lineage, sounding equally great on the hard swingers and the ballads with the delayed beats.

In the '80s, I played with Shirley several times in Europe and New York, as her career gained momentum. At North Sea, I'm there with Charles Ables for two whole sets; you can hear us cradle Shirley's wide beat on the ballad "All Night Long."

After one set at a fancy supper club in midtown with Shirley, Sarah Vaughan and Betty Carter both told me I was playing too loud for a singer. So the next set, I pulled it back. Afterwards, Shirley came up to me and growled, "Billy, are you *for* me or *against* me?"

"Aw, Shirley, people have been telling me that I've been hitting too hard."

She looked me in the eyes and said, "Don't tickle me." The implication was clear.

Shirley and I never dated. Back when I first was working with her, she was an overpowering force and amazingly beautiful, but I knew I couldn't fall in love with Shirley. My first girlfriend, Dolores Cain, was about to become my wife. I met Dolores at Abart's; she had seen me there with Reuben Brown and Butch Warren. I saw her too. As I watched this woman walk past the bandstand, a chill went through me, as if somebody had opened a window.

Since Dolores knew Reuben, she passed him a note with her phone number to give to me. But I was so square that I tore up her number and threw it away! I think I could have been much more popular with the ladies around that time if I had had any idea of what to do. Anyway, Dolores came back in another couple of weeks and met me in person. She said, "Why didn't you call me?" That was it, and after a few years we were married.

Dolores's father was in construction and her family owned their own house, so they were middle-class, in an Afro-American way, although her parents were from the South and very uneducated. They could read, but not well. After going to school, Dolores taught her parents how to read better and how to count. However, her parents gave Dolores a lot of confidence in non-academic ways, and she really took charge when we got married. It was great. All sorts of people came to our big church wedding, where she was in a bridal gown and both our fathers wore tails. She found us a nice apartment, set up house, and soon my first son, Chris, was born.

I owe Dolores a lot. There's hardly a day that goes by when I don't remember how good Dolores was to me. She asked me to marry her with tears in her eyes, saying, "I know you don't want to get married. But I'm asking you to do it anyway."

I said yes. But I also said to her, with an arrogant 22-year-old attitude: "Now, you don't have to do anything you don't want to do. In fact, you can do anything you want to do. But if you once, even once, get between me and the music, it's over."

Dolores got the message and proved it one Sunday afternoon. Both Jimmy Smith and James Brown called our house the same day, to ask me to join their band. Dolores told Jimmy Smith exactly where I was, out in California with Shirley Horn, and I heard from him a few minutes later. But she put off James Brown, telling him I'd be home in a month or whatever, that she didn't know how to reach me. She sent me Jimmy Smith instead of James Brown because Jimmy Smith was jazz and James Brown was pop. Dolores knew what was best for me.

With Dolores Cain, Billy's first wife

3

Deep in the Blues

When I joined Jimmy Smith, I replaced Donald Bailey, who we called "Duck." Elvin Jones gets the credit for making the drums more polyrhythmic, especially on the records with John Coltrane, but this was a community music, where many people made an important contribution. Along with Edgar Bateman, Donald Bailey was one of the other innovative drummers bringing those kinds of polyrhythmic concepts into the music at the same time as Elvin Jones. There was some real African heritage in this approach.

Jimmy Smith made many classic records with Donald Bailey.[1] When Duck plays the slow shuffle on "Midnight Special," he plays the hi-hat on the upbeat with his foot. I still do that once in a while today, and when I do, it's a tribute to Duck. I showed that beat to Grady Tate, and then Steve Gadd played it too. When I play that beat today, someone might say afterwards, "I heard you playing that Steve Gadd beat." No. That is out of order. Steve might get the credit with the commoners, but the royal line goes back to Duck.

Duck didn't like to fly, so he ended up quitting Jimmy Smith when Jimmy started getting more and more popular. Jimmy was picking up drummers on the road, and in Washington, D.C., he expected to get George "Dude" Brown. Dude was a great drummer, a deep swinger, and a bit of a character. Helen Hill told me about how George would get irritated with people who were making noise upstairs in his apartment building, and in retaliation would take out his gun and shoot through the ceiling.[2]

---

1 Jimmy Smith was prolific when recording albums as a leader from 1956 through 1963, the time of his breakthrough; Donald Bailey was the drummer on most of those sessions.

2 Dude Brown played with Jelly Roll Morton in the 1930s and toured with Louis Armstrong in the 1940s.

Jimmy Smith was looking for Dude to play two weeks in Georgetown at The Shadows, but Dude had just left town to play with Illinois Jacquet.[3] Quentin Warren recommended me to Jimmy, and Jimmy said, "Well, we'll try him out for tonight. If he makes it tonight, he can have the whole week. And if he works out for the whole week, he can have the next week."

At the end of the two weeks, Jimmy didn't say anything notably positive, so I figured that was it. But a month or two later—again, thanks to Dolores—he called me in San Francisco to join him in Chicago and officially become part of his band. There was a block in San Francisco with four clubs: The Jazz Workshop, Basin Street West, Sugar Hill, and El Matador. I was at Sugar Hill working with Shirley Horn, but Jimmy found me across the street at the Jazz Workshop, where I was listening to Art Blakey and the Jazz Messengers. In retrospect, I realize that I left Shirley Horn in the lurch, but at the time she was very supportive, treating me like a relative rather than as a sideman, and sending me off to do bigger and better things.

I stayed with Jimmy Smith for about three years at $175 a week. That was respectable money in those days; Herbie Hancock told me he made $300 a week with Miles Davis in the same era, and that was the top band. John Coltrane paid his sidemen somewhere between what Jimmy Smith and Miles Davis paid. We worked all the time, all over the States, and toured Europe and Japan. In those days, we would play the major American clubs for two weeks at a stretch. Going on the road with a name act was a big change. It was what I wanted, but the success came at a price.

One night, after a wildly successful gig in front of a packed house in Buffalo, I walked several miles through the dark to the hotel. I was thinking things over, and I burst into tears because I was so lonely and depressed. At that moment I realized that whatever brings you up will also bring you down.

The next morning I walked more of the town and practiced smiling at everybody. Most of the time, if you smile at somebody, they smile back. In the final analysis, it helps to approach each new event with optimism.

---

3   The Shadows was generally a folk club, but on January 20, 1964, the Jimmy Smith trio (with first-time drummer Billy Hart) was a last minute replacement for the ailing Josh White; folksinger Carolyn Hester was also on the bill.

Jimmy Smith, Quentin Warren, and Billy Hart in the 1964 movie Get Yourself a College Girl *starring Mary Ann Mobley, Nancy Sinatra, and Chad Everett. (Licensed by Warner Bros. Discovery. All Rights Reserved.)*

Jimmy was so popular that he was even featured in a few movies, for example *Get Yourself a College Girl*, also known as *The Swinging Set*.[4] Sometimes we merely pantomimed playing our instruments in front of the cameras, but in *Get Yourself a College Girl* we really played. In fact, the song in that movie, "Johnny Comes Marching Home," is something of a drum feature, I play a few breaks. When we were driving around the lot while making that movie, Burt Lancaster came over to greet us, all smiles, obviously happy to meet Jimmy Smith.

A lot of Jimmy Smith's famous records highlight the blues and have a very swinging shuffle feel. You could put them on your turntable at home and dance. It wasn't just Jimmy: In general, the organ musicians were offering a funky kind of sound, influenced by the blues pianists and Horace Silver, but transplanted to the organ.

While Jimmy started in that funky place, his playing evolved. Jimmy hung out with the great Bud Powell and learned something from Bud. In

---

4 The 1964 MGM film was a musical showcase, but all the other featured acts were white, including The Dave Clark Five, The Animals, and Stan Getz with Astrud Gilberto.

turn, John Coltrane played in Jimmy's first band with Charli Persip, and I believe Coltrane learned a few things from Jimmy Smith harmonically.

The first night, Jimmy started with a solo organ piece, and in that moment, I changed my attitude toward him as a musician. He wasn't just funky! What he was playing reminded me of Gil Evans, or someone with that kind of harmonic sophistication. It didn't sound like an organ, it sounded like an orchestra. This was exciting to me—I was a young cat, and all young cats want to play the most advanced music.

Right out of high school, I went to Howard University, where I studied mechanical engineering, because my father had studied mathematics there. The bassist Wilbur Little thought that was a mistake.

"Billy, you're a musician. Why are you going to college?"

"To have some security," I told Wilbur.

"What?" Wilbur shot back. "There *is* no such thing as security. You could walk out of here and be run down by a car."

Wilbur was probably right. At any rate, I didn't last long at Howard, but I did meet a few interesting people there, like Andrew White.

Andrew White had perfect pitch and had started writing advanced big band charts while still in high school. At Howard University at that time, you only played European classical music: If you were caught messing around with jazz improvisation, you could be expelled. Andrew majored in theory and minored in oboe and got straight As in every class. In the summer of his junior year, he was invited to Tanglewood where he spent time with Leonard Bernstein and Gunther Schuller. He took oboe and European classical music very seriously, but he was also a prodigy in jazz and played the hell out of the saxophone. Eventually Andrew even played bass for both Weather Report and Stevie Wonder.

After we met at Howard, Andrew White and I started working together on the most modern music we could, mainly imitating John Coltrane. In time, Andrew would be internationally known as one of our greatest authorities on Coltrane. He transcribed many Coltrane solos and built a successful business selling those transcriptions.[5] If you want to learn more about Andrew, his relationship to Coltrane, and his early years in D.C., read his book *Trane 'n Me*, which will explain something about his personality as well. Andrew was a very funny cat,

---

5   White's eight hundred and forty transcriptions, *The Works of John Coltrane – Volumes One Through Sixteen*, are housed at the Library of Congress along with his other literary works, compositions, and recordings. He died in 2020.

somewhat aggressive in terms of his sense of humor. He would goof off like a clown, then suddenly turn it around and be so serious that it could seem condescending. A lot of people didn't like him, because he was brilliant and didn't hide it. He laughed all the time, spoke with a southern drawl, and wore extreme high-water pants that showed about six inches of skin over the top of his shoes.

Andrew doesn't give me much credit in *Trane 'n Me*, but I remember helping Andrew found the JFK Quintet for a steady gig at Bohemian Caverns. This was another important D.C. club, run by an older Afro-American cat, Tony Taylor, who really understood the music, and a younger Italian American cat, Angelo Alvino, who didn't know as much but was very energetic. Either Taylor or Alvino thought that having a house band for the club with young cats would be a good idea. The JFK Quintet was given that name by the owners, and that band worked there a lot for a few years.

The pianist, Harry Killgo, was twenty years older than us, and mainly a hustler, who made his money from gambling. Harry told me, "The way you practice the drums is the way I used to practice shuffling cards." [6] There was a big gulf between Andrew and Harry, but Andrew taught Harry as much as he could. Ray Codrington, on trumpet, was an ear player, but very good; you can hear him on Eddie Harris's first recording of "Freedom Jazz Dance." [7] Our bassist ended up being Walter Booker, who was my choice. I knew Booker really well. He lived two blocks from me and was already married with two kids and going to med school. We would have our ups and downs over the years; I could fill this whole chapter with Walter Booker stories.

I was there just at the beginning, but because Andrew was such a prodigy, we could already play "Grand Central," "Giant Steps," and other hard Coltrane pieces. Joe Chambers was also in this mix. I helped Joe get some gigs when he showed up in D.C., and Joe ended up being the

---

6   Harry Killgo's son, drummer/vocalist Keith Killgo, would help Donald Byrd start The Blackbyrds in the 1970s and has led The Blackbyrds since 2012. The original '70s albums have been heavily sampled in hip-hop.

7   The first recording of "Freedom Jazz Dance" was on *The In Sound* (Atlantic, 1965), Eddie Harris with Ray Codrington, Cedar Walton, Ron Carter, and Billy Higgins. Carter then brought the chart to Miles Davis.

final drummer of the JFK quintet after Mickey Newman.[8] Like Jack DeJohnette, Joe Chambers played piano really well, to the point that some people considered both Jack and Joe pianists first and drummers second. I played several matinee trio sets at Bohemian Caverns with Joe Chambers on piano and Walter Booker on bass. That music emulated the harmonically advanced, conversational style of the Bill Evans Trio.

Back to joining Jimmy Smith. Rhythm and harmony go right together; you can't have one without the other, and they affect each other instantaneously. I expected that with Jimmy Smith my role was going to be fully subservient to the gig. Instead, Jimmy's advanced harmonic conception allowed me to keep experimenting with a modern sound, in the manner I had been trying to play with the JFK Quintet or the trio with Joe Chambers on piano. Recently, a few tapes have surfaced of my time with Jimmy, and I was already sort of playing like I play now, breaking up the time, playing cross-rhythms, and so forth. This must also go back to Donald Bailey, who had a conception related to Elvin Jones. I could keep in that direction with Jimmy Smith because Duck had paved the way.

To be clear, Jimmy was just about the only organist who let the drummers get away with this stuff. In most of the organ bands, you had to play more like you were in a pop group. One time the great organist Don Patterson came to hear us, and afterward he came up and asked me with a confused look on his face, "Does Jimmy *let* you play like that?"

Jimmy was a genius with incredible facility on the instrument. His playing was never dull, it was always fresh. The audience loved him. He didn't even need to give them variety. In a certain mood, Jimmy would play four tunes in a row in the same key, at the same tempo, each of them a blues. But the audience would get off on all four tunes.

Unlike most organists, Jimmy always played with two Leslie speakers, which is one reason he was bigger and louder than everybody else. That's probably why Jimmy didn't mind that I was into Tony Williams and Elvin Jones. It almost didn't matter what I did, because Jimmy was so loud.

In Detroit, I broke my third pair of sticks trying to play strong enough for Jimmy, so the next morning I got up early and found the nearest mom-and-pop drum shop. I complained to the owner, "I need

---

8   Carl "Mickey" Newman was the drummer on the JFK Quintet's two LPs for Riverside, 1961's *New Jazz Frontiers from Washington* (produced by Cannonball Adderley) and 1962's *Young Ideas*.

to learn how to play stronger. I'm not in control, and I'm breaking too many sticks."

I don't know who this guy was, but he really helped me that day. Of course, he was trying to sell me some of his inventory as well, and I bought the lot, including a practice pad on a stand and thick parade sticks to be used from a decent height away from the pad. He even sold me metal sticks, warning me that I shouldn't use them too much—and certainly not for speed—because I might get tendinitis.

I asked him what I was supposed to do with all this stuff, and he said, "You practice your rudiments, of course."

"What are rudiments?"

He looked at me strangely, and answered, "Well…like a paradiddle."

He played a paradiddle.

Now, I already knew the paradiddle, because I loved Max Roach, Philly Joe Jones, and Art Blakey, and had learned some of the basic rudiments by ear when trying to play some of their solos. But this was the cue to become more systematic in my studies. I would ask any drummer I met on the road about their favorite rudiments. At the next stop on the West Coast, Roy McCurdy showed me the ratamacue. In Texas, G.T. Hogan showed me a few hip rudiments that weren't even in the books.

Thus began a new chapter in my life, a new way of living, where I'd practice the rudiments for many hours each day, especially while on the road. I had started exercising, so I'd do twenty minutes of paradiddles, then do jumping jacks. Twenty minutes of ratamacues, then push-ups. I could spend the whole day practicing and working out! To save money on hotels, I'd go to the venue immediately after arriving in town and ask around if anyone had a spare room to put me up for a nominal amount. I met a lot of waitresses this way—I mean, a *lot* of waitresses. But the rule was this: Wherever I stayed, there needed to be a door, so I could go in, close that door, and practice.

On the road, I got to interact with more musicians, and some of the experiences could be unforgettable. I was fortunate enough to be in the presence of Jonathan "Papa Jo" Jones in San Francisco for four or five days when I was with Jimmy Smith. I couldn't believe it. I was terrified, and in awe, and excited, all at the same time. In fact, some of those nights I didn't want to see him, because the pressure of standing beside him was just too much.

After a few days of hanging out, Papa Jo actually sat in. The texture was perfect. Even if it seemed a little dated, it immediately got the point across. There was no rushing or dragging or playing too loud or too soft. It was relaxed and radiated self-confidence.

Being on the road with Jimmy Smith was mostly a great experience, but sometimes Jimmy was a bit of a loudmouth, or even downright rude. It could make me uncomfortable, and at times I felt really embarrassed—or worse. When we were on the airplane in first class coming home from Europe, they gave us a seven course meal. But Jimmy told the stewardess, "I don't like getting my food in pieces like this. I want all my food right now! If I don't get it now, I'm gonna blow this motherfucker up." As soon as we landed in Atlanta, the police took us off the plane.

There were also internal tensions in the band. Quentin had been with Jimmy longer than me, and by this point could be pretty disgruntled, especially with how Jimmy would bring in these loud background passages, like a shout chorus, when Quentin was trying to play a solo. The backgrounds were wonderful, but sometimes Quentin would just quit playing his solo when Jimmy brought them in.

Eventually Jimmy fired Quentin, and I recommended my D.C. friend Nathan Page. That's like mistake number 297 in the book or something, because Page immediately starts telling Jimmy about his boy, his favorite D.C. drummer, Bernard Sweetney, another friend of mine. Pretty soon after that, Sweetney calls me to say, "Man, I don't know what's happening, but Jimmy just called me for the gig?"

To this day I don't know why Jimmy fired me. Maybe, thanks to my practicing, I had gotten too confident in keeping up with his powerful sound.

Or possibly I was taking too many chances. After Jo Jones sat in for me, Jimmy looked at me like he smelled something, and said, "Man, that's the trouble with busy young drummers like you—you don't think far enough ahead of time."

I admit that my drum solos had gotten rather avant-garde. I was investigating the new players like Sunny Murray, Milford Graves, Rashied Ali, and Andrew Cyrille. Following their lead, I might take the sticks and throw them at the cymbals in a theatrical statement—although only when I was by myself, certainly not while Jimmy was playing.

Or perhaps Jimmy was simply jealous. While I never touched Jimmy's younger girlfriend, she liked to talk to me a lot, simply because we were close in age and knew the same current references.

I was so shocked when Sweetney called that I immediately got in my car and drove to Jimmy's mansion in Philadelphia. When I got there, Jimmy had a mean look in his eye. "I'm letting you go because it had gotten so weird that, as far as I'm concerned, it almost got physical," he told me. He was apparently so upset with me that he was ready to *fight*.

I had become a real drummer because of this cat. Much of my growth and maturation had come directly from playing with Jimmy Smith. That I had been working with a well-known star was less important than how my playing had evolved. So, not only was I shocked, I was really *hurt*.

There was also the simple matter of economics. Dolores and I were used to getting that $175 a week, and to top it off, our son Chris had just been born. In fact, I remember very well how happy and content I was being a new father, relaxing at home with Dolores and Chris, when Sweetney called with the bad news.

As it turned out, I went out almost immediately with another top band, led by guitarist Wes Montgomery. I was home moping around only for about six weeks between Jimmy and Wes.

San Francisco in the mid-1960s, after Billy got his practice pad

4

Lessons from Wes

It was a sign of changing times that both of the name bands I first started touring with did not have conventional acoustic bass. Jimmy Smith used his left hand and some pedal on the organ, while Monk Montgomery played electric bass.[1] Monk was comical and philosophical in outlook, and liked to talk about playing with Lionel Hampton on a barge floating on the Potomac. Hampton paid him a little extra to jump the rail and dive into the water during the hook of "Flying Home." Monk did that at least twice in a row, and the audience went absolutely wild.[2]

Monk and the pianist Buddy Montgomery had met me on tour with Jimmy Smith, and Monk was the one to tell Wes to call me. That was the band: Wes and his two brothers, Alvern Bunn on percussion, and me.

Wes immediately approached me with some restrictions. The first time I met him, he said, "I want you to ride with me in my car."

On the way to the gig he looked me in the eye and said, "I haven't played any single-line stuff for a few years. I'm just letting you know now in case you can't handle it."

Some of these dynamics are subtle and hard to explain unless you are there living it.

To begin with, Wes was not going to be digging in and playing single-line bebop, not the way we know from that classic album with Wynton Kelly, Paul Chambers, and Jimmy Cobb, *Smokin' at the Half Note*. That LP is definitely American classical music, and that was the last of Wes's albums in that idiom. Now, Wes hadn't sold out, that would be putting it too strongly, but he *had* moved up in the industry and was

---

[1] Monk Montgomery is generally credited as the first musician to specialize and record on the Fender electric bass (on *The Art Farmer Septet*, arranged by Quincy Jones and recorded for Prestige in 1953).

[2] Milt Hinton recounts the story of Monk Montgomery jumping into the Potomac in *Bass Line: The Stories and Photographs of Milt Hinton* (as told to David Berger, 1992).

enjoying a higher class of status. Hell, he grew up working at a milk company in Indianapolis—Freddie Hubbard used to see Wes on the milk route in the early morning—and trying to practice at night. He was entitled to take it easy.

There's a certain tradition of how the music business relates to the social situation of Afro-Americans versus Caucasians in this country. Many times, the innovators are Afro-American. For years, the Caucasians heard the innovation, took it for themselves, and repackaged it with white performers for a white audience to make incredible sums of money. (This is one reason I get irritated when somebody says I'm playing a Steve Gadd beat when the real story is that I learned it from Donald Bailey.) In the '60s, for the first time, there was some change in that process. Jimmy Smith's manager was an Afro-American, Clarence Avant. Avant went on to do a lot of things in the industry: one time I saw him on TV talking comfortably with Bill Clinton. Avant was tight with Quincy Jones, someone else who opened a lot of doors.[3]

Buddy Montgomery was a truly great musician, really just as great, if not greater, than his more famous brother. On one of my earliest gigs with Wes, Buddy came over to me and told me, "Some white lady in the audience said, 'Isn't it wonderful? I understand that Wes Montgomery can't read a note of music.'"

In other words, if the black musicians are characterized as primitives with inborn native talent, it can help sell the music. The white lady in the audience can say, "Isn't that wonderful?"

That's part of the point I'm trying to explain. At that time, you couldn't make any money packaging the Afro-American innovators as intellectuals, but you could make money if you played the game. Clarence Avant was the one to take Jimmy Smith away from Blue Note and over to Verve where he was offered an amazing amount of money.[4]

Creed Taylor was the mastermind. After working at Impulse!, Creed went to Verve and then A&M. He first took Jimmy Smith and then Wes Montgomery and treated them exactly the same way, putting them with

---

[3] Avant (1931-2023) started out as bluesman Little Willie John's road manager before managing Jimmy Smith, Lalo Schifrin, Creed Taylor, and Barbra Streisand. He was an early promoter of Bill Withers through his own Sussex Records and later became chairman of Motown.

[4] Jimmy Smith's new contract with Verve was covered by both *DownBeat* and *The Chicago Daily Defender*. From the March 6,1963 issue of the *Chicago Defender*: "Jimmy Smith to get $200,000 for 9 Verve LPs over 3 years, the highest guarantee any jazz artist has been promised by a record company."

arrangers, big bands, and string sections. (Jimmy and Wes even made some records together.[5]) They would have the same kind of production that a vocalist like Frank Sinatra would have, with arrangements from top people like Oliver Nelson, Don Sebesky, and Claus Ogerman. Eventually, Creed's own label CTI would be the final stage in that process.

Since Jimmy and Wes were being packaged for public consumption, I'm not on too many of their records, even though I was in the touring bands. Creed Taylor liked studio musicians to support his stars.[6] Good studio musicians make a lot of records and can supply whatever is needed in a commercial situation. On those Creed-produced Jimmy and Wes records, the studio drummers were either another mentor of mine, Grady Tate, or Ed Shaughnessy, who soon moved to the other coast and became famous in Johnny Carson's *Tonight Show* band.[7]

On Jimmy Smith's first album for Verve, the big hit was "Walk on the Wild Side," where there's more than two minutes of music before you hear Jimmy Smith play, and then it's Jimmy's most standard repertoire of his bluesiest licks. On Wes Montgomery's biggest hit for A&M, "Going Out of My Head," Wes just plays the melody in octaves, and doesn't even improvise. There's absolutely no single line bebop.

These hits are effective in their own way, but when I talk about Jimmy Smith and Wes Montgomery being geniuses—which they were—I can't show you what I mean by playing you most of their Verve or A&M records.

All this was happening at a time of intellectual and political ferment in the black community. At Howard University I met a few people who were involved in politics, especially Jean Wheeler (whose married name

---

5 *Jimmy & Wes: The Dynamic Duo* and *Further Adventures of Jimmy and Wes* were the product of the same 1966 session produced by Creed Taylor for Verve.

6 The only Creed Taylor-produced album with Billy Hart is Jimmy Smith *Christmas '64*, which has Hart on three of eight tracks. Several Jimmy Smith and Wes Montgomery albums have come out in recent decades with Hart, usually live, but not all discographical information can be trusted. Hart is not on Montgomery's *Live at Jorgies* (the drummer is unknown) or Jimmy Smith *Live at the Village Gate* (the drummer is definitely Donald Bailey). Concert video exists of both Jimmy Smith and Wes Mongomery with Hart.

7 The first black studio drummer may have been Osie Johnson, also from Washington D.C., who recorded innumerable sessions in the 1950's before dying of kidney failure at age 43.

became Smith) and Stokely Carmichael.[8] Jean left Howard to follow Martin Luther King Jr., wrote several important articles on civil rights, including at least one for *Redbook*, and went on a hunger strike while incarcerated. Stokely took me to see Malcolm X speak at Howard.[9] I kept in touch with Stokely; one night in Atlanta we had dinner and went to see a Ray Charles concert, and he drove me back to the hotel. The next day the papers read, *Activist Stokely Carmichael Has Ended Up in Cuba*. He must have gone *straight* to the airport after the hang.

When I talk about jazz as "American classical music," it's a reflection of those civil rights years. It seemed like the establishment was saving the word "classical" for white people, but I believe what John Coltrane told an interviewer in Japan: "The term 'classical music' means the music of the composers and musicians of the country, more or less, as opposed to the music that people dance or sing along with, the popular music. …There are different types of classical music all over the world."[10]

Of course, Coltrane's music had become supremely advanced technically and harmonically in the '60s. But it wasn't just the classical music: some of the dance and pop side of contemporary black music also reflected political concerns. Many people in my social circle were reading Malcolm X and trying to change the world.

But not Jimmy or Wes. They were making serious money participating in the game.

All of that is in the background when Wes says to me, "I haven't played any single-line stuff for a few years. I'm just letting you know now in case you can't handle it."

I could handle it, all right—I wanted the gig, and all three Montgomery brothers were excellent musicians. But the gig *did* come with restrictions.

I loved my ride cymbal. All drummers love their ride cymbal! But after a set at Lennie's-On-The-Turnpike in Massachusetts, Wes came up to me and said, "I don't like your cymbal."

---

8   Carmichael graduated from Howard in 1964 and became a leading organizer for the Student Nonviolent Coordinating Committee (SNCC). In a 1966 speech, he introduced the phrase "Black power" to the American lexicon, and adopted the name Kwame Ture after relocating to Africa in 1968. Wheeler, a Detroit native, left Howard to assist SNCC's voter registration drive in Mississippi at a time when civil rights activists there were being murdered. Wheeler survived and became a pediatric psychiatrist and author.

9   On October 30, 1961, Malcolm X debated civil rights activist and integrationist leader Bayard Rustin at Howard University's Cramton Auditorium.

10 Interview with Kazuaki Tsujimoto in Tokyo on July 9, 1966, collected in *Coltrane on Coltrane: The John Coltrane Interviews*, edited by Chris DeVito.

I thought, *uh-oh*. All I could think to say was, "Wes, just because you don't like my cymbal doesn't mean I can afford to go out and buy another one."

So, he went in his pocket, handed me some money, and said, "Man, go buy a cymbal."

At that, Wes had picked the right place to have me look for a cymbal—just down the road from the club was the Zildjian factory. I went through and played all sorts of cymbals for three hours, but the one I liked was a dirty one in the corner, neglected and laying on the floor. It sounded darker to me, and I liked that. They let me walk out of there with the cymbal for free if I became a Zildjian artist, and I've been with them ever since.[11]

Wes seemed to be satisfied. The new cymbal was brighter than the one I had before, but it was as though he thought he could just tell me what to do and I would do it. He had a bunch of children, and he treated me like I was one of his kids, offering advice on how to be a family man and so on.

I never really fit in with the band of brothers. After a gig, they went back to their hotel and played cards together—bridge, tonk, and poker—and I just didn't care about playing cards. In addition, everyone in the band had to wear uniform clothes. We all got fitted for three suits (dark blue pinstripe, light blue, gray pinstripe) and two tuxedos (black and gray). There were ties to match. One time I actually got fined for wearing the wrong tie with that night's suit.

On another occasion, Wes ran into me on the street when I was wearing full regalia: a bush jacket, black corduroy patches on the arm (mourning for Malcolm X), and moccasins up to my knees. I could see in Wes's eyes that he was appalled that I might be a revolutionary activist when I wasn't in uniform on the gig.

There was also a hand drummer, Alvern Bunn. That was a distraction, of course, because in that situation a hand drummer is just another set of handcuffs for the main drummer. I had to go to Alvern, not the other way around. But it was also a wonderful opportunity, because I learned about Afro-Cuban music from Alvern.

My lifelong interest in learning something about the history of this music started with the stories told to me by pianist John Malachi, who gave me a few gigs in D.C. when I was still just a teenager. (Geri Allen

---

11 The first Zildjian ad in *DownBeat* to include Billy Hart ran in September 1967.

studied with Malachi, and eventually paid tribute with a beautiful composition, "For John Malachi.") Malachi was in the legendary 1940s Billy Eckstine big band with Charlie Parker, Dizzy Gillespie, Dexter Gordon, Gene Ammons, Miles Davis, and others. Malachi told me straight out, "Charlie Parker didn't play no motherfucking changes!" Malachi also said that Gillespie got the name "Dizzy" partly because of the way he wanted to sit underneath Art Blakey's 24-inch China cymbal in the Eckstine band. According to Malachi, Dizzy would tell Blakey, "Hit that cymbal as hard as you can!"

Dizzy was also a competent percussionist with claves or conga, and he acquired some of that knowledge from an indisputable source, the Cuban émigré Chano Pozo. Later on, Art Blakey's Jazz Messengers would play Gillespie's "A Night in Tunisia" every night on tour for decades, and frequently the members of the band would also play percussion instruments. I especially loved the edition of the Messengers with Lee Morgan and Wayne Shorter, and my favorite Blakey album remains *A Night in Tunisia*, with both horn players taking a cadenza at the end of the title track. Blakey would play his same "Night in Tunisia" introduction for 40 years, and I'm glad he did. That drum solo was a masterpiece.

I could relate to Alvern Bunn in the Montgomery band because I loved Blakey and "A Night in Tunisia." Alvern was from the Bronx, where many of the American Afro-Cuban drummers come from, and he taught me a lot, telling me names like the great Mario Bauza, who was the link in the big band era through Chick Webb and Gillespie. While I might have heard the word "clave" before, I didn't really know what it meant. Through Alvern I finally learned the son clave and the rumba clave, and together we listened to *Puente in Percussion*, the Tito Puente album with Mongo Santamaria, Willie Bobo, and Carlos "Patato" Valdes. Alvern called that LP "The Percussionist's Bible."

After a year or so of being on the road together, Wes started complaining again, saying to me, "Billy, what's that you're doin' with your cymbal?"

And I said, "I don't know what you're talking about, Wes."

"You know what I'm talking about."

"Wes, I don't know what the fuck you're talking about."

"OK, Billy, let me put it this way: The shit ain't laying."

Now, how do you put that in words that mean something? "It's not perfectly in sync?" Or, "It's not causing the kind of euphoria that we refer to as swinging?" Well, anyway, the way he put it was: "The shit ain't laying."

He went on to complain about my left hand on the snare, and then about the bass drum. His favorite drummer was Jimmy Cobb, and Jimmy had that perfectly clear cymbal beat. In the studio, Wes used Grady Tate, someone who was an ideal reader and accompanist. Wes was trying to make me be like Jimmy Cobb and Grady Tate. And I guess I have to thank Wes, because I did get it together. It taught me a lot, being disciplined on that level.

It was a valuable lesson, but it wasn't what I wanted to do. I was listening to John Coltrane and Miles Davis and even Ornette Coleman and Cecil Taylor. In the Bay Area, Tony Williams and I had become friendly. Miles Davis was in town at another club, so that's when Tony and I could talk a little bit. On his day off, Tony would come and watch me play conservative sets with the Montgomery Brothers, and then I'd go and watch him play incredibly advanced and creative music with Miles. That didn't help my situation in terms of how I felt about playing with Wes.

I had made up my mind that I would quit and told the guys in the band—though not Wes—that this would be my last tour. A few days later, when I'm standing outside during the intermission, Wes comes out and says, "You know, Billy, you really sound good."

I wasn't gracious or grateful, and replied in a rather grouchy fashion: "Well, Wes, I'm just trying to keep a gig."

"Well, I tell you what, man, you got it," Wes said. "You got this gig." He put me on salary, so I got paid whether I worked or not. I was already making a bit more than I had with Jimmy, and the salary raised the weekly rate to $350. That really meant something to me as a family man, so I stayed around. I might have submitted to Wes and been his Jimmy Cobb and Grady Tate *forever* with that kind of offer on the table.

As it turned out, I was only with Wes for about two years. The last performance was in some big theater in Arizona on a double bill with the Mamas and the Papas. For the first time since I had been in the band, Wes was late for the gig. Then, as we were packing up afterwards, Wes said, "Man, this is the best the band has ever sounded." This was also a first—he *never* praised us like that after a performance.

That was on a Wednesday. I got the call in New York from Harold Mabern on Saturday, June 15, 1968. He said, "Hey, yeah man, it's Harold. Is it true?"

I said, "Is *what* true?"

Harold said, "I just heard on the radio that Wes died of a heart attack." He was only 45 years old.

A little later Creed Taylor called and told me, "The family wants you to be a pallbearer, so we're prepared to fly you out to Indianapolis."

The headline of the *Indianapolis Star* read *2,400 Pay Last Respects to Wes Montgomery,* with a sidebar that noted, "Quintet Members are Pallbearers."

Billy Hart can be seen in front as a pallbearer. This photo ran in the Indianapolis Star. (© James Ramsey USA TODAY NETWORK via Imagn Images.)

5

New York, New York

Whatever people do, the top version exists in New York City—especially when it comes to jazz. During the Wes Montgomery years, Dolores had found a place for us in Long Island. After Wes passed so suddenly, it was time to go out, to try to meet people, to become part of the scene. Walter Booker helped me a lot, and two established drummers playing with Booker, Mickey Roker and Billy Higgins, started recommending me to others. Billy Cobham, who was already active in the studios and with some good bands, also sent me some gigs. Cobham and I had such a good time analyzing Tony Williams and Elvin Jones together when hanging out at Cobham's Manhattan pad.

Both Howard McGhee and Sam Rivers had rehearsal big bands. Jimmy Heath, Hank Mobley, and Cedar Walton were active with smaller groups. This was an elite caliber of musician! I saw the people in that scene frequently performing "On the Trail" by Ferde Grofé, a standard that helped define that late-60s NYC era of serious music. Back in D.C., all the piano players I looked up to played Red Garland's intro to "Bye Bye Blackbird." In New York a decade later, they played "On the Trail."[1]

It could be a little rough. A few times, as I was leaving to go to a gig, my battery was gone, stolen straight out of the car. And while this didn't happen to me, I heard about drummers who opened their cases to find no drums. The professional thieves would steal the drums, but leave the cases, so the victim would drive away from the scene none the wiser

---

1 In June of 1968, Billy Hart played at the Left Bank Jazz Society in Baltimore with Art Farmer, Jimmy Heath, Cedar Walton, and Walter Booker. The repertoire probably included "On the Trail," something that Jimmy Heath played on most of his gigs since his 1964 album *On the Trail*. In *I Walked with Giants: The Autobiography of Jimmy Heath*, Heath explains that this distinctive arrangement was from Donald Byrd. "Donald arranged the tune by placing another song, "Pavanne," as a counter-melody behind it….My recording of "On the Trail" was released before Donald's, so I was given credit for the arrangement. The tune was Ferde Grofé's from the *Grand Canyon Suite*, an American classic."

until a terrible moment of truth. Whatever people do, the top version exists in New York City.

Musically, it could be rough too. Sonny Rollins asked me to play with him at the Village Vanguard. After two nights, his manager called and fired me. I was never as frightened, disappointed, or dismayed as when Sonny decided to make a change in his band mid-week at the Vanguard. He did try to hire me again a few times over the years, but I never felt able to accept the gig, remembering that bad week at the Vanguard.

I tried out with Milt Jackson just after the Sonny Rollins debacle. I thought I knew Milt Jackson because I had the Modern Jazz Quartet records. How was I to know that he often disagreed conceptually with John Lewis and the delicate aesthetic of the MJQ? I tried to play like I would have played with the MJQ, and luckily word got back to me that Milt said: "Billy Hart! I never heard such a drummer that didn't play nothin'. I thought the motherfucker was *dead*."

Between Sonny Rollins and Milt Jackson, it dawned on me that these great New York musicians wanted more from a drummer than subservience. They definitely wanted your opinion. Wes Montgomery had taught me to be subservient almost too well!

For a short time I was in Eddie Harris's band, with Jodie Christian on piano and Melvin Jackson on bass, but that was more of the same, almost a step backwards for me. Eddie was trying to bring a controlled pop style into modern jazz, along the lines of Wes Montgomery, Herbie Mann, and Ramsey Lewis. He was one of the great saxophonists, but he had become intrigued with amplifying his saxophone and looking for a commercial hit.

Melvin Jackson is not a very famous bass player, but for some reason a huge photo of Melvin—really more like a mural—used to grace the entryway of Fasching, a top jazz club in Stockholm. Melvin made only one album, *Funky Skull*, where you can hear me playing in a true pop style, as if I was back at The Spa doing 40 on and 20 off for the dancers. (For the jazz historians, that LP is also a rare example of Chicago avant-gardists like Roscoe Mitchell, Lester Bowie, and Leo Smith on a commercial dance project.) From the records with Eddie Harris, "Movin' On Out" on *High Voltage* gives a sense of his working quartet, where the band plays in support of electronic effects from Eddie's Varitone saxophone.

I didn't need more of that kind of thing. What I really needed was Pharoah Sanders. For a time I was with both Eddie Harris and Pharoah

Sanders, but I quit Eddie when Pharoah had a record date that conflicted with one of Eddie's tours. Eddie was doing pretty well with his career at that point. He asked me, "Man, you're gonna quit me now when I'm at the top of my game?" But I wanted to play with Pharoah more than I did with Eddie. There wasn't a serious contest.

Part of my attraction to Pharoah Sanders was his connection to John Coltrane. Pharoah had been John's choice for a second horn, and Pharoah's own music had continued in the Coltrane line. When I first started learning about this music, my favorite tenor saxophonists were inspired by Charlie Parker. Johnny Griffin played bluesy and fast; then I was impressed by Sonny Rollins. Soon enough, John Coltrane captured me during his solo on "All of You" from Miles Davis's *'Round About Midnight*. I've talked to Gary Bartz about this, and he felt the same way: "All of You" made us John Coltrane fans forevermore.

When I first saw John live, it was through the fan blades at the Spotlite room with Miles. John was back from being with Thelonious Monk, doing that "sheets of sound," or whatever they called it. I watched it happen. John would use a lot of notes, and a lot of what he played came straight from Charlie Parker, but he also always sounded like a romantic singer—a pure rhapsody—and of course he never stopped playing the blues.

I love John Coltrane. At this point, I can honestly say that John is my reason. The church is just a building, but that feeling inside a Black church goes back thousands of years. Coltrane—no matter how avant-garde his late music became—"done get you in touch with *that*." A single note from Coltrane shows you he's in command of a universal, spiritual, and philosophical message.[2]

I was waiting for John to form his own band, but Elvin Jones was a surprise. Bassist Wilbur Little had toured with Jones in the J.J. Johnson group in the late '50s, and laughingly reported back that J.J. Johnson said about Elvin, "Man, this is either the greatest drummer or the worst drummer I've ever played with."

At first, this music was for dancing. In the Afro-American community, dancing is *very* important. I danced throughout high school, when we called our get-togethers at our homes "the rub," as in, "Where's the rub

---

[2] Coltrane's grandfathers William W. Blair and William H. Coltrane were both African Methodist Episcopal ministers in North Carolina. His mother Alice attended Livingstone College, affiliated with the AME Zion church, and played piano accompaniment for Reverend Blair's services.

tonight?" There's a wonderful photo of Lee Morgan and Bobby Timmons dancing together on the LP jacket to *The Young Lions*. Herbie Hancock isn't that young anymore, but I'm sure if you put on a record of Stevie Wonder or some such today, Herbie would immediately get up and move his body in a certain way.

In dance music, the drums basically have to keep a beat. However, after the so-called bebop revolution, drummers were looking to contribute to the ensemble in a contrapuntal fashion. It could be hard to do this with most leaders, who wanted their drummers to keep steady time. Kenny Clarke said that he could tell simply by the leader's expression mid-set if he was going to be able to leave his drums at the gig for the next night, or have to pack them up and go home.

When John Coltrane got Elvin Jones in his band, that was it. The drums were now free. Some of his intensity was surely inspired by Art Blakey. In *Trane 'n Me*, Andrew White argues that John simply could not have got to where he wanted to get to without Jones:

> Trane was structuring his music around Elvin. This was the main source of the symmetry in Trane's music... Breath is life. The music must breathe. Elvin was the breath in Trane's music. ...It was the manipulation of standard devices that established Coltrane as a thorough improvisor as well as a spontaneous creator, but it was the Elvin Jones grammar that brought these elements into clear focus.[3]

Seeing Elvin Jones play with John Coltrane was indescribable. I went every night for a week at the Bohemian Caverns. At the end of the final night, I was looking at Jones taking his drums down. I couldn't move, like I was stuck in cement. I was just watching him. So finally Jones called me up to the drums, and he gave me his bass drum pedal, which had broken. Jones looked me up and down and said, "Don't ask me to show you anything, because if I could show you, we would all be Max Roach."

When Jones told me that, it really made an impression. He was letting me know that despite being one of the most innovative drummers the world had ever known, he saw himself as a representative of a tradition.

I got nervous one matinee at the Bohemian Caverns, because Jones was really late. Was I gonna have to sit in? I went to the bathroom to hide, but I had to pass Coltrane to get over there. I tried to sneak by,

---

3 From *Trane 'n Me: A Semi-autobiography: a Treatise on the Music of John Coltrane* by Andrew White, Andrew's Musical Enterprises, 1981

but Coltrane grabbed my arm and made me stop. "Aren't you going to talk to me?"

I said, "What are you going to do about Jones being so late?"

John replied, "I'm not going to do anything, because I don't want to hurt myself."

At that time I was listening to the album *Coltrane*, with "Out of This World" and "Tunji," two tracks that heavily featured Jones's style. When I asked John about the drumming on those tunes, John told me, "Sure, Elvin worked on his style. But the thing that impressed me the most when I first heard Elvin was his professionalism."

When I looked surprised, John continued, "I noticed the way he could dot the i's and cross the t's."

John didn't say anything about polyrhythms, innovation or intensity. John talked about the tradition.

John also said, "No matter how tense the situation gets, Elvin never tightens up." That was good advice. I have tried to keep that in mind in more chaotic musical settings.

McCoy Tyner was also so impressive. At some point I realized one of the reasons I was going to see the Coltrane quartet was the pleasure of watching McCoy catch up. Not just technically—McCoy always had an immense technical facility—but harmonically. I could see how the band was growing through listening to the piano.

The bass chair evolved in the famous quartet. I first saw them with both Art Davis and Reggie Workman together. Later it was the great Jimmy Garrison, who I had seen in a trio with Bill Evans and Paul Motian. The fact that Garrison had played with both Bill Evans *and* Ornette Coleman suggests some of the qualities Garrison brought to that group. *Everyone* in the band could "dot the i's and cross the t's."

Some people left John Coltrane at *Giant Steps*; other people left him at *A Love Supreme*. Certainly many people left him at *Meditations*. But I hung in there all the way to the end. I loved the last band with Alice Coltrane and Rashied Ali, and "Expression," from the very last session, is one of my favorite ballads.

Later, in L.A. at the It Club, Coltrane sat with me a minute after his set. A lot of people were walking out in disgust, musicians and non-musicians alike. He walked straight to my table and sat down. I said, "John, what are you going to do with everyone leaving during the set?"

"I don't know what I'm going to do," he said. "I just know that I can't stop."

The whole room turned technicolor, like John was a legendary hero in a romantic setting. I told him, "John, you are really beautiful."

John shrugged and said, "I'm just trying to clean up. Imagine if you were dirty for 30 years."

I didn't get to play with John, although he asked me to when he came to Washington one time and was looking for two drummers. I couldn't believe it! He called me at home and asked me if I had my drums. But at that moment, not only did I think I wasn't ready to play with John, I was just back from Japan and actually didn't have them. I also thought I was going to get another chance, because I didn't expect him to die. That was one of those incredible losses of that era: John F. Kennedy, Malcolm X, Martin Luther King Jr., John Coltrane. At one time, I was ready to consider John's passing as part of a conspiracy, where the establishment worked behind the scenes to keep extinguishing the brightest lights. (Once, when we were in the car with Shirley Horn, comedian Dick Gregory told me that he knew the names of the two secret service men who shot John Fitzgerald Kennedy.)

So I missed my chance with John Coltrane, but I did work with Pharoah Sanders. Pianist Lonnie Liston Smith called me to play at Slugs' Saloon in the East Village in Pharoah's band, with bassist Bob Cunningham and vocalist Leon Thomas. For a few years, Slugs' was an important club, a lowbrow joint that was also part of the youth movement. Broadway people and fashion models mingled with college students and the jazz cognoscenti; there was sawdust on the floor, a big hole in the stage, and the club owners and the musicians who played there all chased the same models—or waitresses—and smoked the same pot. Eventually, Lee Morgan was shot and killed at Slugs'.

After setting up my drums—being careful to avoid the hole—I went to look for Pharoah. The club was packed, but I had never met Pharoah before and had no idea what we were going to play. Pharoah looked at me and shook my hand but didn't say anything else. We stood next to each other in silence until the crowd got really restless; they even started slow-clapping in unison in order to encourage the start of the music. Finally, Pharoah turned to me and said, "OK, Billy. You got it."

Well. Trial by fire. I went up there, and started something that could have been an introduction, but nobody came in. I kept playing, like some uptempo time, a few choruses of rhythm changes or something. Still nobody came in. So then I just went for it, playing all out, thinking, "I may lose the gig, but tonight's gig will belong to *me*." Finally, the band comes up on the bandstand and starts playing off whatever I had been playing. And that was my beginning of learning and experiencing how to play *multidirectional*.

Rashied Ali told me that "multidirectional" was what John Coltrane called this freeform feel, where conventional structure was abandoned and the rhythms could cut in any direction. "It's like you're playing fast Latin," Rashied said, and it's certainly true that Rashied, Milford Graves, and Andrew Cyrille had some Afro-Cuban heritage in their conception.

I first heard about this approach from a fellow Howard student, the great saxophonist and composer Marion Brown. He had gone to New York and gotten hooked up with the avant-garde. When Marion came back to campus, he was dressed differently, in a strange colored jacket, and told me, "You know, Billy, I know you're into Tony and Elvin and

such, but in New York, it's some different shit going on. There's a cat named Sunny Murray you need to check out."

That was the next step, the newest music. I bought the records and heard Sunny Murray, Milford Graves, Rashied Ali, and Andrew Cyrille. Sunny gets the credit for inventing the style, although he could also be kind of loud and out of order behind the kit. Rashied was the Lester Young or Philly Joe Jones of that vibe, he held it down with John Coltrane. In the early days, Milford Graves was my favorite. I was entranced by Milford's imagination. Andrew is my friend, and to this very day I am inspired by and learning from the great Andrew Cyrille.

All these multidirectional masters were like magic; they conjured up spirits and ghosts and rainbows. They could give you visions like a psychedelic drug.

That night at Slugs' with Pharoah Sanders was the first time I attempted to play multidirectional myself. It just exploded out of me when they left me onstage alone for so long, and then the band exploded around me.

Not all of Pharoah's repertoire was multidirectional. He always played Tadd Dameron's "On a Misty Night," a serious swinger that Coltrane had recorded with Dameron, where I could show what I learned from Shirley Horn. And then there were the vamp pieces related to Coltrane's *A Love Supreme*. The big hit by Pharoah Sanders and Leon Thomas, "The Creator Has a Master Plan," comes straight from the "Acknowledgement" section of *A Love Supreme*. Elvin Jones plays with the "Acknowledgement" bass line in three distinct ways; I learned them all, and you can hear me emulating all three of Elvin's approaches on that famous recording of "The Creator has a Master Plan," which we tracked for the album *Karma* in February 1969, a week after that first gig at Slugs'.

There really was a collision of worlds in New York in this era. One world was the tradition: "On a Misty Night" and "On the Trail," the line of Charlie Parker, what I call American classical music. Then there were the avant-gardists, the people who believed in multidirectional. A lot of the time, multidirectional music had an overtly spiritual cast. The second night at Slugs', the self-discovery guide *The Impersonal Life* was waiting for me on my low tom, where Pharoah had left it as a gift. I still have that book today.[4]

---

4   *The Impersonal Life* was first published anonymously in 1914; only recently was it revealed that the author was American mystic Joseph S. Benner.

And then there was straight-eighth music, which had come to totally dominate pop.

I believe the straight-eighth style in contemporary music stems from what Charlie Parker, Dizzy Gillespie, and Max Roach took from people like Chano Pozo, Mario Bauza, Tito Puente, and Machito. Their music in the '40s brought the Afro-Cuban clave straight into the forefront, especially in Gillespie's work featuring Chano Pozo, in pieces like "Manteca."[5]

The backbeat had been there, aligned with the shuffle, in a system with triplets. In jazz history books, they write that first there was the swing era, then there was the bebop era. But in between those eras was rhythm and blues, which at that time had a pronounced shuffle rhythm. All the records my parents listened to and danced to, whether it was Jimmie Lunceford or Louis Jordan, had a ternary shuffle. That music highlighted the triplet.

The shuffle is different from jazz swing. As a kid, I listened to Art Blakey play his shuffle on "Moanin'," "Blues March," and other Jazz Messenger hits, and that's how I play a shuffle to this day: like Art Blakey. But there were other, older, and maybe more advanced ways to play the shuffle, even earlier than the Chicago cats heard on the Chess records. One legend suggests that Phineas Newborn's father, Phineas Newborn Sr., was one of the best at the original blues shuffle. Newborn had a bicycle seat for a drum throne and would move his whole body back and forth when he played.

Not everybody can play a shuffle. Only certain people can do it. Count Basie's drummer Sonny Payne could do it, and he probably got it from his father, Chris Colombo, who some people think was one of the first true shuffle drummers.

Again, if you only know the bebop and modern jazz records from the late '40s and early '50s, you don't realize how omnipresent rhythm

---

5 Billy Hart accompanied Dizzy Gillespie, Stan Getz and many other Americans to the 1977 US-Cuban musical exchange in Havana. This 1977 concert was a historic act of diplomacy, the first of its kind after Fidel Castro took power in 1961, approved by President Jimmy Carter and covered by *The New York Times*, *The Washington Post*, *The Los Angeles Times*, and *Newsday*. Hart played with drummers in the Chano Pozo lineage like Oscar Valdés and the members of Los Papines, and commented to Ira Sabin of *Radio Free Jazz*, "It was beautiful. It gave us a chance to see some drummers that are traditionally known as the master drummers, not only among drummers, but, as their fame has spread through Dizzy Gillespie, to all jazz musicians. Now, hopefully, through this concert the political relationship between our two countries will again be able to grow, to enrich this tremendously musical legacy and treasure. I felt like a student playing with them."

and blues was at that time. All sorts of jazz greats played shuffles for dancing and drinking. So when Art Blakey started playing those fabulous shuffles with the Jazz Messengers in the late '50s, it wasn't new—it was just new in the context of this modern jazz band. In that way, you could say Art Blakey was one of the first fusion drummers. His shuffle on "Moanin'" was an appropriation of dance music, just like Tony Willams's appropriation of even-eighths a decade later.

Even-eighths is not just even notes like European classical music. Enter the clave. The clave is not totally binary: the syncopations in the clave imply the ternary as well, which allows the texture of the best straight-eighth music to still radiate the kind of dance-worthy ecstasy we associate with swing. When you listen to Ray Charles's huge hit "What'd I Say," it's in straight eighths, but it's also related to the clave. In fact, the drummer, Milt Turner, is playing something like the Afro-Cuban bolero.

The bass line is a key element when assessing this topic. What the bass player plays in "What'd I Say" is not far from Dizzy Gillespie and Chano Pozo's "Manteca" a decade before. In a beautiful video, Dizzy Gillespie explains how "Manteca" was the first time the bass didn't play a straight four beats to the bar in jazz.[6]

I've been telling my students that straight-eighth music comes from bebop for a few years now. It's always confusing to them at first, because nobody else makes this claim. But I'm just trying to get the events in the right order and give credit where it's due. In the late '40s, black musicians diverged into two camps. Those who wanted to keep steadily working went into rhythm and blues, which begat so-called rock and roll. Those who wanted to be creative individualists went into bebop—or, as I like to call it, American classical music. Everyone knew the same information, harmonically and otherwise—dig how many sax solos on late '40s and early '50s rhythm and blues records sound like Charlie Parker—but one side wanted the joint to keep jumping and the other side wanted the audience to sit down and listen.

Rhythm and blues was always there, but the Afro-Cuban information from Chano Pozo and Machito and promoted by Dizzy Gillespie and Charlie Parker caused rhythm and blues to go from ternary to binary. At first, rhythm and blues was ternary, and it was the clave—along with other associated patterns like the cascara and the bolero—that allowed the music to go binary.

---

6   *The Legacy of Chano Pozo*, directed by Ileana Rodríguez Pelegrín (Efor Films, 2006).

In the end, the word "clave" covers a lot of important territory. The Spanish word means "key," and in music it is almost like the key to life. The heritage of the clave goes back thousands of years. Certainly it goes back to Africa; it also has religious and incantatory associations. Part of the problem with some binary music is an overwhelming emphasis on the backbeat. Even the backbeat is related to the clave, but the backbeat seems pretty simple compared to something as vast as God!

As far as I'm concerned, "clave" is another word for God. It's always been here, and it'll always be here.

It's really up to the drummer to find a way to navigate these waters. In the '60s, many great drummers from my generation and earlier resisted the straight backbeat in the binary system. That was part of what groups like The Beatles meant to us: no swing, and no clave either. They called it "rock drumming," and of course anything that popular would develop its subtleties. Two of the best were Earl Palmer and Idris Muhammad—not that the general public knows their names as well as so many of their white contemporaries. It is unfortunate that the reputation of such musicians as Ringo Starr, John Bonham, Ginger Baker, and Keith Moon dwarfs that of Palmer and Muhammad. I'm not saying that Starr, Bonham, Baker, and Moon weren't great at what they did. My point is this: To really clean up our act in the music industry—not to mention in the arts and society at large—we need to learn our history better and acknowledge the creators. Earl Palmer from New Orleans was the patriarch. Palmer said that the backbeat was always there, since the 1920s or even earlier, but it just got louder and louder.[7]

Along with the even-eighth beat, the guitar took on more prominence on the New York scene. With Pharoah, I played with Sonny Sharrock, who could bear down, but I loved Sonny Greenwich even more. Greenwich was the first person I heard who could play pentatonics like John Coltrane and McCoy Tyner on the guitar. Wayne Shorter rehearsed a few times with Sonny Greenwich, Cecil McBee, and me, but that quartet didn't play any gigs or make a record. At that time Wayne was looking for ways to include Brazilian music in his sound, and a few years later he

---

[7] Billy Hart also admires Ray Lucas ("pop drummer supreme with King Curtis and Roberta Flack") and Buddy Williams ("I met Buddy when he was just a kid hanging around Walter Booker's Boogie Woogie studios, I love him"). Billy also notes that two other greats, Harvey Mason and Steve Jordan, were the first black pop drummers to make the cover of *Modern Drummer*.

helped Milton Nascimento gain traction in America with the famous album *Native Dancer*.

Part of this circa-1970 collision involved two drummers playing at once. With Wes I had already played with a hand-drummer, but soon enough I was playing with other drummers seated at another drum set. John Coltrane had popularized two drum sets for the multidirectional approach, and then Miles Davis had two drummers for *Bitches Brew* and the straight-eighth approach. Many of the first records I'm on had percussionists or second drummers: *Karma* with Pharoah Sanders, *Asante* with McCoy Tyner, *Odyssey of Iska* with Wayne Shorter, and *Zawinul* with Joe Zawinul.

That last session was particularly important, because Herbie Hancock was present. I had already played a swinging tune or two with Herbie and Miroslav Vitous at Walter Booker's pad, but the recording with Zawinul was when Herbie noticed me as part of this younger crowd attempting to blend the tradition, the multidirectional, and the straight-eighth.

Joe Zawinul was an interesting musician. He wasn't just Caucasian, he was Austrian, but that didn't prevent him from studying our folkways and mores like a scientist. His piece "Mercy, Mercy, Mercy," as recorded by Cannonball Adderley, is one of the great gospel-influenced pieces.

I almost didn't make his date, because I had already left the house to go to my regular little gig with Marian McPartland and Michael Moore at the Downbeat on 42nd and Lexington. When I heard the ring, I was almost late already, but I went back in the house and picked up the phone. It was Zawinul, who asked me if I could get to Atlantic studios *right now*. I sent Harold White to Marian's gig and high-tailed it with my second set of drums to Atlantic studios.

The music on *Zawinul* sounds like Weather Report before there was a Weather Report, and one of the Zawinul tunes on the session was "In a Silent Way." Some people—including myself—prefer this recording of that beautiful ballad to the previous one by Miles Davis. When I asked Zawinul what he wanted me to do, he said, "Man, play only what you *have* to play," a comment that still resonates. It's a way to play with intensity and energy, but without overplaying. You are editing your playing. That's one difference between experienced and inexperienced players, perhaps especially in the recording studio.

Sam Jones told me something related about Miles Davis. Sam was only on one record with Miles, *Somethin' Else* with Cannonball Adderley.

This was supposedly Cannonball's record, but Miles really organized the date, to the point that it was almost a Miles Davis record, and of course it was a masterpiece. Sam liked to talk about how Miles made sure nothing was too fast in the studio. For a successful record, you needed to take your time with the tempos.

In this circa-1970 collision, Miles Davis was a key factor—perhaps *the* key factor. But as great and important as Miles Davis is, I worry that we don't talk about Tony Williams enough. First, Tony learned the jazz tradition. Then, he became a protégé of Sam Rivers, who really understood the 20th-century avant-garde composers. (Tony's first two albums for Blue Note, *Life Time* and *Spring*, feature Sam Rivers and really abstract and advanced sounds.) Eventually, Tony dealt out American classical music with Miles Davis at the highest level.

In addition to all of that, Tony was the guy who really understood the even-eighth. He loved Brazilian music, he loved doo-wop, he even loved The Beatles. Tony figured out how to take the clave—especially the New Orleans version of the clave, called the second line—and add it to modern jazz and the straight eighth. You can hear it on Ron Carter's blues "Eighty-One" with Miles Davis on the album *E.S.P.* That was it. That was the whole ballgame, an updated version of the sensual boogaloo Billy Higgins plays on "The Sidewinder." Part of it seemed to be how the eighth note in binary music took the place of the quarter note in ternary music.

Soon, Tony put the hi-hat on all quarter notes the way the older generation played quarter notes on the bass drum. You can hear some of that come together in "Freedom Jazz Dance" on *Miles Smiles*, although that is still ternary. (Billy Higgins did the first recording of "Freedom Jazz Dance" with Eddie Harris.) Next, on "Stuff" from *Miles in the Sky*, Tony's binary beat foreshadows a whole world of whatever we call "rock drumming" in complex song forms. Eventually, on "Frelon Brun (Brown Hornet)," from *Filles de Kilimanjaro*, Tony is playing his flexible and grand interpretation of a James Brown beat, influenced by Clayton Fillyau, Clyde Stubblefield, and Jabo Starks. Everyone plays like this today, but at the time it was revolutionary.

Tony Williams was a big influence on Miles Davis. Tony left Miles to start his own band, with a concept that blended the binary system with the tradition, and brought John McLaughlin over from England to do it. McLaughlin knew about pop music, Coltrane, and the odd groupings of music from India, another concept that would have more and more prominence in the coming decade. When Miles called Tony back to do one last record, *In a Silent Way*, Tony felt that Miles had stolen his concept—and even stolen his guitar player!—which is why Tony plays so little on that album. The previous Miles album, *Filles De Kilimanjaro*, has Tony playing the way he really played. Tony told me he didn't like the word "fusion." He called it "jazz-rock." In my opinion, all of fusion or jazz-rock (or whatever you want to call it) in the early '70s comes directly out of Tony Williams.[8]

Tony Williams is one of my biggest influences. It wasn't just listening to the records. One of the first times I got to talk with him was when he borrowed my drums. We were at the Cincinnati Reds baseball stadium; I was with Jimmy Smith and he was with Miles. Tony's drums didn't arrive, but I had his brand, Gretsch, and it was even the same color as his kit. When he came off the stage, I thought he was going to thank me, but when he got up close, Tony told me, "Man, you gotta learn how to tune your drums."

That made an impression; I thought about that a lot, and many years later systemized my tuning. (My complete drum set-up is included in an appendix.)

John Coltrane had his "Giant Steps" harmonic cycle: John wrote tunes with that sequence, and eventually, almost everything John played was informed by "Giant Steps." For Tony, it was the Swiss triplet. Tony worked that rudiment to death, and the way he could play it could be hard to understand just from listening. One time in a hotel room in California, I said to Tony, "Man, I know that sound on the records. Why don't you show me what that is, 'cause I'm gonna learn how to do it anyway."

Tony said, "Yeah, I know you would, man," and showed me the sticking of his Swiss triplets on the hotel pillow.

I suspect Tony got those Swiss triplets from Alan Dawson. Dawson was a master drummer, and when he took over from Joe Morello in the Brubeck band he showed the world what the right kind of drum solo on "Take Five" could be. I also love the Booker Ervin records with Jaki

---

8   *DownBeat* from May 2, 1957, reports, "WBEE's [Chicago] Herb Kent presented a jazz-rock 'n' roll show, featuring the Ahmad Jamal trio, for teen-agers at the Hyde Park high school auditorium April 13." Another December 22, 1965 article in *Variety* entitled "R&R Evolution: Jazz-Rock And Even Show Rock" declares, "Now it's jazz that refuses to lie down and play dead. First jazz-man to successfully tie the knot with the modern beat was 88'er Ramsey Lewis."

Byard, Richard Davis, and Dawson. He looms large in this music as a crucial guru: countless drummers across the globe have learned from Alan Dawson's Rudimental Ritual.

That very night I talked about before, when Wes complained about my cymbal at Lennie's-on-the-Turnpike, Dawson was there and consoled me afterwards.

"When are these people going let me play the way I want to play?" I asked him irritably.

Dawson replied, "Billy Hart, you'll be surprised how what you want to play will come and go so quickly."

Although all the Boston drummers also stem from Roy Haynes—of whom I speak more later—at that time, Alan Dawson was in charge, teaching a Max Roach-inspired clarity and facility to first Clifford Jarvis, then Bobby Ward, and finally Tony Williams. In the Philadelphia area, Edgar Bateman and Donald Bailey were working on the polyrhythmic independence concept, preparing John Coltrane and McCoy Tyner for the Detroiter Elvin Jones. I brought up Bateman and Bailey in the context of Elvin Jones before, noting that this was a community music where many people made important contributions, and the same applies to Jarvis and Ward in the context of Tony Williams.

Over the years, I got to know Tony pretty well. One of the first times we met, I told him, "I heard about you before you moved to New York. I heard about you from Jimmy Cobb." He responded, "Jimmy Cobb told me about you, too." One time Tony even introduced me to his mother: "This is Billy Hart, one of the greatest young drummers today."

I'm sure Herbie Hancock noticed my familiarity with Tony's ideas, since Tony was one of Herbie's biggest influences, too. When we met on Zawinul's date, Herbie and I could really look each other in the eye; it gave Herbie a reason to consider me part of the forward-moving moment. Herbie called me the next week to come play at his studio/workplace, which was a converted apartment next door to his actual apartment on 93rd street and Riverside Drive. We went quickly through his repertoire, just the two of us: "Maiden Voyage," "Sorcerer," "Dolphin Dance," "Eye of the Hurricane," and so forth. I knew all the tunes, so Herbie hired me for his band.

6

Miles Davis, the Teacher

I had first met Herbie Hancock when I was playing with Shirley Horn at the Village Vanguard in late 1962 or early 1963. He was there to hear Miles Davis play with Hank Mobley, Wynton Kelly, Paul Chambers, and Jimmy Cobb while Shirley's trio (with Ronnie Markowitz and me) was the intermission band. Miles did a lot for Shirley Horn, bringing her up to play in New York and telling everyone about her. He also copped a few of Shirley's chosen tunes, including "I Thought About You," and told his piano players to check out her voicings. Herbie Hancock might have learned a few things from Shirley Horn, and he wasn't the only one. One of the last things Miles played on record was "You Won't Forget Me" with Shirley; when Keith Jarrett recorded that song a year or two later for his Miles tribute album *Bye, Bye, Blackbird*, he played Shirley's voicings exactly.

Jimmy Cobb was from Washington, D.C., but I didn't really know him from when he lived there. I met him only after he started returning to D.C. with Miles or Wynton Kelly. I loved his playing, of course. Everyone thinks of him as a swinger, which he is, but he also had great chops. There's a version of Jimmy playing the drum feature "Two Bass Hit" with Miles at Newport which is particularly smoking.

There was a story going around that Miles made Jimmy drive Miles's car to Chicago so Miles had his ride while working there. Miles took the plane, but Jimmy drove the car all that way to meet Miles. When I asked him why he put up with that, Jimmy told me, "I just like the way that motherfucker plays."

At the Vanguard, I was surprised at how hard the band was working. Miles would begin each set with a very fast tune, usually "Milestones." Miles would stomp his foot *once* and away they went. They did it, but it wasn't easy. Hank Mobley—who we called "Hankenstein," and is one of the all-time greats, but was not always one for playing fast tempos—said to me after the set, "That shit ain't funny!"

When I told Jimmy Cobb I loved the set, he shook his head. He told me he was practicing during the day, trying to get ready for the gig, but sometimes, it left him spent. "I just left it all at practice," he said. "I didn't have nothin' tonight."

Miles was always *up*, and that made him a good match for Tony Williams. When Tony got in the band, Miles played all those fast tempos with Tony like they were made for each other.

At the Vanguard that night, Herbie Hancock was with Freddie Hubbard and Joe Henderson. They were all standing in the back. I told Herbie how much I loved his playing on Donald Byrd's brand new *Royal Flush*, which is still one of my favorite albums, with an amazing feel in the rhythm section of Herbie, Billy Higgins, and my hometown friend Butch Warren. Herbie was flattered that I knew the album and had singled out his contribution. Miles came over to say hi to us and ended up being very displeased with me for not knowing anything about the famous Washington, D.C. boxing gyms. Miles walked away shaking his head, and Freddie, brash as always, said to me, "Punch that motherfucker!" and we all fell out laughing.

You could almost say that after Miles wore out his old band with Hank Mobley and Jimmy Cobb, he was ready for Herbie Hancock, Ron Carter, and Tony Williams. George Coleman was the first tenor player, and George sure sounds great on the live albums *My Funny Valentine* and *Four and More*. However, I heard that Tony didn't like the way George would practice what he would play on the gig backstage before they went on. At any rate, when Wayne Shorter took over from George Coleman, it was four against one. Miles had his back to the wall.

Tony Williams was the ringleader. Herbie will be the first person to tell you that he learned about metric modulation and odd groupings from Tony. Tony was also listening to all the current pop music, from Brazil to the Beatles, and figuring out how to deal with all of *that*.

The younger members of his band dragged Miles in that direction. A lot of people think of it as a pop direction, but personally I think of it more as a straight-eighth direction. In the '60s we saw a change from Cuban music to Brazilian music in the American landscape, and both of those musics influenced the pop vocabulary *immediately*.

Miles Davis, the Teacher

Lenny White taught me a lesson about that. He's several years younger than me, and when I first got to New York, we got close enough to the point where if I had left my drums at one gig, I would call Lenny and he would have his father drive him and his drums over to my house so I could use them for a second gig. That's how young he was! Finally, one time I wanted to use his drums and Lenny said, "Well, you know, I can't do it, man. I got a gig."

I said, "Really? Congratulations!" I wasn't expecting to be impressed, but I asked anyway: "Who you playin' with?"

He said, "I got this gig with Jackie McLean."

Whoops! Yes, Lenny was a comer, no doubt, and ended up being on *Bitches Brew* and Freddie Hubbard's *Red Clay* before joining Chick Corea's Return to Forever. Both Lenny and I once sat in with Pharoah Sanders at the Village Gate on hand percussion, and I realized that Lenny knew a lot more about what he was doing than I did. It became painfully obvious that I was limited in that area. Afterwards, I complained to him about it, and Lenny told me, "You have got to check out more Afro-Cuban music." That was a good lesson.

When you see Lenny being interviewed today, people are always asking him about *Bitches Brew*. In general, if you played with Miles Davis, that's what people want to ask you about. Even I get asked about the records I did with Miles, even though they aren't nearly as famous as *Bitches Brew*—although I suppose *On the Corner* might be the most famous record I'm on, just because it's by Miles Davis. When journalists ask me about *On the Corner*, I sometimes say, "It was the combination of Les McCann and Claude Thornhill." That's true: *On the Corner* was a mixture of popular bluesy dance and intellectual exploration of tone color. But also, since the journalist probably doesn't know much about either Les McCann or Claude Thornhill, we can move on to something else.

At the Vanguard with Herbie Hancock, Miles came up to me and looked me close in the face, so close that our noses were almost touching, and said, "The next time I need a drummer, I'm gonna call you."

He did follow up, but I was committed to Herbie Hancock and didn't do any live gigs with Miles, just a few studio sessions. When I first took out my drums for what became *On the Corner*, I thought I might be the only drummer at the session, but then Jack DeJohnette set up next to me. We started tracking, and I was doing whatever I could to make the two-drum thing work. Miles went into the control booth, and when he came out, he walked over to me and whispered in my ear, "It don't go like that."

That's all he said, and nobody heard it but me. But the fact that Miles actually walked over and singled me out for any kind of conversation drew some attention.

Then we did another take—and you can say, "Another take of what?" and you'd be right, because *nobody* knew what they were doing. After that, Miles listened in the booth before coming over again and whispering in my ear, "Aw, man, just play whatever the fuck you wanna play."

A few takes later, he whispers, "You know any James Brown beats?" Yeah, Miles, I do, and you can hear that beat on the track "Black Satin."

I never listened to *On the Corner*—maybe just once, and never the whole thing. When Herbie told me, "The record we did with Miles is out," I replied, "Man, what the fuck does that sound like?"

Herbie said, "It sounds like what we did."

That wasn't an answer for me, and it *still* isn't an answer for me. Jack DeJohnette has better answers. Jack is much more articulate about how the Miles Davis sessions from that era went and what Miles was trying to do, explaining how it was experimental music, searching for the new, and if anything connected, then that's what went on the record. Somehow, *On the Corner* has gotten a certain amount of notoriety over the years. A few years ago I went to see Robert Glasper play, and Glasper introduced me to one of his friends by saying, "This is Billy Hart, who played on *On the Corner*, which is one of the first hip-hop records."

So, that's interesting. One of these days I really need to sit down with *On the Corner* and try to figure out just how far ahead Miles was from everyone else. On *The Complete On the Corner* sessions, there's a piece that Miles named for me, "Jabali."

Miles was always the teacher. He played with Charlie Parker, and he learned from Charlie Parker, but Bird didn't say much. Dizzy Gillespie was the one to show other musicians what was going on. In the wake of Dizzy's example, Miles took on that role. He also took on a lot of Dizzy's ideas. There's hardly a classic Miles Davis LP from the '50s that doesn't have something to do with Dizzy: "I Waited For You," "Two Bass Hit," "Salt Peanuts," "Woody'n You," "Tadd's Delight," and so forth. In the liner notes to *The Musings of Miles*, Miles says, "You can always learn something from Dizzy Gillespie." When Red Garland and Philly Joe Jones make hits together behind Miles or John Coltrane, those hits are derived from the Dizzy Gillespie big band.

Both Dizzy and Miles played enough piano to be on famous records as pianists: On "Ko-Ko" with Bird, that's Dizzy behind the saxophone solo; on "Sid's Ahead" from *Milestones,* Miles comps for John Coltrane, Cannonball Adderley, and Paul Chambers. Three times, after sets I played with Shirley Horn, Jimmy Smith, or Herbie Hancock, I saw Miles go up there and sit at the keyboard to talk harmony. One of the pictures from the *Milestones* sessions shows Miles surrounding Red Garland at the piano, showing Red the right voicings.

Miles gave me two specific lessons when I was playing at the Village Vanguard with Herbie Hancock. Miles sat right in my corner, the drummer's corner, where the heavy cats hang out to watch the drummer onstage.

First, Miles said, "Billy, start your phrases on four, and don't finish nothin'."

A few years later, I got what Miles meant, when I heard Hank Jones, Ray Brown, and Roy Haynes play together at a festival in Europe. They'd all start something, like a familiar riff or melody, and rather than it coming out where I expected, they'd leave the ending of the familiar riff off—but the music was still swinging as if they were completing the sentences. It was suddenly clear as day to me: Something about American classical music included *not resolving phrases*. In his book *Possibilities*, Herbie Hancock says Miles Davis "played like a stone skipping across the pond," which may mean something similar.

Then, Miles told me, "Sometimes, you can play behind the beat. That shit swings like a motherfucker. Sometimes, you can play on top of the beat. That shit swings like a motherfucker. Sometimes, you play right in the center of the beat. That shit *swings like a motherfucker!*"

Miles was ecstatic describing the center of the beat, grabbing his dick and moving his arm like someone was giving him a hand job. Probably everyone in this music knows about the three places of the beat—behind, center, and ahead—but it was interesting that Miles valued the center so much.

Louis Armstrong phrased a little behind the beat. On "Summertime" with Gil Evans, you can hear Miles's Louis Armstrong quarter notes.

Just a little bit late. Freddie Hubbard, as great as he is and as much trumpet he can play, didn't have that Louis Armstrong confidence with the phrasing. Miles exhibits total relaxed confidence.

In a Silent Way, Bitches Brew, Fillmore, Live-Evil: Those are some of the Miles Davis records people talk about as defining the era. But I'm grateful that I wasn't in his band. Instead, I was in Herbie Hancock's sextet, which was even better. The sextet was dealing with the same moment Miles Davis was—the intersection of tradition, multidirectional, and the even-eighth note—but on a higher level.

Buster Williams deserves a lot of credit. He really hooked up with Herbie musically. You can hear it on their first album together, *The Prisoner*.

The bass is so important. A lot of the swing comes from the bass. I remember one time, maybe I was 20 years old, when I was driving in a car listening to the radio. One of the Red Garland records with Jamil Nasser came on, and I had to pull off to the side of the road to listen and groove with Nasser properly. (At the time Nasser was still known as George Joyner.) Nasser wasn't just playing quarter notes, but a whole lot of syncopation and melody.

Buster Williams also plays bass lines full of syncopation and melody. We met in the early 1960s when we were both working for Betty Carter in Detroit. (That was a memorable trip: On that same tour to Detroit, I met Bennie Maupin and heard Tony Williams live with Miles Davis for the first time.) Buster and I fell in love at first beat, and we've ended up making a lot of gigs and records together. Some people think that Buster Williams and Billy Hart is a historically significant rhythm section.

Ron Carter was great, too, of course. I played with Ron a bit over the years, but not nearly as much as with Buster. These are the Herbie Hancock bassists! You could write a whole book just about Herbie and Ron vs. Herbie and Buster. One time I asked Herbie about these two great bassists, and Herbie looked very solemn, like he was going to make a declaration about his innermost feelings, and said to me, "There *is* a difference."

Buster's beat is really something else. He plays related to the cymbal ride. Accurately. He's more than an assistant—he really has that feel, to the point that if your cymbal isn't correct, he's got it. When Buster was with Billy Higgins, it was truly otherworldly, but Higgins didn't *need* to be there. I've heard a whole unswinging band swing because Buster was playing bass.

Buster has influenced me just as much as Shirley Horn. I guess Buster does that to drummers. In fact, I've heard the great Ben Riley on the radio with Buster and thought it was me: I think Riley and I both adjusted our uptempo ride patterns thanks to Buster. Buster also has the whole harmonic thing *down*. He played with the singers and learned all the tunes.[1] Herbie has that too, and when I was first playing with Herbie, he made sure to check Buster and me out together in the traditional music. I know Buster told Herbie, "Billy has that old-time *swing*."

My experience with Shirley Horn was my original ace in the hole, and working with Wes had made me reinvest in my Jimmy Cobb. After all, I was following in the wake of great swinging drummers for Herbie's music, Mickey Roker, Pete La Roca, and Tootie Heath. We didn't record any of that kind of music in the studio, but live we played "Toys," which was a Hancock swinger first recorded on *Speak Like a Child* with Roker. Roker's first name is Granville, which was his father's name, given to him by a slave owner on the British Isle of Nassau. Roker's cymbal beat had all that Caribbean information, as well as simply something that could swing you to death. We called him "Stroker." When Stroker arrived for a rehearsal with the Duke Pearson big band, the members of the band would all applaud because they loved his beat so much.

One time I ran into Barry Harris at the Japanese consulate. Barry was the keeper of the flame. I don't know if Barry approved of my phrase American classical music, but Barry Harris is *definitely* what I mean when I say American classical music. There aren't too many piano players who are the true classical pianists: Barry Harris, Tommy Flanagan, Hank Jones, Cedar Walton, and perhaps a few others. I'm not sure that even Herbie Hancock or McCoy Tyner command quite that level of expertise concerning the tradition.

Barry Harris told me that day at the consulate that the difference between Sonny Stitt and Charlie Parker was that Stitt played in four while Bird played in six. Now, if you don't know that much about this music, I'm not going to downplay Sonny Stitt's greatness to you. Sonny Stitt was truly, truly great. A bebop *master*. But it's also true that Charlie Parker has something even more rhythmically profound than Sonny Stitt.

---

1   Buster Williams recorded extensively with Sarah Vaughan and Nancy Wilson in the 1960s.

And what Barry Harris told me that day indicated that Bird's phrasing unlocks the ternary. That classical way of generating ecstasy, "swing" or whatever you want to call it, always needs the ternary.

There's a bootleg version of "Toys" with Herbie, Buster, and me from Nice, France that Buster and I have talked about.[2] It's at a high level; we are swinging, and then what happens harmonically between Herbie and Buster is pretty remarkable. They really had a thing together. I'm pretty sure Buster is why Herbie kept "Toys" in the repertoire; on our two little sextet reunion gigs, in 1976 and 2014, we played "Toys."[3]

I needed to catch up. At first, when we got on the gig, once we left the melody, the lights went out. I had no idea where I was, or where anything was. I hadn't been playing with anybody who played advanced reharmonizations and metric modulations like that. Herbie reharms the reharms, and Buster was trying to one-up Herbie. Oh, yeah. The lights went *out*. I didn't have *anything* to hold on to. Each gig was a real adventure.

Herbie had started his sextet with *Speak Like A Child* and *The Prisoner*, the last of Herbie's long line of significant LPs produced for Blue Note.[4] There was a big Gil Evans influence in the sextet. One of Herbie's favorite albums was *Miles Ahead*, arranged by Gil. (I love it too; that opening stack Gil writes for "The Meaning of the Blues" is fantastic.) With three horns, Herbie was going for some of that harmonic richness, and when he added in the Fender Rhodes, there were even more sustained colors.

Pete La Roca was Herbie's first choice for the live gigs with his new sextet with Johnny Coles, Garnett Brown, Clifford Jordan, and Ron Carter. La Roca was late to too many gigs, so Tootie Heath took over. A transition record was *Fat Albert Rotunda* for Warner Brothers, which had a contemporary pop influence. The legendary pop drummer Bernard Purdie is on some tracks, like "Wiggle Waggle," which foreshadows the style Herbie played with the Headhunters later.

---

2   This extraordinary performance of "Toys" in Nice took place on July 21, 1971.

3   Both later Mwandishi performances (after the band ended) took place in New York: The 1976 concert was part of a festival of three Herbie Hancock bands, and can be heard on the 2-LP Hancock release *V.S.O.P.* In 2014 the sextet played the single tune "Toys" at the Great Night in Harlem gala for the Jazz Foundation Of America at the Apollo Theater.

4   Alfred Lion was in charge during what many consider to be the glory years of the Blue Note record label. Herbie Hancock's first albums as a leader were all done for Lion: *Takin' Off* (1962), *My Point of View* (1963), *Inventions & Dimensions* (1964), *Empyrean Isles* (1964), *Maiden Voyage* (1965). The next two were done after Lion sold Blue Note to Liberty: *Speak Like a Child* (1968) and *The Prisoner* (1969). Billy Hart never worked with Alfred Lion.

Not only was Herbie the hot young jazz pianist with Miles Davis, he had invaded the studios. He worked with *everybody* in a studio context: not just jazz-to-pop records with Wes Montgomery and Paul Desmond, but also commercials, soundtracks, jingles, and who knows what. His compositions "Maiden Voyage" and "You'll Know When You Get There" were originally written as commercial jingles; *Fat Albert Rotunda* was based on a television show; I did a few jingles with Herbie myself.

I'm aware that many people would call "Wiggle Waggle" "funk" and Bernard Purdie a great "funk drummer." But, to me, funk was always there: Horace Silver, Milt Jackson, Stanley Turrentine, Ray Charles—whatever that bluesy thing is, it's just an element of American classical music. What "Wiggle Waggle" and Purdie are doing is the pop or dance version of that traditional aesthetic.

When I was first on the road with Herbie, we would open with "Wiggle Waggle." After the second or third gig, his new manager David Rubinson came up and happily slapped me on the shoulder. "Man, I'm so glad you're here and in the band. I've been telling Herbie he needed to get a real rock and roll drummer."

That really bothered me and made me feel like I was part of the old plantation system. This music was *just too good* to be characterized by the latest word from white people. Calling our music "jazz" is bad enough; calling it "rock and roll" is even worse.

I *love* Miles Davis. I *love* Herbie Hancock. But I do put them a little at fault. The immense attraction of money isn't just economic, it's psychological—even sexual. When you see the Beatles, they don't seem that sexy to look at, but it's still some kind of glamorous show, like they're movie stars. So many aspects of American life are affected by corporate decisions and the slow march of capitalism. Making money seems like a subliminal motivation for almost everything.

Tootie Heath played on *The Prisoner* and on half of *Fat Albert Rotunda*. Of course, Tootie could swing hard *and* play straight-eighth music just beautifully. But Tootie left Herbie and went with Yusef Lateef after a big tour fell through.[5] Herbie had made the mistake of entrusting the management and booking to an old college buddy, which was the last time *that* happened. (To be fair to David Rubinson, who I didn't like much otherwise, I don't think Herbie ever had a tour cancel on him again.)

---

5   The Yusef Lateef quartet with Kenny Barron, Bob Cunningham, and Tootie Heath went on to be one of the great bands of the early 1970s.

By the time I got to Herbie's sextet, the front line was Woody Shaw, Joe Henderson, and Garnett Brown. The repertoire was the music Herbie wrote for his '60s sextet plus Buster's song "Dual Force," which they had recorded as "Firewater" on *The Prisoner*. Herbie was also trying out a few of the pop things he had written for *Fat Albert Rotunda* like "Wiggle Waggle," and there were also the classic pieces that Herbie would end up always playing no matter the band: "Maiden Voyage," "Eye of the Hurricane," and so forth.

Herbie was already almost exclusively on electric piano, and certain things were beginning to open up in the music structurally, but it really broke open in the next iteration. Joe Henderson left to start his own band and more or less took Woody Shaw with him, and Garnett Brown preferred to stay home and work in the New York studios. Their replacements were Bennie Maupin, Eddie Henderson, and Julian Priester.

7

Mwandishi

Jimmy Heath's son was Mtume, so named by Maulana Karenga of the US Organization, an important political group connected to the social ferment of the times. The American version of the holiday Kwanzaa was Karenga's idea.

Mtume played congas with Gary Bartz, Sonny Rollins, and Miles Davis and later wrote the hit songs "Juicy Fruit," which was successful with his own group, and "The Closer I Get to You," which has been recorded by Roberta Flack, Luther Vandross, and Beyoncé. I'm on Mtume's album *Alkebu-Lan: Land of the Blacks*, which was recorded live at the East, a cultural center in Brooklyn that only allowed black people onstage and in the audience. When I played at East with Herbie Hancock, they didn't allow Herbie's white wife to attend.

Mtume is a Swahili name. Most Afro-Americans go by a name originally given to them by a slave master. If you take an African name, it's a way to reject the status quo and reclaim your heritage. Tootie Heath was Mtume's uncle, and Mtume named Tootie "Kuumba," Buster Williams "Mchezaji," and Herbie Hancock "Mwandishi" on a 1969 record date, *Kawaida*. As the final version of the Herbie Hancock sextet came together, everyone took a name, mostly assigned by Mtume.

All these names mean something, or even several things:

Herbie Hancock — Mwandishi — Composer
Eddie Henderson — Mganga — Doctor of Good Advice
Bennie Maupin — Mwile — Body of Good Health
Julian Priester — Pepo Moto — Spirit Child
Buster Williams — Mchezaji — The Player
Billy Hart — Jabali — Moral Strength

My name, Jabali, has stayed with me ever since this era.

The first album was called *Mwandishi*, and the band became known as Mwandishi as well, although when we toured, it was always listed as the Herbie Hancock Sextet.

Julian Priester was a little older than the rest of us. He had played with Count Basie, Duke Ellington, and Max Roach, and also knew all the Afro-Cuban music, since most trombonists get to play in Latin bands. On "Sleeping Giant," the music begins with the rumba clave: Julian taught us how to do that and led us on the cowbell. He was also in charge of the horns in terms of how they rehearsed and phrased certain things, which was correct, because he had the experience. By the time of the first gig, the band sounded like it had been together for a year, and that's

Flyer for Mtume's Umoja Ensemble at The East

Mwandishi

because Pepo had rehearsed the horns. That was the kind of respect we all had for him. When Herbie introduced him to the audience, he'd often say that Pepo was "steeped in the tradition."

Woody Shaw had recommended Eddie Henderson to Herbie. Eddie was a medical doctor, and had bought a Ferrari with all the money he was making. (Miles also had Ferraris, while Herbie had his Shelby Cobra.) We were a little surprised when he gave all that up to play music full time, but it also shows how much Herbie's music affected him, that he took a sabbatical to go on the road. Eddie is a genius who always knows just what he wants and how to do it. A particularly impressive example of his playing is on a record not everyone knows about, *Journey* with the McCoy Tyner big band: Try Mganga's solos on "Peresina" and "Blues on the Corner."

Bennie Maupin had already been on *Bitches Brew* and one of Lee Morgan's greatest records, *Live at the Lighthouse*. In fact, Bennie left Morgan to join Herbie. When Joe Henderson had sent Pete Yellin to sub at the last minute, the band rebelled. It wasn't that Pete was white—although I guess that didn't help his case—it was that Yellin was no Joe Henderson. (Pete was actually a fine player, and I made a few records with him.) Anyway, Buster told Herbie, "Call Bennie Maupin." Bennie memorized all the music in the van on the way to the first gig, so that was that. Mwile also believed in eating right, and, for a time, turned the whole band into vegetarians. Bennie was the only one Herbie kept when he broke up our band and started the Headhunters.

Vegetarianism is just one of the higher ways of living that the explored. It was really a kind of Aquarian age commune. Four of us in the band—including our tour manager, Billy Bonner, named Fundi (meaning "expert") by Mtume—had birthdays on the 29th, and those four were the elements: air, water, earth, and fire. Herbie started including the number 29 in the artwork for the sextet albums.

When we went on Ellis Haizlip's TV show *Soul!*, it was on August 29, and it turned out that two people involved in making the show were also born on a 29. So we hung big shiny cardboard "29s" all through the studio as part of the stage set.

Herbie announced:

> *I'd like to relate some facts to you, some very strange facts. Out of this sextet that I have—which, by the way, is the only seven man sextet in existence—four of the men have birthdays on the 29th,*

in four different months. And the other three men have star signs, that—according to astrology—are ruled by the planet Mars, the fourth planet from the Sun.

The show is being taped on the 29th of August. The director has a birthday on the 29th of June, and the stage manager has a birthday on the 29th of November. So, '29' plays a very important part of this particular event.

Herbie keeps going, reading spiritual guidance from my copy of *The Impersonal Life*. Behind the spoken word, the band plays little percussion instruments, evolving into a long version of "Ostinato."[1]

This might have been pretty far out for TV, but it was business as usual for the sextet. Herbie would frequently recite to the audience from the stage at the start of the gig, and the collective percussion improvisation would organically show us which composition we would start with, as if we were taking dictation from a higher source.

We would name certain women we met on the road for principles of Kwanzaa, like Nia or Imani. At the beginning of this memoir, I made it clear that this would be a musical autobiography. It doesn't seem right to write about the non-musical elements, especially without getting permission from all the other people involved. But if I had wanted to write a gossipy tell-all, then the Mwandishi years would be prime material. At the end of the '60s, human consciousness was explored through free love and inhibition blockers. There was a *lot* of sex and a *lot* of drugs. When I look back on it now, I'm surprised we all made it out of there pretty much intact.

Another thing that kept us together was religion. One of Buster Williams's sisters was interested in Nichiren Shoshu Buddhism. She told me about it, I got interested, then Buster got interested, then Herbie, then the whole band. Herbie and Buster are still avid practitioners of Nichiren Shoshu Buddhism to this day. I do it too; I keep the missal with me at all times, and I make sure to chant Nam-Myoho-Renge-Kyo once a day.

When I've seen Herbie or Buster discuss their Buddhism, I've found it beautiful. But I don't discuss it much myself or go to meetings. I'm always inspired by John Coltrane's example. Azar Lawrence—certainly

---

[1] The source of Herbie Hancock's speech from the television program *Soul!* is a very rare audio-only recording supplied by Hyland Harris, taped off the TV set at time of transmission by a member of Harris's family.

a fellow Coltrane fan—can quote *The Aquarian Gospel of Jesus the Christ*. This spiritual text, which covers the "lost years" of Jesus, when he was educated at the mystery schools of Tibet, Egypt, India, Persia, and Greece, seems to be connected to John and what John tried to show us through his music.

You need to give up a part of your ego to play this music at the highest level. On two different occasions, Donald Bailey and Paul Motian told me essentially the same thing about composition. In Duck's case, we were at some Jimmy Smith gig, while Paul had just come from a class lesson in counterpoint, but they both talked about how it mattered less how you yourself played on one particular night. What really mattered was how you could play with others. If you could fit the music so that everything worked, then it was a successful composition.

Of anybody I ever played with, Herbie Hancock is the best example of someone willing to surrender himself to the full band to create a successful composition. When we played together, he was not just playing with whatever I had just played, but was also somehow reading my mind and anticipating what I would play next. At times he guided me like a witch doctor into the better form of whatever I wanted to play.

Everybody else in the sextet felt that way, too, that Herbie could read everyone's mind and support the next event *before that event even happened*. Herbie deserved that name, Mwandishi, meaning "composer." It wasn't just that he wrote the tunes, it was that Herbie enabled the whole sextet to coalesce into a spontaneous evening-length composition.

And all this is *on top* of his piano playing. When Duke Pearson took off to party for a weekend, he sent Herbie Hancock to Donald Byrd as a sub. Duke never got the gig back. Donald Byrd asked Duke Pearson, "Did you *hear* how that young motherfucker plays?"

Of course, Herbie's records with Miles Davis are famous. I will never tire of Herbie on "My Funny Valentine" and "Stella by Starlight" with Miles, giving us that kind of romantic ethos, while the whole of *Miles Smiles* exists on another plane. But really, anything Herbie played is truly great. I love him with Billy Higgins; I love him with Roy Haynes. He is in the middle of *everything*. He played all the European classical music as a kid and then studied Mongo Santamaria just as seriously. Herbie is from Chicago, which is *the* blues town of blues towns.

I joke with students: "There's rhythm, and then there's harmony. If McCoy Tyner was faced with a gun and asked to choose between

With Herbie Hancock

harmony and rhythm, McCoy would choose rhythm. Keith Jarrett would choose harmony. But Herbie would say, 'I don't know. I can't choose between them, I love them both too much, you'll just have to shoot me.'"

The sextet records we made are nice, but in most cases we were playing the songs for the first time in the studio, and some unintentional looseness creeps in here and there. Live, the tunes got both tighter and looser in all the right ways. Herbie was also caught between pleasing his band on one hand and pleasing David Rubinson and the record labels on the other.

I can't fault Herbie for not doing his best: He did do his best, and these will always be some of the most important records I've ever made.

The first album was *Mwandishi*. "Ostinato (Suite For Angela)" is in 15. Herbie got those kinds of odd groupings from Tony Williams. This is the only track with a second drummer. I practiced the 15, and we do the 15, but the second drummer, Ndugu Leon Chancler, shows that he deserved to be there, too. Ndugu was Mtume's man, they were best friends. Later on, Ndugu played with *everybody* in jazz and pop music, and would become famous for his beat on Michael Jackson's "Billie Jean."

Buster could also play electric bass extremely well, and in the Hancock sextet he played both acoustic and electric. One night in Philadelphia, a crew of heavy bassists, Stanley Clarke, Alphonso Johnson, Anthony Jackson, were all in the front row to watch Buster play electric. The live show often started with "Ostinato (Suite for Angela)" with Buster playing that fierce odd-meter groove on electric for up to an hour. (The front line would play percussion for about half an hour before picking up their horns.) A few years later, Buster's own album *Pinnacle* featured a long version of Buster's song "The Hump" with electric bass. That groove was in 17: three phrases of 4 plus a bar of 5. "The Hump" felt really good, and eventually it was sampled by Fugees, A Tribe Called Quest, Showbiz & A.G., Jurassic 5, and All Saints. (Buster had to sue everybody, but in time they all paid up.)

I guess Joe Morello and Dave Brubeck get the credit for odd-time signatures—"Take Five" and all of that—but Morello was really trying to play like Max Roach and barely making it, although he certainly had excellent stick control. These days I give Brubeck a tad more credit

With Herbie Hancock

than I used to, since now I wonder if he wasn't an important influence on Bill Evans.

Max Roach knew about odd groupings: Max did certain things phrased in fives, like the drum intro to "Klact-oveeseds-tene," not to mention his shocking 5+5+6 part on "Un Poco Loco" with Bud Powell. I talked a lot with Billy Higgins about "Un Poco Loco." Higgins said this beat was so important, that Max had even invented another clave. When you look at it like that, it turns out you can rationalize all the odd meters and odd groupings with clave. I make my students buy the Danilo Perez album *Panamonk* so they can learn his odd-meter claves.

Possibly the true source of odd groupings is the classical music of India. Just recently, I learned that Max interacted with Ravi Shankar as early as the 1940s. In the '60s, Max's band featured pieces in 5/4 and 7/4. Even 3/4 is an odd grouping, and in this case Max *was* the first, playing "Valse Hot" with Sonny Rollins. However, when John Coltrane and Elvin Jones put out "My Favorite Things," that was something we all really had to deal with—although Stan Getz wasn't so sure about the way everyone started to mix up the 3/4 time in the wake of John and Elvin. Stan told me, "If you play in three, it's a waltz as far as I'm concerned," singing, "*Boom*, chick, chick," with a big emphasis on the downbeat. I sort of agreed with Stan. In my mind's eye, I can see a scene in the 1700s in France or Spain with people dancing to this sexy waltz and it being offensive or lascivious. In some kind of way, that original waltz was the *funk*.

Also on *Mwandishi* was "You'll Know When You Get There," a jingle Herbie had written for a commercial. While Herbie was in charge, he also brought forth our best ideas, and we all contributed to the arrangement of "You'll Know When You Get There." This way of working was not far from what he had learned from Miles Davis, and the title of the piece references the idea of true spontaneity. Herbie loves to talk about how Miles taught him there are no mistakes, only incorrect resolutions. If you land "wrong," that might actually be "right," if you are attuned to the moment. You will know if you get there.

"Wandering Spirit Song" is one of Julian Priester's great compositions, and one of my favorite tracks from these records. I really love the beginning and the long duo between Herbie and Buster at the end. "Wandering Spirit Song" became the band's anthem, and we would

The Herbie Hancock sextet in concert

play it only at special times. If we'd had a great night, a night that you don't even have to talk about, when we *all* knew that it was a great night, Herbie would say, "Yeah, man, we got our magic back." And then we would encore with "Wandering Spirit Song."

When the sextet played in New York at the Village Vanguard, the members of Weather Report, The Mahavishnu Orchestra, and Return to Forever were all in attendance. Miles Davis himself came five nights out of six.

However, when you compare our music to the other big name fusion bands, including the Miles Davis records of that era, you will notice that as contemporary as *Mwandishi* is, there is a close connection to the tradition—closer than the rest of that fusion music. Herbie, Buster, and I still put that ternary situation front and center, for example on "Wandering Spirit Song."

But we *also* had a commitment to the multidirectional. I was really in charge of that, because I regarded our music as American classical music, and Cecil Taylor, Ornette Coleman, and John Coltrane with Alice and Rashied had produced the latest intellectual advances. I always broke up the time with allusions to this kind of experimental thinking, which I considered an essential ingredient.

Billy and Herbie at the Village Vanguard in the 1980s

Eventually, that would be a real conflict between Herbie and me. Herbie's next drummer was Harvey Mason, who was one of my first students, and I recommended Harvey to Herbie myself. In addition to being one of the great pop and studio drummers, Harvey can play timpani and other percussion with the London Symphony Orchestra on Gustav Holst's *The Planets* and other pieces. Harvey is also someone who never allowed a multidirectional concept to interfere with those who wanted to get up and dance.

"Sleeping Giant" opens the next record, *Crossings*. I might have to get some credit for the first composed melody, as I suggested to Herbie that he take the idea of his classic tune "One Finger Snap" in a straight-eighths direction. There's a drum solo at the beginning, against the Afro-Cuban rhythms led by Pepo. In post-production, Herbie added a low-pitched synthesizer effect to the drum intro, so that the tension grew and grew before releasing into the melody. That was pure genius on Herbie's part, another example of why he is everyone's favorite accompanist. The opening becomes symphonic—a concerto for the drums.

"Sleeping Giant" is another of my favorite tracks from the studio records, but it's still not the whole story, for the piece had a lot of sections and could go to wildly different places in concert. One time, we played "Sleeping Giant" for two and a half hours straight.

For "Quasar" and the rest of the studio material, Patrick Gleeson's synthesizer was added to the tracks, usually in post-production, although soon Gleeson was on the road with us, too.

At times I liked Gleeson's contribution; other times, it was a distraction. Gleeson certainly didn't know anything about Count Basie or Duke Ellington. But it wasn't just Gleeson out there, our sound engineer Fundi would join in on Echoplex as well. We were all high, playing this way-out sextet music with other people on synthesizer and Echoplex. I'd toke an inhibition blocker, hit a drum, and there was suddenly a big delay effect on it, resonating through the hall. It was like a science fiction movie, but we were doing it live. You go through a door and your direction changes. One night, the gig had started, and we were all backstage looking at each other in sort of a relaxed fashion, thinking the other person was onstage, but actually *no one* was onstage yet. It was *totally* insane.

You can see something of a science fiction style in the artwork for the three studio albums. Bennie Maupin's tune "Quasar" would take on another kind of meaning for the band. Internally, we started calling the band "Quasar 429," another reference to our exceptional numerology. "Quasar 429" also sounds like the name of a science-fiction spaceship. We'd happily pilot that spaceship around for hours before landing!

Like "Quasar," "Water Torture" was also written by Bennie Maupin, which caused conflict with the record company. They really wanted Herbie out in front as the leader at all times. When Herbie signed to Columbia, Herbie did the band the honor of bringing the whole sextet to a meeting or two with Rubinson and the record executives. They mostly talked about money, and how if we put Herbie front and center and played more commercial music we could get rich. Sometimes the sextet would double bill with a rock act like Iron Butterfly. One of those Columbia suits asked me, "The drummer of Iron Butterfly is making $700 a night, and Billy Hart with the Herbie Hancock sextet is making $100 a night. Is that fair? Do you want that?"

Herbie himself was touchy about money. His parents were almost well-to-do, or at least upper middle class by Afro-American standards. One time I complimented him on how great the music of the sextet was, and he groused at me, "Are you *really* that satisfied for only $300 a week?"

The truth of the matter was that I *was* satisfied. I understand Herbie's point of view, and even Columbia Records' point of view if it comes to that. But I don't know if it's worth changing great music to make more money. Truly great music is hard to find, and worth protecting at any cost.

When we recorded *Sextant* for Columbia Records, it was a surprise. We had all thought we would contribute new music equally, but Herbie came in and said, "We ain't gonna do any of that," and had three short sketches going in more of a pop direction. For "Rain Dance," we had to play with a vamp generated by Gleeson's Random Resonator. We did it, but I made sure to keep some multidirectional in there, something between Sonny Murray and Tony Williams. Afterwards, Herbie was upset with me. "Why did you do that?" he complained. He really was perplexed. To him it was obvious that I should have played a pop beat.

However, to his credit, Herbie did keep the take. Like Miles Davis—and like me, when I'm in charge—Herbie knows that, much of the time, the first take is the best. When you start arguing about how to approach the music in the studio, it frequently invokes the law of diminishing returns.

"Hidden Shadows" is based on that "James Brown beat" I had played for Miles Davis on *On the Corner*. Herbie asked me to slow it down, so he could learn it, and then trimmed off a corner to make it an odd grouping.

On "Hornets," Herbie had an idea for a fast drum part on the hi-hat. At first I was trying to do it with one hand and couldn't do it. So, after two takes of abject failure, I figured out that you could do it with two hands. This may seem obvious to drummers now, but at that time I hadn't seen anyone play a main cymbal beat with both hands. We always played the cymbal beat with one hand. Herbie was so relieved we could actually get through the tune from beginning to end that he took that take. I begged him to do just one more take, since I had finally figured out how to play my part, but the one we managed to get through was apparently good enough.

I really wish I'd had two more years with that wonderful Herbie Hancock sextet. What we did was great, but there was also untapped potential. From a selfish perspective, if I'd had two more years, I could have evolved my drumming even further.

You can't blame Herbie for breaking up the band, because what he did was right for him. Herbie's other crucial mentor besides Miles was Donald Byrd, and I believe Herbie consulted with Byrd before making a change—partly because Donald was there in person, standing to the side, the day Herbie broke up the sextet. It looked like Herbie needed Donald there in support.

The next Hancock record after *Sextant* was *Head Hunters,* featuring much more of a pop concept. *Head Hunters* was a huge hit record, probably bigger than Donald Byrd's own hit LP *Black Byrd* from the same year. (The drummer on both *Head Hunters* and *Black Byrd* is Harvey Mason.)

Herbie would then go on to make more hit records than anybody in so-called jazz. Somehow he was always attuned to dance music and knew how to connect those dots. Of course, he always played such beautiful piano, too. I *love* Herbie Hancock! But I was pretty upset with Herbie at the time. At one of the last gigs, at Zellerbach Hall in Berkeley, California, Herbie said to me, "Don't be sad, Jabali. It's only through this that we'll get to do what we were destined to do."

We were really all in this together? I glared at him and said, "I hope you get what you deserve."

Herbie swung around, away from me, and started walking down the Zellerbach steps. Looking over his shoulder, Herbie replied, "Okay. Thank you, Jabali, for putting me in my place."

That was basically that, although a year later, Herbie called me on my birthday and said, "I might not have made the right decision."

I really didn't want to hear this and shot back: "You *better* have made the right decision, because look what you've given up."

In time, I've come to appreciate how Herbie has *improved* popular music, raising the general musicianship in many ways—perhaps not unlike Duke Ellington, who was both popular and sophisticated. If you took out Herbie from pop music there would be an irreplaceable hole. People are going to dance no matter what, so it's good that they dance to Herbie Hancock. A few years ago, I visited Herbie backstage at one of his giant festival concerts with an all-electric band and told him I was proud of him. Mwandishi said to me, "Thank you, Jabali, that means something. I feel like calling my wife right now and telling her that Jabali approves!" We were both completely serious.

8

In the '70s with McCoy Tyner

After steadily working with the bands of Jimmy Smith, Wes Montgomery, Eddie Harris, Pharoah Sanders, and Herbie Hancock, not to mention being on record dates with Joe Zawinul, Wayne Shorter, and McCoy Tyner, I was reasonably established on the scene. I've never had much of a problem staying busy—people keep calling me to play, and I love to play. The larger problem was how the scene kept contracting. As inflation went up, the money for the gigs stayed the same, or even went down. I had two more runs with established leaders who could work constantly at a high level—McCoy Tyner and Stan Getz—but after that it would always be a struggle to assemble the patchwork quilt of gigs and tours.

Billy during one week of the early '70s when he didn't have a beard

Playing with Herbie was the highlight: that was perfect, in terms of projecting American classical music in the present tense. When Herbie broke up our band, I was in my early 30s. I was still so young! Looking back on that era now, it's hard to believe everything that happened, and how it all happened so fast.

The first gig I had back in town after Herbie was with the great singer Joe Williams at the Half Note Midtown. That was a beautiful experience, not least because he had Harold Mabern and Buster Williams in his band. Joe told us, "Fellas, I know you think I'm not gonna know where I am. But you're gonna have to trust me." He could go far forward and far backwards in the time and end up right in the pocket.

I was holding it down with Joe Williams, but I hadn't given up my interest in the avant-garde. Anthony Braxton was important, and Anthony's cat was John Cage. Cage was his *man*! Anthony would talk about the relationship of David Tudor to John Cage as if they were as hip as Lee Morgan and Bobby Timmons. I loved listening to Braxton talk about music, and whenever I see Anthony, I always have more questions to ask him. Braxton is a serious force.

Anthony came out of the Association for the Advancement of Creative Musicians (AACM) in Chicago, where part of the concept was simply banding together and getting grants to survive. Muhal Richard Abrams, in his very calm way of being, was the guru of this approach. When on tour in Chicago, I would go to AACM concerts in Hyde Park. They would play a serious program of innovative music in an elementary school cafeteria—and they were doing it! They were finding a way to keep the music moving forward on their own, without having to be dependent on a capitalist society. My first good connection there was Gerald Donovan, known as Ajaramu, who had played with Gene Ammons and Sonny Stitt and was at that time dating a great pianist, composer, and conceptualist, Amina Claudine Myers. Ajaramu turned me on to creative drummers like Thurman Barker, Steve McCall, and Alvin Fielder. McCall and I got pretty tight, especially after Steve moved to New York. But I was friendly with the whole AACM crew, and they all showed up to hear Herbie's band when we played the London House in Chicago for the first time.[1] That was a famous night, the night the AACM avant-gardists dressed in futuristic, African-inspired garb descended on the elite dinner crowd at the upscale London House.

---

1   A month-long stint in November 1970.

In the early '70s, you could find Anthony Braxton and Dave Holland in Washington Square Park playing chess. Braxton and Sam Rivers were Dave's heroes; one got the feeling that Dave would have done anything for Braxton or Sam. I admire Dave Holland very much. He's a smart guy and has a certain kind of humility that's based on strength.

Anthony Braxton, Dave Holland, Chick Corea, and Barry Altschul played together in Circle, doing important avant-garde music. Altschul was naturally multidirectional, but he also could get into an uptempo time space with Holland that was loose and impressive. But then Chick broke up that band to start Return to Forever, which was even more of an extreme shift than Herbie breaking up our sextet to start the Headhunters.

Stan Getz was also in that mix. Chick had written a whole book of attractive modern tunes for Stan, before starting Return to Forever with *exactly* the same book. When Dave joined Stan after Circle broke up, Dave had to play all those pretty Chick tunes with Stan: "La Fiesta," "500 Miles High," and my favorite of that set, "Times Lie." This was a bit ironic, because the break-up of Circle was an unhappy one, with the cult of Scientology in the background. But Dave surmounted all that, and steadily became more visible as a leader, to the point that I felt lucky that Dave played on a few of my own records.

There were so many of my generation that didn't quite get their due. After McCoy and Herbie, people would probably give third place to Chick. I heard Keith Jarrett a bit, but never saw him on the scene. I'm aware that for some Keith is greater than Chick, although for me Chick's command of Latin music is very important. Behind them were two of my closest friends, Stanley Cowell and Albert Dailey. Man, these cats were great pianists. McCoy Tyner himself told me how impressed he was with Albert Dailey.

It was either Dave Holland or Albert Dailey who said Stan Getz was looking for me. Maybe it was both. I remember Albert coming into Slugs' and saying, "Stan wants us," while I believe Dave called me on the phone. When we did hit with Stan I felt really comfortable with Albert and Dave. I enjoyed it so much that when McCoy Tyner called me to play, I told McCoy, "I'm working with Stan now."

A day later the phone rang, and it was Mtume. "*What?!* You're gonna turn down McCoy Tyner to play with Stan Getz?"

Mtume shamed me into calling McCoy back and telling him I would give Stan my two weeks' notice. McCoy was ready for me to join sooner, and seemed bothered that I needed to give Stan two more weeks. Apparently, when John Coltrane called McCoy, he left the Jazztet the very next day, and McCoy reminded me of that fact a few times. However, McCoy probably also guessed that he was paying less than Stan, so he eventually told me, "I would have done things differently, but okay."

Part of why Mtume advised me to go with McCoy instead of Stan was about race. We protected our image and helped our community by banding together. But race wasn't the only factor; there were also musical considerations. Mtume and I loved John Coltrane, and McCoy Tyner seemed to be the next best thing to Coltrane himself. Mtume was so surprised that I would be willing to give up that chance.

Mtume was right, but McCoy's music had also changed.

I can't remember much about *Asante*, the first record date I did with McCoy in 1970. That happened right in that first flush, when everything was going down for me in New York. The Joe Zawinul and Wayne Shorter dates were in August, McCoy was September, and I joined Herbie right around then as well. My old friend Andrew White from Washington, D.C. was there—*Asante* is the one document of us playing together—and so was Buster Williams. I have no idea how McCoy even knew to call any of us; we were all pretty young and none of us had an established name. It was one of Mtume's very first records, and later Mtume told me that he wished he'd had more time to prepare. The fact that I can recall so little about it all must mean that we barely rehearsed before tracking.

On "Fulfillment" from *Asante*, I play four beats with my foot on the hi-hat in an uptempo swing context. It's a bit of a chaotic track, so maybe I was trying to help the band stay together, but whatever I was thinking, this was a Tony Williams technique. If you play the hi-hat on all four beats it's really a straight-eighth feeling, even though you're playing the swing ride beat. Elvin Jones would never do that. Elvin really is about the quarter note. Tony Williams made it about the eighth note.

McCoy played with Elvin in some of the greatest music ever made, but by the time McCoy was leading his own bands in the '70s, there was less Elvin in his concept. It was almost like McCoy was following the Tony Williams line. Certainly all his drummers of that era, people like Alphonse Mouzon, Eric Gravatt, Wilby Fletcher, and Sonship Theus, were trying to imitate Tony. Jazz critics might have written that McCoy was a standard bearer of the tradition while Herbie was selling out, simply because McCoy never played any electric keyboards. But in my opinion, the music of the Mwandishi sextet was actually more ternary than the corresponding music of McCoy Tyner, which had become almost exclusively binary.

Tony Williams himself is essentially above criticism. Sure, he played four on the hi-hat, but there are certain records where you hear him playing four on the bass drum, and I suspect he is doing that to show his respect for the jazz tradition.

Feathering the bass drum is very important. Max Roach played 4/4 on the bass drum. Art Blakey played 4/4 on the bass drum. Feathering the bass drum creates depth and a certain mood. It immediately affects people psychologically. There are subtle versions of it, depending on how smooth the texture is: Is it cotton? Is it silk?

You might not think Elvin Jones does a lot of feathering, but he's doing enough; certainly, when you think about Elvin Jones, you think about his *bass drum depth*. Feathering is not boom, boom, boom, boom. There needs to be a bit of syncopation or even clave in the feathering, something more like a human heart, keeping the music round.

Jo Jones played the hi-hat so beautifully, but they say Kenny Clarke gave us the ride cymbal beat. When he did that, Kenny Clarke was actually playing his ride cymbal like a bass drum. It's the same function. If you don't realize that the cymbal functions the same way the bass drum does with the bass clef of the ensemble, then you're driving a car that is out of alignment. Some people spend years looking for the perfect cymbal to play their dream ride pattern on, not realizing that you can play the ride pattern on the back of a metal chair and make it work, as long as you play it like a bass drum. Kenny Clarke was famous for his syncopated bass drum bombs—and those bombs were certainly clave—but it made all the difference in the world how his cymbal beat related to the bass clef. [2]

I don't feather much. Offhand, I think the only place on record you can hear me playing obvious 4/4 on the bass drum is on Don Byron's *Bug Music*, an album that features repertoire from the swing era. But over the years, when I gigged with the old-school and deeply swinging bassists Milt Hinton, Eddie Jones, and George Duvivier, I offered some stumbling, fragmented approach to feathering, like going to a foreign country and attempting to speak their language. All three of those masters applauded me and encouraged me to keep going.

---

2 In this context, "bass clef" means any instrument fulfilling the traditional bass function.

Maybe it wasn't always enough. When I was first working with Herbie Hancock at the Village Vanguard, word got around that there was a new drummer on the scene, so Clifford Jarvis came down to check me out. He sat right beside me, watching how I played the bass drum. After one and a half tunes, Jarvis got up, said, "Aw, shit," and left. For some people, if you don't have enough of the right kind of bass drum presence, then you're simply not playing the music.

It's one way to look at it. Sonny Stitt told me that maybe Herbie Hancock was a pretty good classical pianist, but Herbie certainly couldn't play no *jazz*.

Tony Williams was above reproach, but not all of his followers were as concerned about the tradition. Azar Lawrence attended the *Trident* session, a 1975 record date that reunited McCoy Tyner and Elvin Jones in a trio with Ron Carter. Azar says that after a take or two, Elvin put down his sticks, looked over at McCoy, and growled, "I don't know who you've *been* playing with, 'Coy, but this is *me*."

McCoy and Elvin probably always felt the beat a bit differently. If you want to swing, it can be good to have some isometric rub. But when I joined McCoy's working band, he made it clear to me that he wanted a strictly contemporary concept, telling me straight out that it was okay with him if I played some rock beats to his tunes. He even used those terms, "rock" and "rock music." For the overall feel, McCoy said that it was perfectly fine to rush, but that there was absolutely no good musical reason to ever, ever, ever drag.

One of my favorite McCoy pieces was the beautiful, relaxed waltz "Contemplation" from *The Real McCoy* with Elvin Jones. But McCoy would never play that for me, almost because he knew I loved it so much. When I was in the band, most of McCoy's music was fast and loud. Instead of song forms, there were vamps.

The other McCoy Tyner record I'm on is *Sama Layuca*, which is better than *Asante*. But I'm a little disappointed by that one too, despite all the great musicians on it: Gary Bartz, Azar Lawrence, Bobby Hutcherson, Buster Williams, and Mtume. Among other things, I vividly remember that I felt great on the first day, but then McCoy called a halt to proceedings on the early side. I asked him to do just one more tune while everything was feeling good but he said no. On the next day, when we did much more tracking, I didn't feel nearly as comfortable. (Of course, just because I felt one way didn't mean McCoy or any of the other musicians felt that same way.)

In the '70s with McCoy Tyner

McCoy was by far the loudest acoustic piano player I ever played with. There was a physical force there that made you grow. I had to use all my knowledge of playing with Jimmy Smith's massive organ sound to deal with McCoy. I warmed up and practiced every day just to go to the gig; if I missed a day of practice he would simply run me over. When I told McCoy, "This takes a lot of energy!" he shrugged and said, "It just takes some time to get used to. You'll get it. Diamonds are made from pressure."

But I didn't prefer that way of playing, it wasn't my natural inclination. McCoy heard when I left a little more space in the music, and one night he came up between sets and said scornfully, "Billy? Just remember you aren't playing with Herbie Hancock anymore."

Azar Lawrence, McCoy Tyner, Alex Blake, and Billy Hart

I was disappointed by that comment, but I tried to stay in there. The working group was with Azar Lawrence and Alex Blake, and we hit it hard every night.

When we were in Boston, Azar told me that McCoy had gone back to New York to rehearse with my replacement, Wilby Fletcher. McCoy wanted to surprise me like he did with Alphonse Mouzon. He told Alphonse at the airport after they landed, "Alphonse, you're through." Boom! It's kind of cruel, but that's one way of not having to deal with it. Okay, you're fired. Bye! I'll never have to see you again after this moment.

I played the week, uptight because I knew McCoy was going to let me go. When he tried to spring the surprise on me, he asked if I wanted to quit right away or finish out two weeks. Since I had time to prepare, I replied, "Well, McCoy, you're the one who hired me. You know how much I'm making. You also know I have a family that I have to support. I'll need that two weeks because I'll need that money."

And he said it again, just like before, "Well, I would have done things differently, but okay."

I stayed in the band, knowing McCoy didn't want me there, and threw my back out in Montreal. The last week was at the Half Note Midtown in New York, and I couldn't sit down during the intermission at any of those gigs; I had to stand up and walk around because my back was stiff from playing.

McCoy Tyner will always be one of my favorite musicians, especially his work with Coltrane. There are a few especially extraordinary tracks not everyone knows, including "Out of This World" from Seattle and an "I Want to Talk About You" at the Half Note that's never been commercially available. But even without John, McCoy Tyner is at the top of any kind of music ever made, and, of course, he was wildly influential. One of the most famous Wayne Shorter records is *Speak No Evil* with Herbie Hancock on piano. Herbie told me he didn't like to listen to that classic date, because he thought he was imitating McCoy too much.

It wasn't only fellow pianists. McCoy Tyner influenced *everybody*. When McCoy finally got sick and passed away, it was almost hard to understand how anyone that strong could ever falter.

When I was in his band, we lived fairly close to each other, and sometimes he would drive me to the gigs. I'd call him "Saud," his Muslim name, and ask him a lot of questions, especially about John Coltrane.[3] As unlikely as it sounds, apparently John really liked to sing light opera and "Give Me Some Men, Some Stout-Hearted Men" while driving.[4] McCoy also said that Coltrane only cared about music, and that he could never be like that. For Saud, the most important thing was family.

McCoy said the industry wanted him to join Miles Davis after he left Coltrane. But he didn't want to do that. After all, he had played with

---

3   Tyner converted to Islam as a teenager in Philadelphia, taking the name Sulaimon Saud.

4   By Sigmund Romberg and Oscar Hammerstein II, from the operetta *The New Moon*, which also included "Softly, as in a Morning Sunrise" and "Lover, Come Back to Me," songs Coltrane later recorded.

John Coltrane, so why would he go with Miles? He didn't need Miles Davis! Or so he thought. Immediately after that exchange, McCoy had some very slow years professionally. McCoy's face darkened with anger when he told me, "They taught me a lesson I will never forget." That might sound like a conspiracy theory, but it's how McCoy felt about it deep inside. "They taught me a lesson I will never forget."[5]

If you are McCoy Tyner—if you are truly that great and innovative—it might really affect you to be shut down like that. Something similar might have happened to Tony Williams. Tony was the true innovator of what he called "jazz-rock," but in the early '70s it seemed like the industry more or less ignored Tony Williams in their rush to give everything to Billy Cobham. I'm not saying Cobham isn't a great musician, but something was out of order. There might have been a similar situation with McCoy Tyner and Chick Corea—less pronounced, but definitely present. There is no Chick Corea without McCoy Tyner.

Another exchange McCoy told me about was revealing in a more purely musical way. As I mentioned in a previous chapter, I watched McCoy play better and better with John. Everyone in that famous quartet got to develop night after night; it was just thrilling to experience that growth in real time. It was a surprise to learn from McCoy that they could be a bit competitive with each other—especially surprising from John's side, for Coltrane had a reputation for being the humblest of musicians.

One night, after McCoy had played (in his own estimation) particularly well, he suggested to John, "I'm beginning to get up there next to you."

John brushed that aside, replying, "No. The piano will never be able to *holler* like a saxophone."

Maybe that's why McCoy played so hard, he was trying to get that piano to *holler*. Well, he got there! Listen to some of what he does on the live album *Enlightenment*, which was recorded shortly before I joined his band.[6] I heard that kind of intensity every night! It was incredible.

I didn't get there myself, but I was with McCoy for only about a year. As with Herbie, I wish I could have stayed in the band longer and gotten

---

5   Tyner – like many in the jazz industry – suffered a terrible slump for a time after 1967, but two popular legends about Tyner's wilderness years were denied by Tyner in later interviews: 1) that he drove a cab 2) that he played for Ike and Tina Turner. (Apparently Tyner did talk to a cabbie about what the work was like, while Azar Lawrence was the musician in the circle who played with Ike and Tina Turner.)

6   McCoy Tyner's *Enlightenment* was recorded at the Montreux Jazz Festival in July 1973 with Azar Lawrence, Juini Booth and Alphonse Mouzon.

a chance to develop my approach further. However, I did do *Man of the Light*, a nice 1976 date with the legendary Polish violinist Zbigniew Seifert in a group with Joachim Kühn and Cecil McBee. Seifert was very influenced by John Coltrane and McCoy Tyner—the title track is even dedicated to McCoy—and it was a loss to this music when he died so young. (The beautiful ballad "Elm," by my long-term associate Richie Beirach, is dedicated to Seifert's memory.) Seifert was very generous with me, and I'm happy with the drum performance on *Man of the Light*, at least in the sense that that's where I wanted to get to when I played with McCoy, in that loud and busy binary style.

McCoy went through a lot of drummers in those years. Weather Report ran on a kind of parallel track—apparently, nobody was good enough for Joe Zawinul and Wayne Shorter until Peter Erskine got there. (Amusingly, I advised Peter not to take the Weather Report gig because of their track record with drummers. It's a good thing Peter ignored my advice.) In the late '60s, there was a phase with two drummers, both with the beat (Miles Davis's *Bitches Brew* and so forth) and the multidirectional (John Coltrane's *Meditations* and so forth), not to mention an explosion of hand drummers all over the scene.

The leaders in charge of the contemporary sound seemed to be looking for something that was hard for any one drummer to satisfy. Wilby Fletcher, my replacement with McCoy, was also who I replaced when I joined McCoy, which gives an indication how unsettled everything was at that time. Musical chairs! I was right there in the middle of all that. Perhaps it was my dedication to the jazz tradition and the expert training I received from Shirley Horn and Buck Hill that kept me working when many other drummers who spent a little time with Weather Report and McCoy Tyner drifted off the scene. When I saw McCoy in later years, he would occasionally say something that indicated he respected my contribution or even that he regretted letting me go.

At first I was feeling pretty bad about losing another gig, but, again, it helps to always treat every event with optimism. The same day as a good record date with trumpeter Charles Sullivan, *Genesis*, Norman Connors called me to say, "Congratulations! You made the *DownBeat* list of talent deserving wider recognition." The next afternoon, when I went to load my drums into the Half Note Midtown for the last week with McCoy, Stan Getz was standing there waiting for me. Stan told me to come back. The gig was mine if I wanted it.

9

We All Have a Stan Getz Story

Billy Hart and Stan Getz

Stan Getz told me he grew up as a poor Jew—"Wearing two left shoes" is exactly what he said. But he became a star with the hit "Early Autumn," while playing with Woody Herman, when he was just a teenager. That kind of early success rarely turns out well. Recently I saw a young blond pop star on TV, acting like a brat, and I thought to myself, "Yeah, that was Stan Getz. Take a talented kid, give him a constant supply of fame, women, and drugs, and see what happens."

The thing about Stan, though, was that he was great. *Really* great. His first quartet record date when he was only 19 years old featured Hank Jones, Curly Russell, and Max Roach. He not only knew the folkways and the mores of the true music, but kept up with the current moment. In some ways, I might have taken him for granted during my four-year tenure in his band—when I've heard him again in more recent years I'm always impressed by how fresh he sounds as an improvisor. I'm on many of his records, and a particularly good one is *The Master* with Albert Dailey and Clint Houston.

Stan was a hell of a teacher, whether he meant to be or not. When I first came back to the band after my time with McCoy Tyner, he put his arm around my shoulder every night and said, "Aw, man! This is the best I've felt since Jack DeJohnette was here. I really like what's going on. You know what you're doing."

After exactly six months, like when the clock struck twelve, he put his arm around my shoulder and said, "Billy, God knows I know what you're trying to do, but it's just not working."

I was insulted and tried to offer something sarcastic in response: "What do you suggest?"

Stan looked at me seriously and said, "Undulate, motherfucker!"

Undulate? What does that mean? I thought hard about that word and even looked up the definition in the dictionary. Apparently Stan wanted a more syncopated way of making the shuffle happen.

At first I didn't accept it, but in time I realized that Stan was right. Jack DeJohnette was helpful. A few years earlier, Jack had come up to me when he had been subbing for Tony Williams in Miles's band, and he said, "Man, I figured out *the* cymbal beat."

The cymbal beat.

He played it for me on the table, and his ride had skips and pauses in the pattern. Jack told me he got it from Tony Williams, especially the Herbie Hancock track "One Finger Snap" with Tony on drums, but it sounded like Roy Haynes to me. In fact, one of the first things Jack ever said in print was about Roy Haynes: that he thought of Haynes as his mentor, and that he called Haynes "Papa Daddy."

Haynes was a big influence on me as well, although I didn't listen to him so much at the beginning. I studied Haynes when I was a bit older.

Back when I was learning to play in Washington, D.C., there was a real emphasis on finding your own sound. I remember overhearing some elders debating Clifford Jordan: Was Jordan his own man yet, or did he sound too much like Sonny Rollins?

When I heard people talk like that it encouraged me to prioritize individuality. When I finally thought I had "my own style," I was feeling pretty confident. But then I heard Roy Haynes and realized that he was already doing every possible thing that I thought was "my own style." I even used to look quite a bit like Haynes, and in the magazines his drum set also seemed like mine.

Eventually, I understood that almost everything comes from someplace else.

Once in a while some young cat will tell me they play "their own music." That way of looking at it can be out of order unless they are truly advanced. When someone asked Tony Williams in a masterclass, "When did you have your own style?" Tony responded, "I never did. I don't feel that way now. I still feel like I'm playing the way that the people that I admire would be playing, if they were me."[1]

Jack DeJohnette is a good example. He plays like Roy Haynes—he gives it up for his Papa Daddy—but he sounds like himself. If you emulate who you love, your individual body turns it into your own thing. The more music you love, the more music you know, the more you can assimilate and shape your own interpretation of the tradition.

Eddie Harris told me something practical about that concept when I was in his band. "I go to check out people that nobody likes."

I asked Eddie, "Why's that?"

He said, "Because they have a tendency to be more original. Remember this, Billy Hart: People have a tendency to only like themselves when they sound like somebody else."

Art Tatum told Billy Taylor he liked to do the same kind of thing, that he would go listen to obscure people to learn other possibilities.[2] But at the time of Art Tatum or Eddie Harris, the basics of American classical music were a given. These days, I have no idea how some of the contemporary concepts I hear relate to the tradition. I have occasionally criticized the great Art Taylor for sounding more like a collection of his influences rather than possessing a finished personal style, but we sure could use a few more Art Taylors around today.

---

1 Tony Williams says this in the workshop held on April 8, 1985, "Zildjian Day" in Dallas, Texas.

2 Billy Taylor recounts this anecdote about Art Tatum in his book *Jazz Piano: A Jazz History*.

Nevertheless, I still advise advanced students to be sure to include at least one device per set that only *they* would dare to play.

On the ending of a dark ballad I might use a bass drum thump I borrowed from André Previn's score to the great movie *Elmer Gantry*. Nobody else I know would do that thump, so that's an example of how I created "my own style." As a ballad winds down, I put down the brushes and pick up sticks for the last eight bars. Nobody else does that, so if you hear that on a record, you know it's me.

Roy Haynes could play with anybody and sound like himself. He worked with the original master swinger, Lester Young, as well as the bebop giants Charlie Parker and Bud Powell. Then he held it down for a long run with the diva Sarah Vaughan, but somehow he was just getting started. He went on to make many great records with the new breed of avant-gardists like Andrew Hill and Eric Dolphy, not to mention being Coltrane's choice as a sub for Elvin Jones. When the music changed in the '60s from being exclusively song-form oriented to an emphasis on pedal-points and texture, a lot of older drummers were left in the dust. Haynes not only kept up, he set the pace. Chick Corea made all his drummers use the same flat ride that Haynes played on *Now He Sings, Now He Sobs*.

On top of all that, he could play the slow blues with total commitment. At Dewey Redman's memorial in St. Peter's Church, Haynes sat in with Joshua Redman, Pat Metheny, and Charlie Haden and gave us a clinic in just the right texture for a medium slow blues.

Haynes knew who he was. I called him a week later to compliment him on how swinging that St. Peter's performance was, and he replied, "Oh, you noticed that, huh?"

At the drums, playing a slow blues is harder than it may appear. Even someone as great as Tony Williams wasn't so comfortable with that style, at least at first. On that dirty blues "Yams" with Jackie McLean, recorded in 1963, you can hear that making the right texture happen is a stretch for Tony, although admittedly he was only 17 at the time. He got it together later. Jeff Watts always reminds me that when I gave a masterclass at Berklee, he played a ton of drums—it was incredible, of course—before I slyly asked that he play a slow, swinging blues. To his dismay, the teenaged Tain discovered that honoring my request was more difficult than he expected.

Everything Roy Haynes plays was connected to the clave. In fact, his swing ride cymbal could almost sound like a cascara pattern. He varied it in the manner that Jack DeJohnette showed me when Jack said he found *the* beat.

To use Stan Getz's word, it's an *undulating* cymbal beat.

There are all kinds of textures, but three that seem to be of a higher level or class are Billy Higgins, Philly Joe Jones, and Kenny Clarke. The people who love these drummers stop talking about any kind of European concept of technique, and they talk about texture: how it feels, how it falls.

Upbeats are very important. Billy Higgins had a word for his special way with upbeats, which he called "the Lift." With students, I play Higgins on Lee Morgan's "Hocus Pocus" to demonstrate "the Lift." It is easy to see why many great musicians called Higgins "the Magic Carpet."

There's a euphoric sensuality to laying back in certain situations, but if you don't want it to slow down, you play more upbeats. More shuffles.

Articulating two and three at the same time is a technique as basic to African music as the scale is to European music. A 2:3 polyrhythm produces a texture that people respond to emotionally. The ternary couldn't be more important!

All of this undulation helps project something at softer volume for acoustic music. Lester Young told his drummers he just wanted a little "ti-ti boom." Yeah. Pres didn't say play soft or play simply, he said something that already sounds like clave or swing, "ti-ti boom."

I don't know how much my playing *really* changed after Stan told me to undulate. Washington, D.C. drummers have a real commitment to the blues shuffle in their ride cymbal beat. That was Jimmy Cobb, that was Stump Saunders. I was always going for that myself, and I still do. "Undulating" just let a little more air in, gave my cymbal beat a bit more space. Vinnie Colaiuta once talked about hearing me with Stan in *Modern Drummer*:

> *There are a lot of situations I've learned from, even from doing a movie date and having to sit in a room with a full orchestra. It was tough trying to make something sound like it's really smoking, having to just barely touch the drums because the sound was leaking into all the string mics. I just tried to do that by playing with a certain amount of mental intensity. Probably the most amazing drummer I've ever seen doing that was Billy Hart. I saw him playing with Stan*

Getz once in Boston, and I couldn't believe how somebody could burn so hard at such a low volume level.[3]

I can't be sure, but the way Vinnie is talking suggests that he heard me after I followed Stan's advice. What I *can* say for sure is that before I worked with Stan, I was on a few records a year, and after I worked with Stan, I was on dozens of records a year. Ethan Iverson tells me that I'm on well over 500 records, and apparently you can even make a convincing case that I'm the *most* recorded drummer on LP and CD playing small group jazz with extensive improvising.[4] That's hard for me to believe, but when I look back, it's certainly true I was in the studios a lot. One time, between back-to-back record dates for Steeplechase, I didn't go home, I just curled up and slept beneath the studio piano.

When Stan Getz really got into a groove, he would lift his foot off the floor, like he was putting his foot in lukewarm water. He floated in the music, and the rhythm section would float with him. He was a great musician, but he wasn't a great man. Occasionally, when I tell my Stan Getz stories—and anyone who played with him has plenty of stories—listeners are shocked by his dark side. Maybe this is because Stan's gift was lyricism. When he played a ballad, everyone fell into a trance. It wasn't just the audience; the *band* fell into a trance.

For a ballad, Stan didn't want the band to undulate or float, he wanted something stiffer. If the rhythm section played way on top of the beat on a ballad, then Stan could lay back and be romantic on top. On one occasion we were performing "Lover Man" at a big outdoor concert at the Umbria festival in Italy in front of thousands of people. Stan was being so romantic! I was totally lost in the music. But then—right after one of his gorgeous, lyrical phrases—Stan took the horn out of his mouth, turned around, and screamed at the rhythm section so that everyone heard it for miles around, "The motherfucking tempo is slowing down!"

I've said above that I won't be telling many gossipy stories in this memoir, but I'm going to make a quick exception for Stan Getz. People always ask me, "Tell us some Stan Getz stories!" and perhaps the stories are too good not to share.

Stan performed at many upscale places. The Catamaran was a glamorous spa in San Diego situated on a small lake. After the gig one night, two men robbed Stan in his room. Stan fought back and they

---

3   From *Modern Drummer* (October 1993), by Robyn Flans.

4   The third appendix has a partial discography of Hart's work as a sideman.

ended up pistol-whipping him pretty badly. A little while later, bassist Clint Houston was walking around the grounds, enjoying the night air, and saw that the door to Stan's room was open. He investigated, found Stan unconscious and bloody on the floor, and called an ambulance. To make sure everything was going to be okay, Clint got in the back of the ambulance to ride with Stan to the hospital. Halfway to the hospital, Stan comes to, looks at Clint in disgust, and says, "You're just trying to keep your gig, you motherfucker. You're fired."

The way he let Joanne Brackeen go was almost as bad. Her father was dying, but he kept talking her into playing a few more gigs. "What are you going to do? It's too late. He's too sick. Play my gig." Then when he died, "Okay, Joanne, he's dead already, he's not going anywhere, play two more nights and then you can go to the funeral." She finally went back home to join her family. Sadly, Stan liked her sub, Andy Laverne, and never hired Joanne again.

Everybody who played with Stan was a good musician. I always got along with Joanne Brackeen; she's a great composer with startlingly progressive tendencies. I had a nice hook-up with bassist Niels-Henning Ørsted Pedersen as well: Joanne, Niels-Henning, and I got into a groove with Stan on his 50th birthday concert in Denmark, *Stan Getz Gold*.

Stan was competitive with everybody and everything. After he came back from playing with a reunion of the Four Brothers, he told me casually, "It was great, I tore Zoot Sims a new asshole." Somehow he thought he had the right to say, "You know, even Sonny Rollins is afraid of me." On that tour of Denmark, he set his sights upon the promoter's wife.

Stan was incorrigible about women. On an international flight, he took notice of a certain stewardess. He was up in first class with his wife and came back to coach to give me a note to hand off to that stewardess. "Don't open it," he warned me, but of course I ignored him and read it anyway. It read: "I'm Stan Getz. I'm with my wife, so you will think I'm a dog, but you are so beautiful and life is so short. Here's my phone number." The stewardess took the note and called him later.

Part of Stan's enormous fame came from his recordings of Brazilian music, starting with *Jazz Samba* with Charlie Byrd, and then *Getz/Gilberto* with João Gilberto, Antônio Carlos Jobim, and Astrud Gilberto. (Stan got his hands dirty there as well, for Astrud left João to have a short affair with Stan.)

These days, people sometimes ask me if Getz's huge success with Brazilian music was cultural appropriation. As far as I understand it, no—especially since Stan apparently helped the whole economy of Brazil. Stan told me that when he went to Brazil for the first time, they were so grateful for his support that they set him up in a nice house with seven women, from "blackest of black to whitest of white" (his exact words) plus a jelly glass full of cocaine.

I had been aware of bossa nova for exactly as long as Stan Getz. In the early '60's Stan's quartet came to my old stomping grounds, Abart's, with Pete La Roca on drums. Charlie Byrd, a local guitarist who had traveled to Brazil, got talking with Stan. In the corner of the club, I literally overheard Charlie Byrd tell Stan Getz about bossa nova![5]

Afro-Cuban music had been influencing American pop and jazz since day one, but many American musicians responded positively to the Brazilian bossa nova because of its fresh harmonic perspective.

Jelly Roll Morton liked to talk about the "Spanish tinge" for jazz. Rhythmically, the Spanish tinge is obviously clave. Jelly Roll was in that crucial port city, New Orleans, which is where the American version of the clave, the second line, comes from. All drummers from New Orleans get a special badge. Nobody was greater at the rhythmic feel of American classical music than Billy Higgins, and whenever I asked him where he got his magic from, Higgins credited studying with Ed Blackwell, one of the *most* special of all the special New Orleans drummers.

But Jelly Roll's Spanish tinge might not just be clave—it might also be harmony, as in chords that first came from a guitar, not a piano. When Miles Davis and Gil Evans did *Sketches of Spain*, it was a natural fit, almost like they'd been playing that kind of music even before they made that record. So much of the modal jazz of the '60s seems to be a bit Spanish somehow.

Bossa nova was softer than what came out of the Cuban and Puerto Rican populations in New York and the Bronx. It was the West Coast cool school side of things. In a parallel situation to jazz, the darker-skinned people in Brazil were the innovators, but most of those who traveled to this country and got famous, people like Gilberto and Jobim, were white Brazilians. Bossa nova epitomized that life of sitting by the swimming

---

5 Buck Hill's first recordings were with Charlie Byrd in Washington, D.C.—1958's *Jazz at the Showboat* and 1959's *Byrd in the Wind*. (*Byrd in the Wind* includes an uptempo swing version of the Brazilian ballad "Copacabana.") Byrd recorded 1962's *Jazz Samba* with Getz in Washington, D.C.

pool with a glass of champagne. Perfect for romance. Perfect for Stan Getz.

I have a huge collection of Brazilian music on LP. Some of those records are really deep and authentic; others are more casual. Astrud Gilberto wasn't a truly great singer, but her album arranged by Gil Evans, *Look to the Rainbow*, is certainly enjoyable.

Of the many great Brazilian drummers and percussionists, Milton Banana got to the American audience first, playing drums on *Getz/Gilberto*. I also listened to two important innovators, Edison Machado and Dom Um Romão. Edison hit the drums hard; he was something like the Elvin Jones of that style. Certain American drummers might have been a bit condescending to bossa nova at first, thinking that it was pretty dainty, but Edison showed us how the style really comes from the samba, which originally happened in the streets of Brazil with huge drums and a whole parade of people dancing. At Carnaval, there might be dozens of drummers together playing the batucada in a fast and fervent style.

It's impossible to name everybody, but João Palma, Airto, Portinho, and Duduka Da Fonseca influenced a lot of people. My personal favorite might have been Paulo Braga; another great is Edu Ribeiro, who knows all the history and who I still talk with and learn from today.

I loved the wonderful singer, composer, and guitarist João Gilberto from the beginning, and first played with him at Charlie Byrd's club the Showboat in the '60s. At that time, I was just imitating what I *thought* the bossa nova beat was, like what Milton Banana played on *Getz/Gilberto* and what the American cats played on *Jazz Samba*.[6] Most American drummers at that time were in that same boat.

Rhythm is at least equal to harmony in the scheme of human evolution. It's just that the European concept, since it was so devoid of rhythm, related harmony to emotion so clearly that it used to seem like the only way to do it. At this point, we know differently—rhythm can give you that same emotional value.

A decade after I first played a basic bossa beat with João, I got another chance to deepen my studies. João and Stan put aside any former differences in order to record a new album, *The Best of Two Worlds*, a major studio production introducing the singer Heloisa Buarque de Hollanda, also known as Miúcha. Stan and João toured together a bit to promote that LP, and just recently, the archival recording *Getz/*

---

6   Buddy Deppenschmidt and Bill Reichenbach, Sr.

Gilberto '76 appeared, featuring performances with Joanne Brackeen, Clint Houston, and me at Todd Barkan's Keystone Korner. On that live album you can really hear my hookup with João.

We rehearsed for *The Best of Two Worlds* at Shadowbrook, Stan's mansion in Tarrytown. Shadowbrook was formerly owned by Irving Berlin; George Gershwin visited as well. I hated driving up there to rehearse for days on end, but João made up for it by teaching me the partido alto.[7] The African community, religion, and culture is stronger in Bahia than anywhere else in Brazil. João is from Juazeiro in Bahia, and that is also where the partido alto comes from.

At Shadowbrook there was a ping pong table. João loved to play ping pong incessantly and made everyone play with him. In those days I was pretty good at ping pong myself, but competing with João was a chore. When you slammed the ball, João would hit it in such a way that it would go up to the ceiling before coming back down. The game slowed

João Gilberto, Billy Hart, and Todd Barkan. (Courtesy of Todd Barkan.)

---

7 The partido alto is a samba rhythm considerably older than the bossa nova.

down to a crawl, you would lose focus, and eventually João would just beat you without much effort, bouncing the ball up to the ceiling again and again. That was irritating, but during these ping-pong games, João would discuss how to play his music.

Basically, João played partido alto on the guitar. But when I started playing that beat with him, he said, "Now, don't play it so stiff like that." João didn't speak much English, but he was able to tell me clearly: "Billy, play like the rain."

I loved that, of course, and "play like the rain" is something I still tell all my advanced students. On *Getz/Gilberto '76*, I am accompanying the way João taught me. Rather than just repeating the partido alto over and over again, I would play it against what João was playing. I also had some kind of harmonic attitude, relating the drums to the song, not just keeping it in a stationary place like a studio drummer.

João excelled at creating an intimate feeling with the audience, so I used a special small balloon stick, just the size of a pencil, on the drum, while playing the ride pattern with a brush on the leg of my pants. There's a nice picture of João, Todd Barkan, and me after one of the sets at the Keystone Korner. I remember that moment well: João had just told Todd, "Get Billy whatever he wants!"

One thing to Stan Getz's credit: his biggest hit was "The Girl From Ipanema," and people wanted that wherever we went, but he never played it *once* in all the years I was in his band. Instead, his repertoire was modern and very hip, including pieces by Wayne Shorter and Ralph Towner and many standards updated with a fresh twist.

Stan will always be one of my important teachers. Not every Stan Getz story is about something competitive and nasty; he also could speak lovingly of his experiences with so many important players. From Stan I learned of the Boston drummer Tiny Kahn, who "would tie your solo up with a nice little bow."[8]

He also had extrasensory perception in terms of what was going on. One time I took in the first half of a Boston Symphony Orchestra concert featuring the music of Olivier Messiaen. (Woody Shaw, Herbie Hancock, and Tony Williams were all feverish Messiaen fans, so I also listened to Messiaen whenever I could.) My favorite conductor, Seiji Ozawa, was in charge and Messiaen himself was there. They smoked it; I could hardly

---

8   Kahn (1923–1953) can be heard in good form on *Jazz at Storyville* with Getz in Boston on October 28, 1951.

sit in the seat I was so excited by the concert. At the intermission I ran back over to play with Stan. Maybe I was influenced by the concert at the gig? I didn't really think I was doing anything different, but at one point Stan took the horn out his mouth and looked over at me. "My god, Billy, *what* are you hearing?"

Stan was furious when I wanted to miss a night in England to play a reunion with Herbie Hancock in New York, and he wanted to fight about it. "I know you want to play with Herbie Hancock more than me!" he yelled. Yeah, Stan, that's true, why are you making a big deal about it? (That concert was a retrospective of Hancock's bands, and ended up being recorded and released as the first album called *V.S.O.P.* I wasn't originally going to do it, but Herbie said, "You've got to do it, the night of the gig is the 29th!"—playing into the Mwandishi lore of the number 29.)

For some reason Stan started getting into it with me about whether I was smiling enough at him or not. But then when I smiled at him— admittedly, not my most unforced smile—his reaction was, "You know, Billy, you don't have to *Tom* for me."

Eventually, I started looking in hotel mirrors and having two-sided conversations with myself about how long I was going to put up with him. At the Actor's Club in LA, I finally decided it was time. We had been playing for two months straight and there was a month off before we were planning to start again for another month. Enough was enough. When I sat next to him backstage on a plush couch out of some kind of politeness, Stan sensed my meaning. "Alright, man," he said. "What the fuck do you want?"

I replied, "Stan, I'm finished. I'm through."

He growled back, "Are you going to honor your commitment to the next month? Or are you going to quit like a fucking dog?"

I said again, "Stan, I'm through."

10

Striking up the Band

Elliot Meadow was from Scotland. He started by being a roadie for Count Basie, but worked his way up to being a prominent player in the jazz industry. Everybody in the Herbie Hancock sextet knew Meadow. In 1977, Meadow told me it was time and negotiated my first record as a leader, *Enchance*, on the A&M Horizon label.

The packaging on the label was producer John Snyder's idea—artwork, photographs, commentary from the musicians, a separate set of liner notes from Stanley Crouch, reproductions of two scores, and a transcription of Eddie Henderson's solo on "Layla Joy." One of the people quoted was my close friend, James Lott:

The music on this record represents many centuries of paths, struggles and dreams. Being at once rooted in our history and our destiny, the music is creative energy through which we move. Like us, the music moves linearly, spirally, or in jumps. Yet, always interpreting the ever-present, sometimes mysterious, order that dominates the cosmos.

> *Widen the movement*
> *Open the song*
> *Remind us who we are*
> *Dance on, players.*

Lott was a mathematics professor from Atlanta, where I met him on tour with Jimmy Smith, but he was also into the music. For a time he was in Manhattan, teaching at Hunter College, and John Coltrane became a personal friend. John would ask for Lott's serious opinion after sets at the Half Note, and John even gave Lott an alto saxophone that Lott could play in an avant-garde fashion. Lott was extraordinarily intelligent, charismatic, and philosophical.

Occasionally I'd pick up the phone and Lott would be there, saying, "I'll be brief."

I'd say, "Yeah?"

"Do you know what women are?"
"No."
"They're our teachers," he'd explain, and hang up.
Every time Lott would say something like that, it was true.
Phone rings:
"Hello?"
"I'll be brief."
"Yeah?"
"Do you know the highest form of intelligence in the universe?"
"No."
"The highest form of intelligence in the universe is love."

I am influenced by Lott to this day and still quote him when I can. He once sent me a letter that was headed, "Shit mope is auto boy." That turned out to be a mixed-up version of, "This poem is about you."

Lott ended up being close with bassist William Parker, and Parker helped organize a memorial when Lott died in 2018. Because James Lott never made a record, his name is barely known outside of his close circle of family and friends, but he was nonetheless an important part of my musical life.

Hannibal Marvin Peterson and James Lott shared something in personality: Southern, spiritually guided, intelligent, and able to bring other people around to their point of view. In that era Hannibal and I were tight. Hannibal was pure fire on the trumpet, but I also wanted lyricism, which is why Eddie Henderson joins Hannibal on *Enchance*. Eddie plays melodically on "Layla Joy," while Hannibal blows the walls down on Dewey Redman's tune, "Corner Culture."

"Layla Joy" was the first tune I wrote and the first one to be recorded. The title was revealed at the very end, just after we finished the take: A phone call came in from happy father Ed Williams, saying there was a new child on this earth and her name was Layla Joy.[1]

I hear things and can whistle them well. If someone else plays the chords on the piano, I can say whether they are right or not, and sometimes I give certain poetic words or even specific musical references while working out the harmony. "Think of what Herbie Hancock plays at the beginning of 'Stella by Starlight'" is something I've said to a pianist.

---

[1] Ed Williams was a DJ whose WLIB program "Maiden Voyage" (named for the Herbie Hancock composition) had wide reach. Williams also supplied liner notes to the Freddie Hubbard Atlantic LP *The Black Angel* and narrated the spoken word LP *Afro-American History Highlights: The True Story of the Black Man's Achievements*.

Of course, there's a lot of leeway there, which is why my tunes sound so radically different in the hands of different bands. I like the way my tunes have evolved; Duke Ellington's tunes didn't stay the same over time, either.

But I probably wouldn't have tried to compose any melodies if it weren't for Dave Holland. When I called Dave for *Enchance*, he asked me about my music. "Well, Dave, I can't even find middle C on the piano. Maybe every now and then I might hear something in the shower."

I was being a little sarcastic, but Dave replied, "Well, man, you better get back in the fucking shower, because I'm not doing this date if you don't write something."

Dewey Redman helped me with "Layla Joy," and that's his chart reproduced in the notes on *Enchance*. I had met Dewey when I visited San Francisco for a week with Shirley Horn, the same week I left Shirley in the lurch when called away by Jimmy Smith. Jimmy Lovelace was one of the great drummers, especially for vocalists, and he lived with another drummer, Art Lewis (nicknamed Sharkey), in Happy House, 729 Oak Street, later immortalized in song by Ornette Coleman. A lot of people were around the jam sessions at Happy House, including the Englishwoman Caroline Joy Hadley, who became an editor of *Car & Driver* magazine and for a time dated Bobby Hutcherson. Caroline gave me good advice when she told me, "Happiness is just a momentary high. You'll always be happy or sad, so what you need is peace."

At Happy House, Dewey Redman was playing totally avant-garde, with many extended techniques. Later, when I heard him with Ornette Coleman's band, Dewey had mastered that comparatively smooth bluesy thing that characterized Ornette. Ornette and Dewey were both from the same part of Texas, there's no doubt about it.[2]

I wanted Cecil Taylor to play piano on *Enchance*, but that wasn't going to happen, so I called Don Pullen. I didn't know Don, but he nailed the music. Since I couldn't get Ornette and Cecil for my record, I got Dewey and Don.

Oliver Lake was my man, and he still is—we're neighbors in Montclair. I had met Oliver in St. Louis when he was involved with B.A.G., the Black Artists Group, but it was the LP he made in New York, *Heavy Spirits*, that convinced me I should get him for my own record. On the opening tune on *Enchance*, Oliver's "Diff Customs," we played free. But with Buster

---

2 Both were born in Fort Worth, Texas; Coleman in 1930 and Redman in 1931.

Williams there, it wasn't just free, it was groovy, too. Dave Holland and Don Pullen also contributed memorable tunes in varied styles. On Hannibal's "Rahsaan is Beautiful," Michael Carvin plays percussion. In this era, both Hannibal and Carvin were close to my teenage son, Chris; when I was on the road, they would hang out together.

I was really comfortable on that record date, and the combination of personalities was really interesting. I don't think those musicians have played together much before or since—it was a real one-off.

A lot of people were surprised that my first record would be so avant-garde. Stan Getz couldn't believe it, saying to me, "What the fuck was that?"

Enchance made a few "best of the year" lists and then sort of vanished. I was hoping to get a follow-up, but John Snyder's replacement, Tommy LiPuma, wouldn't return my calls. Eventually, when I was working with Stan outside the Horizon offices in LA, I walked over and talked my way past the secretaries and saw LiPuma in person. LiPuma told me to my face, "Billy, to tell you the truth, I just don't like your kind of music."

Fair enough. But if you do make something of quality, it has a chance of staying relevant. When I did a gig of the *Enchance* music many years later, Don Pullen wasn't alive, so I called Craig Taborn. Craig told me, "Of course I'll do this gig with you, Billy! I know every note of *Enchance*."

My next two records would be for Gramavision, owned by Jonathan F. P. Rose, whose family was important in New York real estate—Frederick P. Rose Hall at Jazz at Lincoln Center is named for Jonathan's father. When I met flutist and composer James Newton there was some shared vision between us. The musicians in Newton's circle included people like Anthony Davis, Abdul Wadud, and Pheeroan akLaff. In that world, there was a real dedication to finding a bridge to contemporary European classical music, and I appreciated that perspective. For example, their bassist, Rick Rozie, was in the Hartford Symphony. A lot of their first records were on India Navigation, which was a well-meaning but bare-bones affair owned by Bob Cummins, a lawyer who helped musicians. Several on the India Navigation roster eventually moved over to Gramavision, which had an important run of documenting creative and interesting music in New York. I'm on a couple of Newton Gramavision LPs including *Luella* (1984) with violinist John Blake and pianist Kenny Kirkland; the glamorous sound world of *Luella* leads directly into my releases *Oshumare* (1985) and *Rah* (1988).

Some people really like *Oshumare*. Billy Drummond told me he thought it was one of the best records of the whole era; Ethan Iverson really loves it too. Dave Holland is on both *Enchance* and *Oshumare*, and even Dave asked me, "How did you like this one, man? This was a lot better, right?" But I didn't agree with him, especially now. *Oshumare* felt almost a little commercial after *Enchance*. Of course, the music and the style were my choices, but, looking back, I appreciate the first blast of avant-garde more than the comparatively conservative follow-up. Still, as with *Enchance*, the musicians on *Oshumare* are a group of people not usually associated with each other, and they all certainly do play very well!

Mark Gray is an excellent studio musician in addition to being a talented jazz pianist. I met Mark on a Hubert Laws date, and he became part of the social system I had with my first wife Dolores, Hannibal Peterson, Carvin, Lott, and so forth. Mark contributed to *Enchance*, but is more visible on *Oshumare*, taking a synthesizer solo on the opening "Duchess." For a time, Mark was the one to help me put my songs in proper order, and on *Oshumare* they are "Duchess" and "Lorca." Going forward, many of my compositions would reflect my family. "Duchess" is for the grandmother who bought me my first drum, and "Lorca" is for my son, who is now a well-respected drummer living in California.

James Newton had hired Kenny Kirkland for his record, and I was impressed right away. I then checked out the ECM records Kenny made with Miroslav Vitous and thought the way he was playing was romantic and multidirectional.[3] The Kirkland legend has grown over the years, and at this point we all know he was one of the true greats of his era. When I called him for *Oshumare*, though, in my mind Kenny was mainly a romantic player—I hadn't heard him with Jeff Watts yet.[4] The waltz he contributed to the date, "Chance," is really beautiful.

Mark played keyboards and Kenny played piano, but there are also two guitarists on the album, Bill Frisell and Kevin Eubanks. I had a dream with two guitarists playing together. It sounded like a harp, and I knew that John Coltrane suggested that Alice Coltrane start playing the harp. Upon awakening, I thought I should get two guitarists for my next album. When the Gramavision opportunity arose, I started asking around, and bassist Marc Johnson told me one of the guitarists needed

---

3   *First Meeting* recorded May 1979 and *Miroslav Vitous Group* recorded July 1980, both in Oslo.

4   Kenny Kirkland and Jeff Watts were a significant high-energy partnership in the bands of Wynton Marsalis, Branford Marsalis, and Kenny Garrett; they also appeared on each other's records as a leader..

to be Bill Frisell. I asked Marc what Frisell sounded like. Marc frowned, thought about it, and replied, "I can't tell you."

That was good enough for me, so I called Bill for the date, and his piece "Waiting Inside" was strong and evocative. Dave Holland recommended Kevin Eubanks, who also came from a serious musical family. [5]

I had heard Branford Marsalis with Art Blakey and had also played a week in Ron Carter's band with Wynton and Branford. (The repertoire for that pianoless quartet ended up on Ron's album *Etudes* with Art Farmer, Bill Evans, and Tony Williams.) At that time, Branford reminded me of Wayne Shorter a bit, like in his fine solo on Dave Holland's fast jazz tune "Cosmosis."

Steve Coleman was obviously already on his own path, although he got a lot of direction from the important drummer/composer Doug Hammond. When I saw a performance of Doug's band with bass, cello, and Steve, I really liked Steve's conception. In recent years Steve and I have been more in touch—he's a perpetual student, just like me.

Kenny Kirkland, Bill Frisell, Kevin Eubanks, Branford Marsalis, Steve Coleman: these are all important and influential names now. In particular, Steve's original concepts dominate the creative scene, but at the time they were all simply young cats who I thought had potential.

Violinist Didier Lockwood was a last-minute addition. Just a few days before my date, I participated in Didier's Gramavision recording *Out of the Blue* with Gordon Beck and Cecil McBee. Probably thanks to my grandmother Viola, I always maintained an interest in romantic European classical music, which means the violin. John Blake was wonderful with James Newton, and then I loved the sound of Didier right away. Didier brought something special to *Oshumare*—try what he plays on "Lorca"—and I was so pleased with the addition of violin that I would feature Mark Feldman in my first working band a few years later. Manolo Badrena played hand drums on a few tracks, giving this date a truly contemporary flavor.

Oshumare was a relaxed session and features a mysterious painting from Ornette Coleman's collection on the cover.

The follow-up, *Rah*, is a memorial for my brother Ronald Alfred Hart, who died suddenly of a heart attack in Hawaii after a basketball game. (*Rah* is R.A.H., his initials.) Three pieces on this LP were specifically

---

5   Kevin Eubanks has two musical brothers, trombonist Robin and trumpeter Duane; their uncles were Ray and Tommy Bryant.

composed for Ronald. "Motional" is for the way he moved in sports (he was a beloved football and basketball coach at Howard University and elsewhere); "Reneda" is the combination of his two daughters, Ronda and Renee; and "Naaj" means "sun" in the West African language Wolof.

"Ra" (like "Rah") can mean sun as well, and I had meant for the cover to the LP to be a sun. But John Blake beat me to a sun-themed cover for Gramavison, so we went with a picture of a cymbal that still looks a bit like a sun.

Some of the circumstances surrounding the recording of *Rah* were a bit rushed. It was supposed to be Kenny Garrett and Branford Marsalis, but Garrett went with Miles Davis and Branford never showed for the rehearsals. In a panic I called Dave Liebman for heat and Ralph Moore for lyricism. Eddie Henderson returned on trumpet, sounding great as always, and Dave's wife, Caris Visentin, thickened the texture with oboe on his song "Junque."

One of the highlights is Kenny Kirkland's wonderful, ferocious solo on "Reneda." At that time, my four favorite bass players were Buster Williams, Dave Holland, Cecil McBee, and Eddie Gomez, and *Rah* featured both Eddie and Buster—including a couple of Eddie's Spanish-influenced, romantic, lyrical bass solos.

Bill Frisell and Kevin Eubanks were back again from *Oshumare*. It worked, but neither album really features the two guitars playing together like a giant harp the way I first dreamed it. Still, the two Gramavision LPs are a nice snapshot of the times, and they both came from that dream of two guitars.

Enchance, *Oshumare*, and *Rah* are all strictly studio dates. The first band of mine that played gigs was *Such Great Friends* (1983) with Billy Harper, Stanley Cowell, and Reggie Workman, which evolved to *Great Friends* (1986) with the addition of Sonny Fortune. When a Japanese promoter asked me to put a band together, I suggested some of my favorite musicians who were already familiar with Japan. I never intended to formally lead that group, which was a collective.

Reggie was a bit older. He had worked with John Coltrane and Art Blakey and went on to be active in all sorts of fields, including being a pillar of jazz education at The New School. Stanley Cowell knew the whole history and played it his own way. Billy Harper was coming out of Coltrane—a lot of power and commitment to the gospel ethos—a true Texas tenor. Sonny Fortune was similar, an incandescent force but on alto.

For Harper and Fortune, Coltrane was like a religion, and that was okay with me. Coltrane was my religion, too. Harper was more quiet, but Fortune loved to talk about music. When Sonny Fortune called me on the phone, if one of us mentioned John's name, that was it—we would discuss him for two or three hours.

It's not easy to be in a collective. In the end certain people take charge, and that's probably right—usually those people are doing all the administrative work. I enjoyed both versions of Great Friends, but not every internal interaction was smooth sailing. Those two Great Friends records also have lesser production values, the albums solely under my own name sound much better.

The next two records were for Arabesque and continued in the same vein as the Gramavision albums. The head of Gramavision, Jonathan F. P. Rose, told me he liked me, but that he couldn't support more releases unless I took a band out on tour. When Daniel Chriss asked me to record for Arabesque, I looked for musicians that might actually be able to go on the road. The same basic line-up is on both *Amethyst* and *Oceans of Time*, and together they are my most forceful statement as a leader, where I was calling all the shots and writing a lot of music. As with all my albums up to this point, it was a diverse cast of people who may never have played together otherwise.

John Stubblefield was a soulful tenor player but also a proficient arranger and composer. He was from Arkansas, and his heart was in

Santi Debriano, David Kikoski, John Stubblefield, Billy Hart, David Fiuczynski, Mark Copland, and Mark Feldman

the blues. Stubblefield was also a member of the AACM, at least for a time, and I was attached to the idea of someone like that in my band. At the opposite end of the spectrum, Mark Feldman was a rhapsodic violinist who loved European classical music but who also spent time on the road with country star Loretta Lynn. On Stubblefield's tune "King of Harts," first the composer plays, then Feldman plays. They couldn't be more different, but they both fit my music.

Having all this guitar and piano on these Gramavision and Arabesque records gives them a somewhat symphonic atmosphere. David Fiuczynski is well-known for his rock group, the Screaming Headless Torsos, but I saw him in Ben Perowsky's band, where he impressed me with his improvising. Fiuczynski sounded enough like my dream of two guitarists for me to call him cold—no wonder he goes by "Fuze." On his fiery "Melanos," Fuze pulls out all the stops.

Dave Kikoski is a more obvious choice; his talent speaks for itself, and at that point he had been playing with Roy Haynes for several years. I met Kikoski on a nice Ralph Moore record date with Buster Williams, *623 C Street*, where he impressed with his facility—he had that kind of McCoy to Herbie to Chick thing we all like, but he did it in his own way. Try his tune "Shadows" for Kikoski in a more reflective mood.

Bassist Santi Debriano is from Panama and has a lyrical and modern conception. I always hire an acoustic bassist, but that bassist also needs to understand the history of the electric bass coming from a Latin perspective. Santi takes a really beautiful solo on "Amethyst." Marc Copland guests on synthesizer on two tunes; Marc and I had been playing trio with Gary Peacock.

For the second Arabesque date, *Oceans of Time*, Chris Potter was a guest artist, because he had subbed for Stubblefield on a few gigs. Chris was already a star at a very young age. I liked the two tenors in the front line and afterwards tried to continue that when I could. Craig Handy filled in for Stubblefield at the reunion gig in Healdsburg.

The name of the title track, "Oceans of Time," is from a line in the movie *Bram Stoker's Dracula*, where Gary Oldman says, "I have crossed oceans of time to find you." Women can't resist the archetype of Dracula, and in the end, I *am* a romantic! Apart from the meaning in the movie, I like "Oceans of Time" as a phrase, suggesting all kinds of music and rhythm, which is also why it became the title of this memoir.

Musically, my song "Oceans of Time" is based on certain family whistles that my parents used when calling Ronald and me in for dinner.

My father's whistle was fast and short, while my mother's was more bluesy. We'd be playing down the hill with a bunch of other little kids, but when we heard those whistles, we knew it was time to go in and wash up.

This group played in New York and toured Japan. I always meant to get back to the *Oceans of Time* band—it really seemed to be the most like me of all the bands I led. But the phone always kept ringing for any group but my own.

By this point, I was well into long-term associations with Dave Liebman and Richie Beirach. These two really go together, feeding off each other musically for over 50 years now. Their original Quest group was with George Mraz and Al Foster, but when Al left to play with Miles Davis they got me, and when George went with Tommy Flanagan they got Ron McClure.

In the final analysis, Quest is really Liebman and Beirach's band, but they bill it as a collective, and we all play like we are leaders. In some ways, Quest was the most comfortable I felt since the Mwandishi sextet, at least in terms of a band that gave me a chance to develop my drum language on the gig in real time.

Liebman had played with Miles Davis and Elvin Jones and was coming out of that post-Coltrane thing. (He and I are on Miles's *On the Corner* together.) Beirach was too, but he was also committed to modernism in the European manner. At the time, I felt the lineage was: McCoy,

Quest: Richie Beirach, Billy Hart, David Liebman, and Ron McClure

Herbie, Chick, and then Richie. Richie taught both Kenny Kirkland and Joey Calderazzo a lot, and, in fact, one time when I heard Kenny on the radio, I thought it was Richie Beirach.

Ron McClure had a lot of experience—he'd played with Wynton Kelly and Thelonious Monk—but he also was ready to experiment. Ron's flexibility is his greatest feature, and the music can change direction under his guidance. A lot of Liebman's music is on a pedal point, and Ron can mix it up.

All three—Liebman, Beirach, McClure—are significant composers.

When we were at our best, Quest almost pulled off a coup, both musically and in the music business, as *the* next important acoustic jazz sound. Our first studio document, *Quest II* from 1986, has something delicate and multidirectional next to burning jazz pieces and the occasional driving even-eighth beat. Ethan says he can hear my mature drum concept come together on *Quest II*, and maybe he's right. For about five or six years Quest was very busy, especially in Europe.

Internally, there was a certain amount of discussion about how we were being passed over by the American jazz critics in favor of David Murray and the Marsalises. Whether or not that was true, Quest lost momentum and went on hiatus for many years in the '90s; during that time I played more with Dave or Richie separately than together. Dave put together several more projects that had high-level tours; the fact that bright lights Michael Brecker and Joe Lovano agreed to work for Dave in the Three Tenors indicates the level of respect they had for him. In fact, Brecker told me directly, "I'm here to study with Lieb." In time, Quest reunited, and we've occasionally played together again since 2005.

I first heard about Ethan Iverson from trombonist Christophe Schweizer, who told me, "There's this young pianist who can sight-read *anything*." (Schweizer would eventually arrange some of my music for *The Broader Picture* with the WDR Big Band.) In 1998, I ended up making one of Ethan's first albums, *The Minor Passions*, with Reid Anderson on bass. I was comfortable in that music, especially with Reid, who I thought was a great bassist. Over the years, several notable people like Nasheet Waits and Rodney Green checked out *The Minor Passions* and reported positively on my performance. Even then, Ethan was trying to showcase my conception at the drums.

It was a surprise to everybody when Ethan, Reid, and a drummer who had stayed in Minneapolis, Dave King, broke through and had commercial success with The Bad Plus. I didn't admire their overwhelming emphasis on binary thought, and teased Ethan, "It seems like you are putting more Elvis Presley in your music now."

The Bad Plus was such a hit that Ethan managed to get his own week at the Village Vanguard in a quartet with Mark Turner, Ben Street, and me. Ethan knew Mark and Ben from their work with Kurt Rosenwinkel, who was a leader of contemporary thought for Ethan's generation. The week at the Vanguard was nice, and I enjoyed everyone's playing. In fact, I enjoyed it so much, I called *them* for my next gig two weeks later in February 2004, a little performance in a town I had just moved to, Montclair, New Jersey. Mark, Ethan, and Ben played a bunch of my tunes and the gig went well.

Ethan met with me soon after and said, "Billy, the quartet was good at the Vanguard. But when you were the leader, where we played your tunes and you addressed the audience, it was much better. You are the best musician in the band. If you want this to be your quartet, let's do it."

In recent decades this has happened with some frequency. Someone will make me the nominal leader and we'll do a record and a tour. It's always fun to get the kudos without doing much of the administrative work. At first, I thought this was what Ethan was proposing, so I said yes. In time, the quartet has proven to be the most durable and longest-running ensemble I've ever been with. We haven't gigged *quite* as much as I would've liked, but there have been at least one or two tours a year and consistent local runs at the Vanguard, the Jazz Standard, Birdland, Dizzy's and other good New York venues. There was one album for High Note (*Quartet*), and three for ECM (*All Our Reasons*, *One is the Other*, and *Just*). A live recording for Smoke is in the works, to be called *Multi Directional*.

With the quartet, I was able to return to the avant-garde style of *Enchance*, the multidirectional line. Dave Liebman had something to do with that, too, having hired me for a new recording, *John Coltrane's Meditations*, and I found a few new things to play that I really liked. With Richie Beirach in Quest, there was already a more lyrical approach to multidirectional music than the full-on fire of the post-*Ascension* churn. Phil Markowitz, Liebman's pianist of choice in the Saxophone Summit and *John Coltrane's Meditations*, kept that going with a big assist from the great Cecil McBee.

I can see Beirach, Markowitz, Gray, Kirkland, Kikoski, and Copland as all connected to each other harmonically. Ethan is different and has a totally unique way of harmonizing my melodies, somewhere between Thelonious Monk and a Hollywood film score. Ethan helped me put together my most epic multidirectional composition, "Song for Balkis," which opens our album *All Our Reasons* in a 13-minute performance.

It was meaningful to be in Paris and play "Song for Balkis" with my daughter Balkis in the audience. "Lullaby for Imke" is for my second daughter, mothered by my second wife, Tracy. Imke went to Oberlin and now lives in LA; we are in steady contact and she's surely the apple of my eye. "Teule's Redemption" is for my first son, Chris, who I still see daily when I'm home. I'm sure Chris could tell you some stories about me I don't want you to know. Lorca is the only musician of the bunch, he's a fine drummer doing well on the West Coast, and "Toli's Dance" is for Tolliver, the son who keeps some distance.

I tried to be a good family man, but I didn't know everything that was possible. When I took every gig I could, I always gave the money to my family. But that also meant I wasn't around as much as I should have been. In my musical peer group, this was common. Some of the younger players have shown me a different way to live, like two members of my quartet, Mark Turner and Ben Street, both of whom are excellent parents.

With Tracy Resnick-Hart and daughter Imke Hart

With son Lorca Hart

Mark is the quartet's ace in the hole. Everyone knows that he is one of the finest—if not *the* finest—tenor saxophonists of his generation, yet somehow he keeps coming back to play in the quartet. He's incredibly influential, and I can't tell you how many young tenor players I've heard imitate Mark Turner. We've had the very highest level subs for Mark: Josh Redman, Chris Potter, Dayna Stephens, and Walter Smith III. Josh and Chris are stars. They can tell a story and put the audience on the same page in a way that is undeniable. Dayna and Walter are more like Mark, a bit more mysterious and elliptical. But it will always be Mark's gig if he wants to keep doing it.

Some of what makes Mark Turner unique is his interest in Lennie Tristano, Lee Konitz, and Warne Marsh.[6] I played with Lee quite a bit in the '70s but never paid much attention to the Tristano school otherwise, although Liebman studied with Tristano, and both Wayne Shorter and Herbie Hancock credit that school as an influence. I did notice that when Mark Turner started playing in my band, Lee Konitz was suddenly at all my gigs to see Mark. I really love Mark's 5/4 tribute to Tristano, "Lennie-Groove." So many people have played "Lennie-Groove" that it's almost like "Giant Steps" for that generation of musicians.

---

6 Pianist Lennie Tristano was an innovative bebop musician who (unlike most jazz musicians of that era) also taught precepts of improvisation. Saxophonists Lee Konitz and Warne Marsh were his most famous students.

Ben Street really believes in the tradition. I do too, but I may have met my match with Ben Street. We both search for logical solutions to the most "out" music: that there is always a way to make the avant-garde presentable. He has also worked with the modern historian of the clave, Danilo Perez. I can play *anything* with Ben and he will hear it and make it work.

With Ben, I noticed how he loved Jimmy Garrison. Garrison's work with John Coltrane remains underrated. My peers didn't always keep Garrison's contribution in the forefront. Indeed, the bassists in this chapter so far—Dave Holland, Buster Williams, Eddie Gomez, Cecil McBee, Ron McClure, and Santi Debriano—are not so much in the Garrison line, except perhaps for Buster, who shares that gritty Philadelphia lineage. (Jymie Merritt was one of those Philly bassists. One time, Lee Morgan turned around to look accusingly at Merritt, who had gone fully into a moment of breaking up the time with unexpected double-stops. Merritt responded to Morgan's glare by yelling, "It's too late, Lee!" as he stayed inside his abstract bass patterns.)

The younger generations have done something to bring Garrison back into the music. I was impressed when one of the biggest bass stars of his era, Larry Grenadier, told me that he was trying to get to Garrison. The

Ben Street, Billy Hart, Mark Turner, Ethan Iverson at the Village Vanguard, 2019. (Photo by Desmond White.)

bassists who have subbed for Ben in the quartet, Thomas Morgan, Joe Martin, and Joe Sanders, all know their Garrison as well.

At first I was taken aback by the sparse approach employed by everyone in the quartet. Mark's solos would begin slowly, Ethan would lay out, Ben's low thumps could make Garrison sound busy in comparison. I was used to my peers, like Quest, the *Oceans of Time* band, or the music on *Great Friends*, where we fervently played thousands and thousands of notes in the post-Coltrane tradition. But since the quartet was so sparse, the texture allowed my drumming to speak clearly. For the first time, I also started setting up many of the pieces with unaccompanied drum solos. Ethan insisted on including many blues pieces, to the point where I've been surprised at how much of a blues band the quartet has become. Mark, Ben, and Ethan have all expressed appreciation at how playing in my band gives them a chance to learn about the tradition.

If the quartet features my softer and bluesier side, then The Cookers, which has been active since 2007, is where the modal fury remains. That's almost the reason for that band, to keep the passion from an earlier era alive. Trumpeter David Weiss is like Ethan, he organizes the band and books the tours. Internally it is fairly ective, with everyone contributing compositions and telling stories. Our first record, *Warriors*, was made in 2010, and features a high energy version of "The Core," a piece by Freddie Hubbard, someone who David knew very well. "The Core" was first recorded by Art Blakey's Jazz Messengers on the famous album *Free For All*, and to some extent I am in the Blakey role in the Cookers, playing multi-horn charts accurately and supporting long horn solos that tell a story. The names of the musicians in the history of the Cookers make up a roll call of the very best: Eddie Henderson, Donald Harrison, Billy Harper, Azar Lawrence, Craig Handy, George Cables, and Cecil McBee. I look up to them all as mentors, teachers, and composers.

In 2016, my old friend Jessica Felix honored me at her Healdsburg festival in California. Jessica has great taste, loves the music, and has done a lot for jazz on the West Coast. Her presentation "40 Years of Billy Hart" included the *Enchance* repertoire in a group with Eddie Henderson, Oliver Lake, Joshua Redman, Craig Taborn, and Dave Holland; the *Oceans of Time* repertoire with Craig Handy, Chris Potter, Mark Feldman, Dave Fiuczynski, and Cecil McBee; and the standard line ups of Quest and the Quartet. It was just fabulous of Jessica to give me that opportunity.

My discography covers a lot of terrain, but one area that has not been documented is the percussion ensemble. In the '70s, Horacee Arnold put Colloquium III together with Freddie Waits and me. We did a few workshops and gigs but never recorded. On another occasion, Milford Graves put together an epic Harlem performance of multidirectional drummers with Rashied Ali, Beaver Harris, Ed Blackwell, Andrew Cyrille, and me. More recently, Andrew Cyrille and I have played duo and trio with guest saxophonists including Dave Liebman, Joe Lovano, David Ware, and Gary Bartz; Andrew and I also performed together at the memorial for Paul Motian. It doesn't happen often, but when the opportunity arises, I love working closely with other drummers and putting the spotlight squarely on the drums.

Colloquium III: Billy Hart, Horacee Arnold, and Freddie Waits

11

Dramatis Personae

In Duke Ellington's memoir *Music is My Mistress*, there are pauses, "Dramatis Personae," that string together anecdotes featuring important people.

Here are some of my own Dramatis Personae...

Al Foster and Philly Joe Jones

I was born in 1940 and see myself in the class alongside people like Tootie Heath (1935), Billy Higgins (1936), Louis Hayes (1937), Jack DeJohnette (1942), Joe Chambers (1942), Al Foster (1943), Billy Cobham (1944) and Tony Williams (1945). That's one decade, 1935–1945, and one hell of a lot of great drumming.

I first met Al Foster at the Howard Theatre when he was playing with Oscar Brown, Jr., when Al was still a teenager. Al knew bebop perfectly—he would sub for Max Roach in the late '60s in Max's own band—but he also acquired some serious Afro-Cuban information, absorbed naturally when growing up in Harlem bordering on the Bronx. Although Al got famous playing with Miles Davis, he always wanted Miles to play more like the straight-ahead jazz we grew up with, rather than the vamp-heavy electric style Miles featured in the '70s and '80s.

Al and I shared a trial by fire together. In 1977, Philly Joe Jones called Al and me for a gala event with his band at the midtown club, Storyville. I was honored to be asked, but also terrified. When you watched Philly Joe sit at the drums—or even the way he talked and walked offstage—it felt like you were watching a great Shakespearean actor delivering a famous soliloquy. The word "elegant" covers a lot of it. One time Elvin Jones told me, "I savor Philly Joe Jones like a fine wine."

When I got there, everyone in the drum world seemed to be in the audience. The way we set up, I would play first, then Philly Joe, then Al.

That was okay, I thought. If I played first, then at least I didn't need to follow Philly Joe like poor Al Foster.

We all know Philly Joe is great, but that night he transcended everything I thought possible. Whatever I played, he did sort of the same thing but much better. Eventually, in despair, I thought, "Okay, I'm going to play my Max Roach stuff." That was like feeding red meat to a lion, and Philly Joe *really* got going.

At the set break we had to sit up there as all these legends talked about how great Philly Joe was. Even Papa Jo Jones spoke for quite a time. Finally Max Roach got up to speak. Oh no! I didn't know that Max Roach was in the audience, and there I was, playing my Max Roach licks. Max took his time to set up and moved the microphone so that he could stand right in front of me, still seated at the drums. Finally, Max addressed the audience at some length, telling them about the importance of innovation, and how one needed to have one's own sound. All the while Max was speaking, he was reaching behind his back to *gently tap on my high tom-tom*. It was disastrous.

Al and I didn't say goodbye to each other that night, we just skedaddled. A year or two later, we ran into each other, and he immediately began, "Billy, I think we have been disrespecting the cats. We need to have our own shit. I'm giving myself five years to have my own material at the drums, and if I don't find it, I'm gonna hang it up."

I thought Al already had a personal sound, but there's no doubt that he found even more unique touches after taking this vow—his work with the hi-hat has been particularly innovative. A few years ago, I went to hear him at Smoke, and the minute he started playing, I felt my whole body relax. The texture was so correct. I had been hearing all these great young drummers, and they *are* great, but being in the room with Al Foster's sound was like therapy.

We just lost Al as this book went to press. I surely regret that I won't be able to enjoy that therapy again.

Freddie Waits, Joe Chambers, Freddie Hubbard, Joe Henderson

Freddie Waits was brilliant even as a young musician, playing not just drums but also flute and the full percussion family, including all the mallet instruments. In that last capacity, he was perfect for Max Roach's all-percussion ensemble M'Boom. He also played marimba on one of the records we made together, Bennie Maupin's *Jewel in the Lotus*. He was Southerner from Mississippi, but there was also family in Detroit, and Detroit is where I first met him, when he was a member of the Motown Revue, working for Choker Campbell. This put us in a similar category—we both played pop music at a high level at a young age. I did my turn at the Howard Theatre in D.C., but Freddie acquired much more touring experience. He's also on some famous Motown records, including some of Stevie Wonder's first hits. He got to New York a couple of years before me, and played with McCoy Tyner, Lee Morgan, and many other modern jazz greats. We were close and shared many ideals; for example, we were both singer's musicians. Freddie Waits told me how he just *loved* playing with Ella Fitzgerald.

Joe Chambers is another important drummer, heard on many great '60's albums by Wayne Shorter, Bobby Hutcherson, and so many others. In terms of a drummer responding to harmony, Joe is the peak, and he was also influenced by his brother, the important composer Talib Rasul Hakim. Let's not forget that while Joe Chambers had a wonderfully modern conception, he was a blues musician, just like Freddie Waits. As I mentioned earlier, I tried to help him out in those early D.C. years and even let him sit in on my own gig with Fox Wheatley to play a tune with Freddie Hubbard, who was visiting town with Art Blakey. The night Joe played with Freddie on my drums was the reason Hubbard brought Chambers to New York.

Jam sessions were frequent and important in those early days. The two tenor players I sort of "missed" at first were Dewey Redman and Joe Henderson. I heard Dewey in San Francisco and Joe at a Washington, D.C. session, and neither really made an impression. But then, of course, I heard their records and quickly changed my mind. In fact, those two in particular are tenor players you can recognize in just two notes. Two notes! That's all you need with Dewey Redman or Joe Henderson.

Both Wayne Shorter and Joe Henderson studied the music of John Coltrane. But I think Joe took other things from Sonny Rollins. John Coltrane is my favorite, but some people have suggested that Sonny Rollins knows even more about the tradition than Coltrane, especially the rhythmic understanding of Cuban and Caribbean music. That might be true. At any rate, when Joe Henderson moved to New York, he played a lot with Kenny Dorham, and KD surely taught Joe some of that traditional Charlie Parker-era material.[1]

In the '80s, I did two substantial tours in all-star quintets with Freddie Hubbard, Joe Henderson, Michel Petrucciani, and either Buster Williams or Charlie Haden. I didn't play with Charlie much, but of course I recognized his contribution. A few times when I have asked good bassists about what they were playing, especially things like pedal points that I really liked, they said they got it from Charlie Haden.

Charlie's regular group in his later years was Quartet West, and once or twice I subbed for Rodney Green. When we rehearsed Ornette Coleman's "Lonely Woman," Charlie asked me to play a fast swinging ride cymbal beat against the texture. I did it, but Charlie stopped me. "It's fast, but not quite that fast," was his lesson.

The first all-star quintet tour with Hubbard, Henderson, and Petrucciani was with Buster Williams, and at that time Buster was really the only person I knew well in that group. I had played with Joe in Herbie Hancock's band, but I never played with Hubbard before and only knew him a bit socially. Petrucciani was a complete stranger. I liked him, but for a little man he had an ego the size of a giant. I guess there were a lot of big egos on that particular bandstand! It was a George Wein production, and we started at the big festival in Nice, which began as La Grande Parade du Jazz before being rebranded under Wein's JVC imprint.

At soundcheck, before we played a note, Hubbard told me, "Just so you know, I'm used to *loud* motherfuckers. So *hit* those drums."

I said, "What about Buster?"—meaning, I don't want to drown out a great bassist.

Hubbard said, "Fuck the bass player."

When we played the gig, we started with a fast "Rhythm-a-ning" and Hubbard took the first solo. He played loud and high. Obviously, Hubbard's attitude was, "*I* am the leader, musically and otherwise."

After a gig or two, Hubbard came and found me, saying, "Okay, I know what you mean about Buster, Buster sounds good…"

I said, "Yeah?"

"…but I'm still the trumpet player."

---

1 Kenny Dorham played with Charlie Parker throughout 1949; the studio records include "Passport," a relatively obscure Parker rhythm changes melody that Joe Henderson eventually recorded in trio with Charlie Haden and Al Foster. The front line of Dorham and Henderson can be heard on several early 1960's Blue Note LPs including *Page One*, Henderson's first album as a leader.

Meaning, *what I say goes.*

Changing gears for Joe Henderson after Freddie Hubbard was a challenge. We'd be up there, bashing away for Freddie, and then Joe would start, kind of smooth and quiet in comparison. Joe was very un-theatrical and unassuming in his approach—he never buckled his knees or went for house. While I was playing above my capacity to be fluid at that dynamic for Freddie, bringing it all the way down for Joe Henderson didn't seem right either.

After a few days of this, I went behind Hubbard's back and addressed Joe directly: "Hey, Joe, it's all loud and chaotic, Freddie always solos first, sometimes it seems like the time is getting turned around. I don't know exactly what to do."

Joe looked at me and said, "Frankly, Billy, sometimes I like dealing in that zone."

Okay, that meant Joe was in agreement with this unmusical approach. The next night I went completely overboard, playing anything that came to mind as loud and fast as I could. Immediately after the gig, I felt dirty and unethical, like I had betrayed myself. But Joe Henderson ran to catch up—he never looked for me before—put his arm around me, and said, "Billy! I knew you had it in you all the time!"

Both Arthur Blythe and Roy Hargrove complained to my face that I wasn't loud enough. On one occasion Richie Beirach said, "Drown me out!" During the first few years of the Cookers, David Weiss would suggest that I was "letting the band down" if I wasn't producing high-energy drumming all the time. It's one way of doing it, but it's not always my first choice.

Dexter Gordon, Dizzy Gillespie, Sonny Stitt, John Tchicai

Some leaders are notoriously hard to satisfy. I had the exact same conversation about downbeats with Dexter Gordon and Dizzy Gillespie a year or two apart. Dexter was on the road with Tootie Heath in Scandinavia. When I ran into him over there I suggested that he must be happy with Tootie, who was such a great drummer. Dexter replied, "Yeah, but Tootie doesn't play enough 'ones.'"

Later, when I saw Dizzy in London and complimented him on *his* great drummer, Mickey Roker, Dizzy said the same thing. "Mickey doesn't play enough 'ones.'"

At the time, I thought that these two old men, Dizzy Gillespie and Dexter Gordon, were just not hip enough to understand phrasing over the bar line. But then I had a valuable lesson with Sonny Stitt.

Stitt was one of those gladiator types who enjoyed a cutting session playing fast tempos. On a gig somewhere in Jersey in the late '70s, Sonny called something really fast, the speed they used to call the "Max Roach tempo." I could play a fast tempo, but I wasn't flexible, I was stiff. Stitt heard me flailing around back there and came around and talked to me during Jim McNeely's piano solo.

"Okay, youngblood, watch me."

Stitt looked me in the eyes and both said and mimed, "One. One… One. One…One…One."

It wasn't every downbeat, but it was quite a few of them, and they had kind of a nice, staggered feel. All of a sudden it was clear as day to me, and I have never had a problem playing fast tempos since.

Stitt was showing me how the "one" was important. I already knew this from Shirley Horn, who played big ones as a part of her style. That "one" of hers went straight from the piano down to the center of the earth: Listen again to "I'm Old Fashioned" from *A Lazy Afternoon*.

Beat "one" is like "once upon a time," the beginning of the story. It's the overture. When Dexter Gordon and Dizzy Gillespie criticized Tootie Heath and Mickey Roker for not playing enough "ones," they must have been thinking of the kind of 1940's big band music that Dexter played with Billy Eckstine and Dizzy had with his own big band. That kind of music always has a curtain-raiser or an overture. If Tootie or Mickey had tried playing with Dexter or Dizzy as if they were powering a big band rather than a small group, there probably would have been no problem.

It's hard to please everybody. The drummer is usually in the hot seat. I was enjoying working with John Tchicai, who was an avant-garde legend, famous for his lyrical solo on Coltrane's *Ascension*, but then Tchicai told me, "Billy, you aren't playing free. Just play free."

"I'm not playing free?"

"No, you are just playing against the time."

It's true that someone like my friend Andrew Cyrille is more of a pure improvisor, whereas I am more of a pattern player. Still. Is "just play free" actually a style?

Frank Foster, Walter Davis, Jr., Larry Young, Horace Parlan, Slide Hampton, Art Farmer

My one shot working in a regular big band was a year or two with Frank Foster in the 1970s. When Thad Jones and Mel Lewis took off from their regular Monday nights at the Vanguard to go on European tours, Frank Foster's Loud Minority would fill in. Frank was a lovely man; talking to him felt like talking to a gentle uncle.

While Frank Foster may be best known for his long term association with Count Basie, he was also a truly contemporary player who worked a lot with Elvin Jones. The story goes that Miles Davis asked Frank to join his band before Coltrane. A musician the caliber of Frank Foster could cross genres with real authenticity. People like Count Basie, Ella Fitzgerald, and Teddy Wilson performed Frank's most famous song, "Shiny Stockings," but Frank also recorded "Shiny Stockings" in a modern trio setting with Elvin Jones and Richard Davis. His minor blues waltz "Simone" is a staple of the NYC scene even today.

I'm not on any of his big band records, but the Loud Minority disk with Elvin Jones, *Well Water*, gives a sense of Frank's wonderful '70's big band and the high level of musicians on that scene from that era, many of whom are not so well-remembered today.[2]

The small group Frank Foster records I'm on feature Mickey Tucker, a pianist who is definitely overlooked now. I really liked Tucker's 1979 record date *The Crawl*, where I got a chance to play the real deal with Marcus Belgrave, Slide Hampton, and Junior Cook.

Tucker was in the lineage of Walter Davis Jr., who had a lot of contact with the giants. We called Walter "Humphries," and a few of the great tunes he wrote for Art Blakey are still heard once in a while. Jackie McLean is one of my other favorites, and the record *Let Freedom Ring* has beautiful McLean tunes, beautiful Davis piano, and some really spectacular Billy Higgins drumming. Humphries wasn't the only musician of that generation who had some pretty esoteric theories; he once told me quite seriously about the man in the center of the Earth who piloted the planet.

This reminds me of the organist Larry Young, whose album *Unity* with Woody Shaw, Joe Henderson, and Elvin Jones was magnificent,

---

2 Frank Foster's big band recording *Well Water* was recorded in 1977, but not released until 2007 on Piadrum Records. The soloists include Cecil Bridgewater, Bill Saxton, and Mickey Tucker.

innovative, and influential. Young didn't say much, and if you asked him how he was doing, Young would just look at you and intone the word "bong" slowly like a bell.

"Bong....bong....bong..."

I played with Roland Hanna with the Mingus Dynasty band. That was great, but then when Horace Parlan replaced him, it made a difference. Parlan could really play the blues and swing at the highest level, despite being crippled in his right hand from polio as a child.

Another underrated giant in this music, Slide Hampton, wrote the arrangements for Eddie Jefferson's 1977 *The Main Man*, one of the few albums that shows me almost as a kind of big band drummer, setting up the hits in longer arrangements. Kenny Washington always tells me that *The Main Man* is one of his favorites, and I've heard other people say that it is simply Jefferson's best record.

For a year in 1983 I was back to more truth when the Jazztet returned to gigging. Tootie Heath got me in there with the Jazztet—Tootie was the original drummer for that legendary group featuring Art Farmer, Benny Golson, and Curtis Fuller—and we did an epic tour of the Pacific Rim from Singapore to Melbourne with Mickey Tucker and Ray Drummond.

Ray Drummond, Mickey Tucker, Benny Golson, Billy Hart, and Curtis Fuller.

Some people might think of Art Farmer as a softer, Miles Davis/Chet Baker kind of trumpeter, but I always found him very exciting, with chops that rank with Dizzy Gillespie, Fats Navarro and Clifford Brown. A good video of my own drumming is a set with Farmer, Fred Hersch, and Dennis Irwin. Farmer is *burning* on that, too.[3]

Art Farmer also plays like an angel on a ballad, and I think he got some of that tenderness from Benny Golson, one of our great composers. Golson wrote for Farmer like a European opera composer writing for a favored diva.

Curtis Fuller was great with the Jazztet, but I loved him most with Art Blakey in those Jazz Messenger bands from the early '60s alongside Wayne Shorter. A real bad boy. Jimmy Garrison and Curtis Fuller shared something amusing and irreverent in terms of their personality.

I wasn't in their league, but I loved hearing Fuller or Farmer or Golson tell stories from their checkered past—a lot of stories that I unfortunately can't include here!

Kenny Barron

I first met Kenny Barron when he was touring with Dizzy Gillespie and I was on tour with Jimmy Smith. At that time, more than a few people told me, "Herbie Hancock is cool, but he's no Kenny Barron." Man, did Kenny sound great playing bebop with Dizzy. That was maybe the drunkest I've ever been. It was Kenny's birthday and we were just smashed on the Norman Granz tour bus. Somehow we got to naming our favorite tunes to each other, like a hundred tunes in a row. "Stella by Starlight!" one of us would say, and we would both drunkenly moan in ecstasy. "Invitation!" the other would respond, and we'd moan some more.

Kenny is one of the few from my generation or younger whom I would call a "classical pianist" in the mold of Barry Harris, Tommy Flanagan, Hank Jones, or Cedar Walton. The only person who I heard after Kenny who truly had that together was Mulgrew Miller.

Kenny's composition "Sunshower" has become one of the most-played pieces from that era. I was there on the first recording of "Sunshower" in 1975, on the Sonny Fortune date *Awakening*, where Kenny almost shyly brought it out in response to Sonny's request for more material from the band.

---

3 *Art Farmer: Jazz at the Smithsonian* (Shanachie Entertainment, 2005), recorded live in 1982.

At one point, Kenny and I played a stretch in Las Vegas with the fine blues singer Queen Esther Marrow. The repertoire was mostly blues, but Marrow actually got her start singing the *Sacred Concerts* of Duke Ellington. On bass was Bill Salter, who was from a different area of the music. Salter had toured with Harry Belafonte and Miriam Makeba and wrote hit songs like "Just the Two of Us," "When You Smile," "Mr. Magic," and "Tradewinds" with Ralph MacDonald.

Manfred Eicher, Charles Lloyd, Geri Allen

There's no doubt that the Mwandishi sextet had a profound impact on all its members. Each of the horn players made albums back then that were somewhat in the Mwandishi line.[4] Bennie Maupin's *Jewel in the Lotus*, from 1974, is the first Manfred Eicher record I'm on, and remains the only ECM record featuring Herbie Hancock.

The Jewel in the Lotus is a hell of an LP, and I've heard people say that they prefer it to Herbie's own Mwandishi records. Bennie's spacious compositions were a perfect fit for the new kid on the block, Manfred Eicher.

The famous "ECM sound" is influential to the point that I have been handed charts in a New York rehearsal where the tempo is written, "Like ECM." No other record label has had that kind of power.

Naturally, ECM is therefore also controversial. Some drummers think there are not enough drums on the ECM mixes, or at least that Manfred prioritizes cymbals over drums. For those musicians, there's not enough bottom or groove in his approach.

Manfred really loves and understands European classical music: strings, nocturnes, impressionist soundscapes, choral music, and so forth, and he essentially asks his jazz artists to put more of that European perspective in their music.[5] You just can't go in and play for Manfred

---

4   Albums made by sextet horn members that are obviously influenced by their time in Mwandishi: Eddie Henderson, *Realization* (Capricorn, 1973), *Inside Out* (Capricorn, 1973), *Sunburst*, (1975, Blue Note); Julian Priester, *Love, Love, Love* (ECM, 1973); Bennie Maupin *The Jewel in the Lotus* (ECM, 1974). Interviews with all members of the sextet can be found in Bob Gluck's book *You'll Know When You Get There: Herbie Hancock and the Mwandishi Band*.

5   In conversation with Ethan Iverson, Manfred Eicher (born 1943) cited Miles Davis *Kind Of Blue*, Bill Evans *Sunday at the Village Vanguard* (especially the track "Jade Visions") and the trio records of Jimmy Giuffre with Paul Bley and Steve Swallow as jazz albums that notably influenced his way of thinking when Manfred was a teenager. These are all comparatively moody and poetic LPs, especially when compared to Miles Davis's *Milestones* or any hard bop record of the era by Art Blakey or Horace Silver.

like you're going into a NYC club like Smoke, swinging on Horace Silver or Cedar Walton repertoire. Manfred thinks of himself as a member of the band, and that can be distracting, though I like some of the things he's said to me over the years at sessions. During my own date *All Our Reasons*, Manfred mimed playing along with my brushwork in a way that made me smile.

And I certainly appreciate Manfred's attitude toward the cymbals. It's there on *Jewel in the Lotus*, but comes more to the forefront on the Charles Lloyd records I made for Manfred,[6] and then of course on my own ECM releases. I just love the way my cymbals sound on those records.

Charles Lloyd and Manfred Eicher are both interested in "world music." This is not straight-eighth music with an Afro-Caribbean or a Brazilian element, but straight-eighth music that is inspired by specific dances from other places in the world: Greece, the Middle East, the Balkans, Turkey, China, Japan…

John Coltrane predicted the future of jazz when he named pieces "Olé," "Africa," and "India."[7] Many of the innovations since Coltrane have drawn on Spanish, African, and Indian sources. But Coltrane folded those sounds into his own established music. What Charles Lloyd promoted was a more obvious version of drawing on these diverse world music inspirations, more like folk dance music, or people playing drum rhythms on pots by a fireplace in a distant land. Likewise, if you look at the ECM catalog, Manfred has been at the forefront of combining improvisors with world music.

Don Cherry had a lot to do with the world music concept. When I met Bobo Stenson, who is an important ECM artist in his own right, it turned out that he had worked with Don Cherry and considered him one of his most important influences.

Charles Lloyd first burst on the scene with records made with Tony Williams and Jack DeJohnette. I was still in Washington, D.C., but my friend Walter Booker had already moved to New York. Word came through that Jack was going to leave Charles Lloyd to go with Miles Davis, and I sort of wondered if I could get on that Lloyd gig. I asked

---

6   Charles Lloyd ECM records with Billy Hart: *The Call* (1993), *All My Relations* (1994), *Canto* (1996), and *Lift Every Voice* (2002).

7   Coltrane was clearly thinking about what was later called "world music" in 1961. *Olé* and *Africa/Brass* were recorded in May studio sessions, "India" in November at the Village Vanguard.

Booker about it, and Booker said, "I don't know, man, I think you need to come up here and stand in line."

I moved to New York a few weeks later. But it wasn't until many moons had passed that I finally played in Charles Lloyd's band, off and on for about nine years. On the first day of rehearsal, I came in and was looking for the sheet music. Lloyd said to me, "In my band, you don't need any paper. Just keep the dance in the music."

The first few years I played with Charles Lloyd were the best, when it was a steady band with Bobo Stenson and Anders Jormin. I was stepping in for Jon Christensen, one of the quintessential ECM drummers. (When those NYC cats write "like ECM" on a chart, they mean, "like Jon Christensen and Jack DeJohnette.") Bobo and Anders are friends, and in fact, Anders might be my favorite European bassist. Anders made a solo bass record with brass quartet interludes, *Xeiyi*, that is well worth seeking out.

Charles Lloyd sets up a system where he hires the best musicians to really improvise in dance-like contexts, and it works. One of the better videos of me that circulates is a 2002 clip with Lloyd, Bob Hurst, Geri Allen, and me.[8] On that clip, Geri has a real physical energy, almost getting close to McCoy Tyner.

I also played in Geri's trio at the Village Vanguard and elsewhere, and Buster Williams and I joined her for the *Mary Lou Williams Collective*, which was recorded right at Geri's house nearby in Montclair. (Andrew Cyrille is also present on some of the tracks.) When Buster and I played with Mary Lou in the 1970s, the repertoire was mostly standards,[9] so it was a great learning experience to explore her own compositions like "The Zodiac Suite" with Geri. Geri Allen's stature keeps growing since her tragic early death in 2017.

Clark Terry

Clark Terry called me to play a few times. One week in 1979 was with Barry Harris, and that was really beautiful, just about the only time I had the chance to be on the bandstand with Barry. I'd look over at Barry

---

8   From the San Sebastian Jazz Festival ("Jazzaldia"), directed by Angel Luis Ramirez and broadcast on Spanish TVE 2.

9   A terrific bootleg exists of Mary Lou Williams, Buster Williams, and Billy Hart at the Philharmonic Hall in New York on June 30th, 1973. The set list includes "Autumn Leaves" and several blues pieces.

at the piano, and his hands would float in the air between gorgeous bebop phrases.

When it was time for the record date the next week for Norman Granz, Oscar Peterson was playing piano and the repertoire had shifted to all Fats Waller compositions.[10] It was impressive to be working with these famous masters, but Oscar didn't really make me feel welcome—he just turned his back to me and delivered his virtuoso piano material.

In addition to playing the hell out of the trumpet, Clark can sing, like his famous "mumbles" on a blues. I can sing some "mumbles" too. Most of us from that era can do that kind of thing, although in my case my vocals come out more like Coltrane or another '60s kind of sound.

Hal Galper, the Brecker Brothers, Bob Moses

Hal Galper worked with Sam Rivers and Tony Williams in Boston, and I heard a version of that group with Henry Grimes at the Vanguard in the late '60s. A Sam Rivers tune they played that night, "Cyclic Episode," is still one of my favorites.

One of my first steady gigs in New York in '68 or '69 was with the married vocal duo Jackie Paris and Anne-Marie Moss. Paris had sung with Charles Mingus and had a few hit records, and Moss had replaced Annie Ross in Lambert, Hendricks & Ross. The rhythm section was Hal Galper, Gene Perla, and me. Hal and I got to talking, and we've kept talking over the years. He's gotten more visible as an educator, and once in a while I become aware of the two of us being on a kind of long-distance committee where we praise Ahmad Jamal to our students.

Ahmad's trio with Israel Crosby and Vernel Fournier is a perfect entry point to discuss the basics of American classical music. That trio is the transition from the Dizzy Gillespie big band to the Miles Davis Quintet, and, of course, it is so damn swinging besides. On "What's New," you can even hear Ahmad, Israel, and Vernel foreshadow '70s soul music. It's all connected through Vernel's use of the second line, not just on "Poinciana," but everywhere else in that great Jamal trio.[11]

Hal Galper's music with Michael and Randy Brecker has attained something of a classic status, at least in terms of '70s jazz. I'm on *Reach*

---

10 *Ain't Misbehavin'* (Pablo), recorded in March of 1979 with Chris Woods on woodwinds and Victor Sproles on bass.

11 "Ponciana" and "What's New" are heard on Ahmad Jamal's *At the Pershing: But Not For Me*, with Israel Crosby and Vernel Fournier, recorded in Chicago in 1958.

Out! from 1976, where Michael plays a really beautiful and lyrical solo on "I'll Never Stop Loving You."

That was the Michael Brecker I loved. Michael took a lot from Stanley Turrentine. He went to Turrentine, asked questions, and got answers. Michael's overwhelming success in the pop world using some licks from Turrentine reminded me of the way The Rolling Stones and The Beatles were inspired by musicians who recorded Chicago blues for Chess Records.

I preferred Michael as a jazz player, and remember Michael standing in the pouring rain while watching a whole set of Stan Getz. As good as he was, Michael could make mistakes about some notes in the repertoire. I heard Keith Jarrett make some mistakes in the notes, too. Certainly they didn't seem to know all the introductions and interludes. I judged Michael Brecker and Keith Jarrett for that: Why didn't they think the notes of a Dizzy Gillespie, Horace Silver, or Benny Golson composition mattered as much as the notes in Bach or Beethoven? Randy Brecker may have known more about the tradition than his brother—I'm always happy to play with Randy.

Bob Moses is on the other Galper/Brecker records, and Bob has ended up being a big supporter of mine, hiring me for his own albums and helping get me an appointment at New England Conservatory. Bob made a lot of important contributions playing contemporary music with Galper, Steve Swallow, Pat Metheny, and Gary Burton before going completely multi-directional. He has taken Ra Kalam as his spiritual name and no longer buys commercial drumsticks, instead looking for appropriately-sized tree branches and cutting them down further with a knife.

Paul Bley and Hank Jones

For a time I was basically the house drummer for Nils Winther and Steeplechase Records. The first one was Galper's *Reach Out!*, and then I brought Buck Hill, Shirley Horn, Reuben Brown and others to record for the label. When Nils eventually gave me my own date in 2009, we agreed to call it *Sixty-eight*, the number of Steeplechase sessions I'd done up until that point. Coincidentally, I was 68 at the time. *Sixty-eight* is not my most considered album as a leader, as I essentially turned that session over to my talented students.

Nils and his label have provided a great service documenting the music, but most of the sessions have been done quickly. Two of the fastest I did were with Paul Bley. When I got to the first session, Paul said, "We're going to do one take of everything, and we aren't going to listen back to the takes either." Naturally, I don't remember much about the music, although since Bley was such a unique musician, people have brought up those records from time to time.[12]

Paul had played with everyone from Charlie Parker to Charles Mingus in the '50s, was the first piano player for Ornette Coleman, and he certainly knew his own worth. I stopped into Sweet Basil one time and Paul was sitting at the bar. I asked him how he was doing and he said he had played at Basil the previous night. When I casually remarked how I wished I had heard it, Paul immediately agreed: "Yeah, man, you *should* have been here, I played my ass off!"

I didn't tour with Paul, but he did call me for a one-off with Gary Peacock at the Montreal Jazz Festival. I set up my drums and was hanging out in the anteroom with Paul and Gary, wondering what we were going to play. At some point Paul leaves the conversation and—to my surprise—goes out on stage and starts the set. I look at Gary, who treats this as normal, I guess, and talks to me more for another fifteen minutes. Then Gary leaves the conversation and goes onstage. I was pretty unsettled, but I waited ten more minutes and finally joined Paul and Gary. Their music was totally spun left and free form. When the set ended there was a standing ovation.

When we walked off the stage, I said to Paul, "Man! I didn't know what to do or when to come on!"

Paul smiled and said, "You came at just the right time," and Gary nodded in agreement.

I kept trying to understand his concept, saying, "There was no rehearsal!"

Paul replied, "I usually like to rehearse *after* the gig."

Like Paul Bley, Hank Jones made a lot of records very quickly, but there the resemblance ends. I had to *concentrate* when I played with Hank. The fine Danish bassist Mads Vinding and I were in one of the editions of Hank's Great Jazz Trio, where we made five volumes of *Great Standards* and an additional session with a second piano player, Kenny Drew.

With some of the older players, like on that Clark Terry/Oscar Peterson record, I felt like I needed to stay quietly present and not rock

---

12 *My Standard* (recorded December 1985) and *The Nearness of You* (recorded November 1988). Trivia: *The Nearness of You* was one of Ethan Iverson's favorite records as a teenager, and one of the reasons he started collecting records with Billy Hart listed on the jacket.

the boat. Clark might say something to me like, "Man, my rhythm section was really swinging last week," and I'd check the listing, and it was some really old-school, totally solid cats. That was the gig, and there's nothing wrong with that. True swing is hard to do.

But Hank didn't request anything and I didn't feel like I needed to play a special way, or at a special dynamic, either. When I played with Hank, I heard at least three generations at once, and if I thought too much about my own playing, I was going to miss something. He told me his biggest influences were Teddy Wilson and Art Tatum, but especially Teddy Wilson—that was his man. Next, he was already in New York for three or four years when Charlie Parker and Bud Powell hit, and Hank learned that music and even recorded with Charlie Parker. When I heard Hank play "Autumn Leaves" with Cannonball Adderley and Miles Davis, he sounded like a modern player to me, not a Teddy Wilson kind of player. But Hank wasn't done growing, as shown by The Great Jazz Trio with Ron Carter and Tony Williams.[13]

In fact, that all-star band was Tony's idea! I originally assumed it was Hank's idea, but both Hank and Tony told me that the Great Jazz Trio was Tony's invention. That was my one little argument with Hank, not on the bandstand, but in conversation. I said, "Man, it must have been great playing with Tony Williams."

Hank looked at me thoughtfully and said, "Tony would stop playing sometimes."

I thought about it, and realized that I had heard Tony stop once in a while with Herbie Hancock or other people, as a way to further orchestrate the music. I countered, "Well, that was part of Tony's style."

Hank replied, "Why'd he have to stop playing??"

We went back and forth on that a bit before I realized I'd better shut up. That was the one time I saw Hank Jones approaching something like getting angry, when we discussed the spaces Tony Williams could leave in the music.

I'd just listen and try to swing with Hank Jones. There was Herbie Hancock in there, Ahmad Jamal, James P. Johnson. He could handle any situation and seemed to have perfect finger control. Hank was respected, but I don't know if he was respected *enough*, considering how great he was.

---

13 Hank Jones recorded with Charlie Parker several times starting in 1949, with Cannonball Adderley and Miles Davis in 1958, and with The Great Jazz Trio starting in 1977.

Joe Lovano and Tom Harrell

In the early 1990s, one of the better bands I was in was a piano-less quartet with Joe Lovano, Tom Harrell, and Anthony Cox. That music was both swinging and searching, and we recorded live at the Village Vanguard—and then the record company sort of did us dirty by packaging our set with a comparatively conservative Lovano quartet with Mulgrew Miller, Christian McBride, and Lewis Nash recorded a year later.[14]

The rise of Wynton Marsalis has been controversial. There are definitely good things about Wynton and what he's given the music. I played some great bebop gigs with the legendary altoist Frank Morgan in the 1990s, after his release from San Quentin. Someone like Morgan would never have had a second act if Wynton hadn't revitalized a standard acoustic approach to jazz.

At the same time, you can't go back to the past. There's something about American classical music that is always contemporary. Even in my band with Ethan, we argue about the repertoire sometimes, because Ethan is getting all Wynton Marsalis on me, saying we should swing, while I'm asking him to bring in some of the ideas he played in the Bad Plus.

Joe Lovano loves Ornette Coleman as much as he loves John Coltrane or Dexter Gordon. On this Lovano record, the set with Harrell, Cox, and me is a good mix. But then, the other band is playing in a post-Wynton style. They are all great musicians, by the way. I love Mulgrew Miller, Christian McBride, and Lewis Nash! And they play good with Lovano, of course. But the message to the consumer was almost, "Don't worry about the creative sounds, because we have the other kind here as well." It would have helped both bands if they had been packaged separately, not together.

I've worked with Tom Harrell quite a bit and am on a few of his records. Tom is not just a great player, but one of our greatest writers, and more recently he has been a good mentor to younger musicians. Mark Turner toured with Tom Harrell for a few years, and I could tell how good this was for Mark.

Bobby Hutcherson

The first record I made with Bobby Hutcherson was Harold Land's *A New Shade of Blue* in 1971. That's a long time ago—I don't remember it

---

14 The two Joe Lovano groups recorded in March of 1994 and January of 1995, together the sessions were released on Blue Note as the 2-CD set *Quartets: Live at the Village Vanguard*. .

well, but a lot of younger musicians have asked me about it. The album has had some kind of renaissance I didn't really expect, although back in the day Billy Higgins told me he really liked it. Buster Williams is there; we were on tour with Herbie Hancock, and I guess our youthful enthusiasm for playing together is palpable. We were working in Santa Cruz and the recording was in L.A., so Buster and I had to commute every day by plane in order to make the gig on time.

Not so many people ask me about *Enjoy The View* from 2014, which was Bobby Hutcherson's last studio recording before passing away. Bobby was already wearing a mask connected to a portable oxygen tank wherever he walked, including while tracking. It was a somewhat artificial "all-star" record with Bobby, David Sanborn, and Joey DeFrancesco. We rehearsed in the recording studio, and when the smoke cleared, most of the takes that ended up on the record were, to my mind, more like rehearsals than performances. Sanborn overdubbed most of his solos. Nonetheless, it was moving to be next to Bobby Hutcherson.

Joey DeFrancesco really knew a lot about this music. Of course, Jimmy Smith was his god, and, just like Jimmy, Joey could get to the audience in any single tune. On that date, Joey wrote a tune that is kind of like Thelonious Monk or Tadd Dameron, "Don Is"—a wordplay on the producer, Don Was. I couldn't help myself and went for a total Philly Joe Jones imitation. That track remains an enjoyable listen.

Taj Mahal

A lot of the record dates I participated on were more like gigs, one and done, without much impact in the community or in the business. In 1984, Steve Swallow and I were on a long set of sessions for *Conjure: Music for the Texts of Ishmael Reed* organized by Kip Hanrahan. That LP has never come up in conversation, but blues great Taj Mahal was on some of the tracks, and he gave me a piece of advice that stuck. The music was more of a pop situation, and Mahal told me, "I want the drums to sound like an iron fist in a velvet glove."

I thought about that phrase and decided that it especially applied to the snare drum. When I hit that snare drum in a backbeat situation, it is supposed to be exactly that: an iron fist in a velvet glove.

12

Professor Hart

Teacher and mentor

My father was philosophical in outlook, always questioning the bigger picture. I don't know why married people do what they do, but, despite my father's radical tendencies, he followed my mother into Catholicism.

Thanks to my parents, I studied the catechism, sometimes alongside a good friend of mine, the trumpeter Ambrose Jackson. Ambrose and I played together behind pop acts at the Howard Theatre; later he worked with Marion Brown and Steve Lacy in Paris. When we were in high school together, he was an altar boy and had valuable insights into the church.

By the time we got to college, Ambrose had decided that Catholicism was one of the leading causes of atheism, and I agreed.

Religion made much more sense to me when I started embracing other spiritual disciplines as part of the '60s revolution. I now say that in order to swing, you need to believe in God.

The generation that was just a bit older than me really embodied spirituality. Two of my favorites were Bobby Timmons and Lee Morgan. In some ways, what really set apart hard bop from bebop was the way those musicians went back to the call-and-response of the black church. Charlie Parker, Dizzy Gillespie, and Bud Powell had some of that gospel thing, of course, but Lee Morgan and Bobby Timmons emphasized it that much more. Morgan and Timmons *personify* that approach.

Freddie Hubbard always liked to put his best foot forward and brag. Apparently, Hub would get drug that people loved Morgan's blues playing. Hub wanted more respect for his own harmonic ability, at least when compared to Morgan. But people couldn't help it. Everyone just *loved* that bluesy, churchy, gospel thing that Morgan had!

Whatever the church thing is, it's elemental. The drum is also elemental. The drum must have been one of the first instruments—they used the drum to communicate, for harvesting, for healing, for naming babies, for going to war. They used the drum to praise God.

There is no stronger example of a church musician than John Coltrane. He was *serious* about religion.

All religious music has value. Some of the Latin chants I sang in the Catholic church seem not far from late Coltrane, like *Meditations* or *Expression*. However, the official or governmental organizational side of things is where it gets tricky. When Ambrose told me that Catholicism was one of the leading causes of atheism, I knew *exactly* what he meant.

I took no shame in avoiding the draft for Vietnam. Whatever I was going to do, I was not going to be shipped off to fight the white man's war. It was the one time I did heroin. Stump Saunders's younger brother Billy was an addict and was thrilled to fix me up a shot. I was sober enough to get on the recruitment bus taking us to Fort Meade. But by the time we got to the barracks, it was hard to get off the bus, and then I was walking at a much slower pace than everybody else. People kept yelling at us, "Move along, recruits!" or "Get in this line!" but it all went completely over my head. I was in a daze, finally found a place to sit down, and drooled on myself a little bit. They finally got me in front of somebody in authority and I apologized, "I'm sorry sir, I'd really *like* to enlist, but I am a pathetic drug addict."

The sergeant or whoever he was looked at me for a few moments, and finally said, "Get the fuck out of here."

I don't remember how I got home that day, but I didn't end up in the army.

I quit the Catholic Church and avoided the draft, but the one institution I've ended up having something to do with is higher education. My associates Dave Liebman and Richie Beirach were always interested in teaching, and on the road with Quest we would do workshops in Europe. My previous book, *Jazz Drumming*, a collection of audio tracks with transcriptions and commentary, was a product of that era. But I wouldn't have really considered a career in the colleges except for what happened to my mother.

I had remained close to my parents. Whenever I had a gig in Washington, D.C., I'd stay in my room in their house, and they were very supportive through the years. One of the clippings my mother kept is amusing, from the February 27, 1966 issue of *The Washington Post*, where John Pagones writes:

> *One night I was talking with a cabbie, who happened to be a jazz fan, about a local drummer named Billy Hart. Billy used to be the drummer for the Shirley Horn Trio but left the group and I was wondering what happened to him. The cabbie kept on giving me the weirdest look. By one of those incredible coincidences it turned out the cabbie was William A. Hart, father of the aforementioned Billy.*
>
> *It turned out that Billy is now the drummer for jazz organist Jimmy Smith. He filled in when Smith played here two years ago at the Shadows and Smith kept him. Billy has also appeared in the movie, How to Stuff a Wild Bikini, which may possibly lead to other movie parts.*

(We checked, and I'm not in *How to Stuff a Wild Bikini*, although we may have done something that ended up on the cutting room floor, in one of several sessions with Jimmy Smith in Hollywood.)

My father went quickly, too young. He felt something in his leg one day and told a doctor about it; they checked him into the hospital, and he was gone by the weekend as the result of an aneurysm. I did manage to drive down and see him before he died. Everyone thought he was going to recover, until he didn't.

With my mother, it was a long and grueling affair. She drove herself to the hospital, checked herself in, and stayed there for more than a year in slow decline until she finally passed.[1] She'd always had a problem with asthma, and in time her asthma fatally interacted with pulmonary disease. I stopped whatever I was doing to go be by her side in the hospital. The one thing I learned from this terrible experience was: Always get out of the hospital. Never stay a single night in the hospital if you can avoid it.

This was in 1991. Around the same time, bassist Tom Knific and saxophonist Trent Kynaston found me a decent-sized grant to teach a semester at Western Michigan University (WMU). The year before, I had done a gig with Gust William Tsilis where Knific played bass. Knific and Kynaston had been planning to ask a practitioner to beef up their curriculum at WMU, and they ended up calling me. We would eventually make a few records with Stephen Zegree on piano, who was known for his contribution to jazz choral music.[2]

For the first time since the early '60s, I didn't tour. Each week, I taught at WMU for three days before flying to Maryland to finish out the week at my mother's side.

Doing the workshops with Quest, Caris Visentin transcribed a few of my drum patterns—or really the patterns I had learned from Art Blakey, Philly Joe Jones, or Max Roach—for a handout. That's what was in my bag for the first day of teaching, that handout. Over the years, the printed material I give my drum students has come to fill a big binder. I'm always trying to balance the tradition, which you need to be a finished artist, with what's happening now, which is what you need to get gigs. Sometimes I feel like I'm learning from my students, who bring me names like J Dilla and Dafnis Prieto, while I counter with names like Baby Dodds and O'Neil Spencer.

The traditional/contemporary discussion can be framed as ternary/binary. One of my handouts offers a tree with two branches. On the ternary branch of the tree, we start with Baby Dodds, then go up—Paul Barbarin, Zutty Singleton, Gene Krupa, Chick Webb, Buddy Rich, Papa

---

1   William Alfred Hart passed away in May of 1979, Ira Loretta Hart in July 1992.
2   *Firebird: Western Jazz Quartet Featuring Billy Hart* (recorded May 1992), *Blue Harts* (1995), and *Sabine's Dance* (2000). With Knyaston and Knific only, *Home Bass* (1998) and *West of Everywhere* (2001).

Jo Jones, O'Neil Spencer, Sid Catlett, Kenny Clarke, Max Roach, Art Blakey, Roy Haynes, Shadow Wilson, Denzil Best, Philly Joe Jones, and Billy Higgins, culminating with Elvin Jones.

On the binary branch, we again begin with Baby Dodds, then jump to Earl Palmer, Clayton Fillyau, Idris Muhammad, Zigaboo Modeliste, Al Jackson, Clyde Stubblefield, Pistol Allen, Benny Benjamin, Ray Lucas, Bernard Purdie, and Tony Williams—although here it's easier to keep adding more contemporary players like Steve Gadd and Vinnie Colaiuta after Tony. This particular handout is over a decade old and needs updating—it stops at Dennis Chambers, while now it should go at least to Marcus Gilmore.

Both sides start with Baby Dodds, who was in that port city, New Orleans. American music is American because America had all these different cultures in one place. On the musical side, New Orleans could not be more important for the melting pot.

Many black slaves in America were not allowed to keep their drums; in fact, playing a drum could be an act punishable by death. However, in New Orleans, some of the slaves could keep their instruments, and they even had a day off on Sunday. At Congo Square in New Orleans in the 1800s, the cultures mingled on Sundays: African, Brazilian, Cuban, European, even Native American. Around 1900 it came to a boil, and there began to be something like what we could call jazz—and also something like the modern drum set.

I chose Baby Dodds to begin my tree, but he was not the only one. Once again, this was a community music, where many people made an important contribution. In my lessons, I always mention Donald Bailey and Edgar Bateman along with the much more famous Elvin Jones, and I always mention Clifford Jarvis and Bobby Ward along with the much more famous Tony Williams. So, Baby Dodds is my choice, mainly because you can hear some beautiful solo drums and talking Dodds recorded in the 1940s. But he was not the only one.

They made me comfortable in Western Michigan, and in 2008, Kalamazoo Mayor Bobby Hopewell established May 28 as Billy Hart Day. My university career expanded, and I now teach at Oberlin, New England Conservatory, and Montclair State University as well.

In some ways, it seems like the explosion of jazz education proves that the legacy is finally being noticed, at least in the schools. American classical music is about one hundred years old. European classical music is more like 500 years old, but the speed of change has gone faster and faster thanks to the industrial revolution and then the technological revolution. I would have liked to have heard some of the people before Jelly Roll Morton and Louis Armstrong who weren't recorded, like Buddy Bolden or Scott Joplin.

Maybe Bolden didn't want to record because he didn't want white people to steal his material. That's one thing I've heard about Bolden, and I'm not sure if it's true. But if it *is* true, Bolden's concerns were borne out by the way things would go down in 20th-century music.

For a long time, the visible faces in the forefront of jazz education were white, and there was kind of a feel-good attitude about it all. But at Oberlin, the person who started the jazz program was Wendell Logan, who had a different perspective. There had been other important black teachers like David Baker and Billy Taylor, but Baker and Taylor—as great as they were—played the game. They probably *had* to play the game. It was a new day when Logan got in there and tried to put things in more of a proper order at Oberlin. Sadly, Logan passed just after the opening of the Bertram and Judith Kohl Building, a facility at Oberlin specifically for jazz. I enjoyed listening to Logan's "Gullah Island Suite," which was inspired by ring shout. We could know more about Logan's contribution as a composer.[3]

Music on paper is important, and sight-reading is important, but reading is hardly the *only* thing. There's no music on paper that has that much to do with the blues or the sound of the black church.

This puts me in conflict with some of my peers, who see sight-reading and bits and pieces of paper as the best way to teach jazz. Jamey Aebersold is the king of all that. In fact, Aebersold once called up Dave Liebman and bitterly complained about my teaching. I guess I was pretty direct in a masterclass at an Aebersold camp in Louisville. I probably said something like I might usually say—that the students should learn a dozen blues tunes and a dozen rhythm changes tunes, they should be able to sing the melodies and the bass lines without looking at sheet music, and so forth.

---

3   Logan (1940-2010), soprano saxophonist and trumpeter, grew up in Thomson, Georgia, earned a PhD at the University of Iowa in 1968, and taught at Florida A&M, Ball State, and Western Illinois University before joining Oberlin's faculty, where he instituted a Jazz Studies major in 1989. He is the author of *Primer for Keyboard Improvisation in the Jazz/Rock Idiom* (1980), a Guggenheim Fellowship winner (1991), and a former composer-in-residence at the Rockefeller Study Center in Bellagio, Italy (1994).

In my view, reading music is almost an excuse *not* to learn the basic repertoire. *Know the music.* There's no other way. Start with the blues and rhythm changes.

I never say, "Have fun," or "It's easy." Whatever I said in Louisville, Aebersold called Liebman to bitch about how I was too discouraging. Aebersold probably felt I was costing him money, that teachers like me would stop people from buying his books or attending his workshops on how to play jazz.

That's pure capitalism, the kind of economic incentive that aligns with the Catholic Church and the war in Vietnam. The people at the top make the money while the people far below experience hardship. I'm not comparing the small potatoes of Jamey Aebersold to the Catholic Church or the war in Vietnam—but all that money in jazz education is perhaps not so far from the way Sam Phillips and Colonel Tom Parker made Elvis Presley a star by imitating black music. At any rate, I did appreciate how Wendell Logan tried to put things in more of a proper order. Everyone should know the true source of the rhythm in this music is African, just the way we know George Washington founded the country. There is *no* debate.

My teaching has gotten more refined over the years. After hearing a student combo play, I begin by declaring that the rhythm section is a *rhythm* section. It's not a harmonic section or a melodic section, it's a *rhythm* section.

Then, of course, most students have *no idea* of the tradition. Mel Lewis told me, with no doubt in his mind, "The Beatles fucked up jazz." I agree with Mel, at least when I look at all these student drummers who don't know a single basic thing about swing.

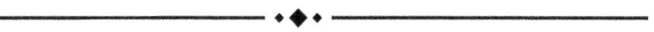

Highlights from my educational materials

Ride Cymbal. There's the quarter note, and there's the upbeat. Both are present in the jazz ride cymbal beat. The upbeat is not an eighth note, it's the last note of a triplet. However that division—swing, or whatever gives a certain kind of euphoria—is often written as binary instead of as ternary. This goes back to whenever people started writing it down, and somehow the disparity between the notation and the way it is played has never been fixed. The word "syncopation" is a valid word, just like "metric modulation" or "hemiola" or whatever the various European terms are. But there doesn't seem to be a word to cover the ternary in the upbeats of the ride pattern.

It's not *really* a triplet, either. The spacing can vary widely from one professional drummer to another. It's mysterious. There's a certain authenticity that comes with being inside the community.

Rhythm Changes. Apart from the blues, most of the standard repertoire for American classical music is a 32-bar song form, AABA. Within that, the most popular form is rhythm changes. Count Basie! Duke Ellington! Charlie Parker! Bud Powell! Dizzy Gillespie! Thelonious Monk! Art Blakey! Miles Davis! Sonny Rollins! They all played rhythm changes in their own way. A drum student should learn at least 12 of those famous variations and be able to sing the diverse root movement of the harmony.

Going to the bridge is also very important. I like to teach two classic patterns, really any two will do, and then use just one for the A sections and one for the bridge. If you stay in that slow alternation for a time, AABA, one pattern for the A section and one for the B, it will do something for your concentration.

It's interesting that "rhythm changes" comes from a song by George Gershwin. It's also interesting that the famous theme of "I Got Rhythm" may have been borrowed from the work of a comparatively unheralded Afro-American composer, William Grant Still.[4]

Rudiments/Vocabulary. Rudiments are a European element. They come from Italy, France, Switzerland, Scotland, and other places.

Rudiments are a baseline of drum set technique. When I saw Miles Davis on a Herbie Hancock gig just before he called me to be on *On the Corner*, I was standing at my drum set. Miles whispered in my ear, "Let me hear your roll."

The topic of a drum roll brings up Art Blakey again. Blakey studied with Chick Webb, who was comparable to Art Tatum at the piano: pure perfection. (Both Max Roach and Art Blakey literally told me that "Chick Webb was the Art Tatum of the drums.") More than once, Art Blakey

---

[4] Gershwin's *Girl Crazy*—the source of "I Got Rhythm," "Embraceable You," and "But Not For Me"–opened in 1930, the same year Still completed his *Afro-American Symphony*. In measures 12-15 of the third movement, flute, piccolo, and oboe play a strikingly similar, syncopated melody to "I Got Rhythm." Eubie Blake claimed Still came up with the line while playing in Sissle and Blake's *Shuffle Along* years earlier.

put his arm around me, pulled me close, and whispered, "Chick Webb would make me roll until the tears started rolling down my cheeks."

Eventually Blakey would be famous for his press roll. There was a nice local drummer in D.C., Fats Clark, a big guy who had a lovely soft touch at the drums. Fats said to me, "I heard all this talk about Art Blakey's famous press roll. I was sort of skeptical, so I went down there to hear Blakey play. I sat down close to the drums and crossed my arms, unwilling to be easily impressed. Sure enough, Art made the press roll, and I was the first one to stand up and start clapping."

Most of the better drum books concern rolls and other rudiments. Piano players can read through Scott Joplin and George Gershwin; drummers have people like Charles Wilcoxon and Marvin Dahlgren.

Rudiments and the associated drum music also have an emotional or theatrical element, especially on the snare drum. When we go off to war or praise the queen, the drums provide a ceremonial touch. Most of what we do comes from dance or folk music, but that rudimental feeling is also important.

Philly Joe Jones played a lot of Wilcoxon, and he told me he got that book from Max Roach. When I asked Philly Joe to explain that further—because he was from Philadelphia and Max was from Brooklyn—Philly Joe laughed and said, "I used to get on a bus to get to Max's house from Philly."

I've heard Elvin Jones play Wilcoxon themes as well. When Philly Joe or Elvin quote Wilcoxon, they phrase those themes a little more dramatically than they appear on the page.[5]

Marvin Dahlgren was my friend, and I was very impressed with his book *4-Way Coordination*, written with Elliot Fine. He gave both Elvin Jones and me a copy of this book when it was still in manuscript form way back in the early '60s. Dahlgren talks about melodic counterpoint and harmonic counterpoint at the drum set. Yeah!

After Shirley Horn told me she loved French and Russian composers—thus validating my grandmother Viola's perspective as well—I began going to a few symphonic concerts. Marvin was in Minneapolis where he was principal percussionist in the Minnesota Orchestra. One time he invited me to a concert of the Mahler 6th symphony and the Rachmaninoff 2nd

---

5   Wilcoxon's books include *Modern Rudimental Swing Solos for the Advanced Drummer* (1941) and *The All-American Drummer: 150 Rudimental Solos* (1945).

symphony. During that concert, I remember wiping my face because it was wet—and that's when I realized I was crying.

Mahler and Rachmaninoff are European music. For that matter, so are drum rudiments. All of that can be supremely beautiful. But Denardo Coleman told me that his father Ornette warned of a familiar pitfall, where many regard the European model as the highest level for music. That's like what Coltrane said: "Every culture has a classical music."

I asked Chick Corea once about the quick-moving clarity of his music—a clarity that bordered on *icy*—and he said he got it from the study of European classical music. All the drummers who played Chick's fusion music had to have superior rudimental control.

But Chick also went into the Spanish-speaking communities and got the clave. The clave is a big part of what made Chick Corea who he was, not just the European classical music.

The Second Line. In America, the clave showed up in New Orleans as the second line, which is the direct translation of African rhythm through India, Brazil, Cuba, Puerto Rico, and the West Indies to the drum set. Now, what makes this version of the clave so different from the clave as heard in so many different Spanish-speaking musics? In my opinion, it is the blues, which is another African influence. Again, all cultures seem to have The Universal Rhythm, 3:3:2, which is also half the son clave. You add some blues to that on a Sunday afternoon in Congo Square, and you're really getting somewhere!

African Rhythms. This is a vague phrase, but what I mean is drum repertoire in 3 and 6. The bembé pattern is famous, and it can be helpful to phrase 4/4 swing with the bembé. I'm still looking for more esoteric 6/4 patterns in my own playing. In my own quartet, I play some fairly advanced permutations of "African rhythms" on Ethan's song, "Neon."[6]

In general, it's good to practice one thing for a long time at a stretch. Working on one rhythm for an hour is when you can notice if you have a tendency to rush or drag.

I don't believe in the metronome. In fact, if people play with perfect time, I might think it's *too* perfect. Again, this is because I believe in the

---

6   See *Billy Hart Quartet* (HighNote, 2018), track 9.

African approach. They invented the metronome in Europe, but all the rhythm was so much stronger in Africa, where there was *no* metronome.

If it feels like things are dragging, it can be helpful to play more upbeats. If things are rushing, it can be helpful to play more downbeats.

From my point of view, it's up to everybody in the band to play the time. Even the horn players—for that matter, even the singers! But, of course, the time is an especially important concern for everybody within the rhythm section.

I didn't play with Horace Silver much, just one record date later in his career[7], so I don't know what it was like to play with him on the bandstand in his prime. But on the record date, he told me, "Just make sure I don't rush."

Now, Horace Silver is one of the greatest, but I was disappointed by that comment. Why shouldn't the piano player take responsibility for how the time feels?

Another band I played in had one bassist where everyone complained that the time was dragging just a bit. We changed the bassist—and then everyone complained that the time was rushing just a bit. Well, *I* didn't change. I do whatever it takes to keep the conversation happily moving along within the rhythm section.

Stan Getz and I had a conflict about that. Clint Houston and I are together on a few of Stan's best records, but live, Clint could be hard to play with. He was originally inspired by the busy approach of Scott LaFaro, and then he showed Stanley Clarke some of that, to the point that Clint thought he deserved some of the credit accorded Clarke. Clint would play on top of the beat in a busy binary manner when the song was just a mellow fox-trot. It was like he was trying to prove that he should have been in Return to Forever rather than swinging with Stan. When I broke up the time in the right places in gentle waves in response to the harmony, he would "twang" the bass string against the neck to show his irritation. Maybe Clint would have preferred a metronome to a real drummer? It drove me crazy.

After some of that, Stan came to me and looked me in the eyes. "What's goin' on back there, Billy? Is it the bass player?"

Oops. Well, I certainly was not going to sow dissension in the ranks, so I lied. "No, Stan, I don't know what it is."

---

7   Horace Silver's *Music to Ease Your Disease* (1988) with Clark Terry, Junior Cook, Ray Drummond, Billy Hart, and Andy Bey is on Silver's own label Silverto.

"Well, I don't care," Stan shot back. "As far as I'm concerned, *the time is the drummer's responsibility.*"

As usual, Stan had a point. If it comes to a really dire situation, I can enforce the time like a studio drummer. But really, for the best results, everyone in the rhythm section should listen to each other and roll with whatever is happening.

───────────── ◆ ─────────────

My handouts go on for pages. One overall model for practice:

Discipline + Humility = Concentration

Under that phrase are two sets of four basic principles. The first four are:

Clarity. This is the basic organization of your technique. In all the great drummers, no matter the style, their articulation is always totally clear.

Projection. It doesn't matter if your ideas are great if they can't be heard. One time in the studio I played something pretty hip with the brushes and didn't hear it in the playback. I asked the engineer about it, and he said, "If you want to hear it, you're gonna have to play it." That was a good lesson.

Undulation. That's the direction from Stan Getz, to play the ride cymbal in a wave. In a hospital room, the heartbeat monitor needs to fluctuate on and off; if the machine goes to a steady, dull tone, we know we've lost the patient.

Placement. Certain things seem to be extra swinging if they are placed behind the beat. Elvin Jones defines this concept, for example in his famous fill going in the Wayne Shorter solo on "Witch Hunt." The beautiful way Barry Harris and Leroy Williams play upbeats together is also notably "late" in terms of the time.

In binary music with a backbeat, placement might be called "pocket."

───────────── ◆ ─────────────

The next four principles I read about from Antonio Sanchez. I instinctively liked these concepts, and Sanchez is also a good model for my students if I'm thinking about contemporary drummers. I took the principles from him, but the comments are my own interpretation:

Dynamics. It's vital to consider dynamics in acoustic music. If you're playing electric music, dynamics are less important. As I've said before, adding in more clave can bring out more intensity in a softer dynamic for acoustic music.

Interaction. An ensemble needs to be on the same page, playing a unified approach. Sometimes that means the rhythm section and the soloist move together like a school of fish. But when I was first learning with Reuben Brown and Butch Warren at the house gig at Abart's, I liked to play back and reinforce whatever Reuben was doing—until Reuben begged me, "For God's sake, Billy, do *anything* but that!" Sonny Fortune called imitating each other on the bandstand "nursery rhymes." Somewhere between never doing "nursery rhymes" and doing it once in a while is part of the vocabulary. It always sounds great when Red Garland and Philly Joe Jones are playing hits together.

Orchestration. Max Roach took the general concept of rudimental playing and spread those rudiments melodically around the drum set.

Motivic development. In pop music they call it the "hook." In gospel music the feeling builds and builds; John Coltrane uses that kind of motivic preaching technique when building his epic solos. Thelonious Monk is another good example of motivic development.

Of course, the above principles are in service of larger questions.

Many improvisors hate to repeat themselves. But Herbie Hancock once suggested to me that we should repeat ourselves more often. When I pressed Herbie on that comment, he said, "No matter how obvious it is to the musicians, it's never obvious enough for the audience."

That was interesting, in part because of the choices he made after breaking up our sextet. Herbie's probably right, but in questions about music or aesthetics, the moment you think you've found the answer is frequently the moment you realize the contrary is also true.

That's another one of my principles in teaching: Prove me wrong or prove me right. Either way is okay with me.

13

The Big Picture

I've been uncomfortable giving my opinions throughout the writing of this memoir. When teaching, giving opinions is inevitable, but I try to temper my stronger comments with the tagline, *"for me,"* leaving room for greater masters to speak in case they disagree. I might have put *"for me"* at the end of every opinion printed in this book, if Ethan had allowed such a literary transgression. It's like when Elvin Jones told me, "Don't ask me to show you anything, because if I could show you anything, we would all be Max Roach."

Billy Hart and Max Roach, perhaps around 2000

The road to racial equality is long. As great as some white jazz musicians are, they don't always see the whole picture. A recurring opinion that gets tossed around by certain musicians is that Max Roach doesn't really swing or have a good feel.

When you criticize somebody, you have to have some clear basis of what that criticism means. Max Roach was Charlie Parker's choice, so that should conclude the discussion. But let's try to get a little deeper.

All meaningful art causes an emotion. How does that happen? Some people are born with something powerful, some people study. For some musicians, rhythm is strong; for others, it's harmony. "First thought, best thought" is a nice phrase—*if* you can think. Can you learn to compose a memorable melody, or does that gift come straight from God? The kind of passion required to create on a very high level should be either spiritual or sensual. But we also need street smarts and book smarts. Is Franz Liszt a better piano player than Thelonious Monk? Just this past week I danced along to Chaka Khan's backbeat and sang along with the conclusion of Stravinsky's *Firebird Suite*.

I'd never want to be in the position of deciding what to take and what to leave out. In a perfect world, I want to be part of it all: soulful, intellectual, traditional, contemporary, the community, the concert hall.

During my brief college career at Howard, I was asked to write a short essay about who I was, where I was from, and what my future held. After pondering the topic, I wrote down just two words: "I am."

"I am" includes *all* the history and *all* the choices.

"I am" could have been the title of this book.

My favorite musician, John Coltrane, declared, "I am." His work covers all the bases: That wonderful disc of gentle romantic ballads, *John Coltrane and Johnny Hartman*, sits right next to the spiritual guidance of *A Love Supreme* and the extreme exploration of *Interstellar Space*.

Part of what goes into meaningful art is the history of the people that created it. What causes inspiration? McCoy Tyner told me, "Diamonds are made from pressure." I'm still learning about Afro-American history. When a good documentary about the Civil War, Reconstruction, or the Civil Rights era turns up on the television, I sit there watching in *awe*.

Max Roach was certainly subjected to a lot of pressure when generating his contribution. Despite all that, he took care of the intellectual side. He put it all in academic order as a real scholar of the instrument: not only physically but socially. He was aware of *everything*.

The Big Picture

Some musicians don't want a drummer who is a thinker, they want somebody who beats on trees like a gorilla. That's like the white lady who told Buddy Montgomery, "I heard that Wes Montgomery can't read music, isn't that wonderful?" Similarly, the old-school crew of George Coleman and Sonny Stitt have a backhanded compliment that means a drummer should just have a happy good time and present no intellectual depth: "No fool, no fun."

Then there's the virtuosity side of the equation. If criticizing Max Roach's feel isn't enough, certain people like to praise Buddy Rich as having more chops than Max did. Maybe that's true, but is virtuosity the only thing that's important? Who's more soulful, Buddy or Max? Who played better with Charlie Parker? Who played with Clifford Brown and Sonny Rollins? Listen to Rollins, Max, and Oscar Pettiford on "The Freedom Suite" and tell me again that Max Roach is less than *perfect*.

I never heard someone who could really swing say anything negative about Max Roach. It's the people who are less confident that dare to speak up out of turn.

If you overhear someone trustworthy giving an opinion to someone else, it makes a difference who they're talking to. I don't say the same things to everybody—I dole out my wisdom according to the level of the recipient. One of the challenging things about writing this memoir was trying to imagine who might read it, because I say different things to different people in conversation.

Benny Golson and Roy Haynes passed away during the final stages of this book, and I looked up to both. Whenever I was lucky enough to have a conversation with Golson or Haynes over the years, I never gave my opinion about anything—I was just listening for what they had to say.

However, if I'm in a room with young students fumbling through a classic Golson composition or setting up a flat ride to emulate Haynes, I might ignore words like "jazz" entirely and suggest that Golson and Haynes are part of "a sociological development demonstrated through music," in an attempt to raise their awareness.

I can do that musically as well. One of the great Coleman Hawkins compositions is "Mop Mop," which is call and response, like the black church. The call is, "Boo-dle a dee. Boo-dle a dee; Boo-dle a dee, dee!" The response is, "Mop mop!"

In front of certain hip audiences, I can play the call and they will give the correct response without a prompt. In front of other audiences, they have no idea. It is what it is. As Herbie Hancock said, "You'll Know When You Get There."

As soon as the slogan "Black Lives Matter" came up, a certain group of people immediately responded, "All Lives Matter." That's an ignorant response. That's just like saying Max Roach doesn't swing.

Max Roach swings his ass off!

Max was also the first composer for solo drum set, and one of his iconic pieces is "For Big Sid," which uses "Mop Mop" as the starting point, after Big Sid Catlett's amazing drum solo on the famous recording of "Mop Mop" with Louis Armstrong at Symphony Hall (called "Boff Boff" on that release). Everyone in America should know "Mop Mop" and "For Big Sid."[1] These works are absolutely essential to the very fabric of our culture.

After I left Stan Getz and started playing with anybody and everybody, it could be a heavy lift. A lot of times I was the only Afro-American musician on the bandstand or in the recording studio. Many of the other musicians present were great, some less so. In every case, I try to balance the musical equation successfully, and at times this has meant pulling rank. But when I pull rank, I might not be doing it just for musical reasons, but also to teach something about the history. If I'm the only Afro-American person for miles around, then I need to represent for my lineage.

A young white student once complained to me that it wasn't fair that all the greatest jazz drummers were black. Not *fair*? What's fair got to do with it? Does this kid want to grow up under the same conditions that oppressed Max Roach?

Capitalism is another aspect to manage, especially since politics and capitalism usually end up one and the same. Some people run with a slogan like "Black Lives Matter" and try to monetize it for personal gain. I was there for the ferment of the 1960s, and not everybody remained committed to the cause for the right reasons.

One needs to accompany the world the way you accompany a musical group. Sometimes it needs more sway, sometimes it needs something less yielding. You can't fix a weak group no matter what you play, but you don't need to betray yourself or your values, either. "I am."

A few people have named their children "Jabali" after me. They had no connection in a family sense, but they apparently appreciated what

---

1   On *Drums Unlimited* (Atlantic, 1966).

I and the name "Jabali" stood for: "moral strength." Or maybe they just liked the sound of the name. Either way. "I am."

I appreciate the younger musicians so much and have tried to keep up with fresh innovations. In every generation the vocabulary changes. The brilliant Marcus Gilmore seems especially important, in terms of whatever the contemporary styles are. At this point, the classical music of India seems to be as influential on the current scene as the classical music of Africa. When Danilo Perez successfully transformed the clave into odd groupings like five and seven, that made a difference.

While the only way to know what's going to happen in the future is to have some knowledge of the past, it's also all too easy for an older cat to criticize a younger cat. I'd rather learn from a young cat, for they, of course, are really what's happening. Whatever is "new" has a kind of automatic validity, though in some cases the capitalist system promotes some people too far too fast. At any rate, just as I was always deferential to my elders, I ask questions of the great younger players and try to gain insight into how they think and what they practice. For over twenty years now, if you called me and got my voicemail greeting, that message has been a 7/4 clave I learned from Jeff Watts.

At the risk of sounding like just another elder complaining about the kids, I will say that I wonder about the continuance of swing. Swing in a deeper sense, not just checking some boxes and playing in a superficially straight-ahead style. It's not just knowing certain patterns; there needs to be a deeper reason for why you're trying to swing. "Nobody plays any of the hip shit anymore," Al Foster said to me a couple of years ago, and I kind of knew what he meant.

I need to bring up Buster Williams again, and the way Buster plays time. Whatever *that* is, it used to be the baseline of what you needed to play American classical music. When teaching, I call it the ternary, but it isn't just a triplet—it's something else, it's really a different way of thinking. You can hear it on all those great records from the '40s, '50s, and '60s. It's still here, but you can't find it so easily. Nasheet Waits has it, but even he is not that young of a cat anymore.

Some people think the ternary is less advanced than the binary, simply because the binary seems to be more contemporary. In this case I'll pull rank and flatly declare that those people just don't know what is advanced and what isn't. In my final analysis, swinging consistently is the hardest thing to do. Swing is based on what was played centuries ago in Africa, a rhythmic significance that's built on a very heavy intelligence. When you play it accurately, people respond euphorically.

There's no point in worrying. It's important to always be moving forward. James Lott told me, "The greatest form of human intelligence is love."

I remain profoundly grateful for all the music I've made on all the stages of the world. Art is communication, and the exchange definitely goes both ways. When I address the audience at the conclusion of one of my own gigs, I say to them, "Thank you for the way you've inspired us tonight."

Billy with son Chris Hart, in Billy's backyard, Memorial Day 2025. (Photos by Ethan Iverson.)

Appendix 1. Other Drummers Discuss Billy Hart

> *Kush Abadey, Nasar Abadey, Barry Altschul, Jeff Ballard, Johnathan Blake, Obed Calvaire, Terri Lyne Carrington, Billy Drummond, Peter Erskine, Bill Goodwin, Hyland Harris, Eric McPherson, Allison Miller, Lewis Nash, Adam Nussbaum, Bobby Previte, Jorge Rossy, Damion Reid, Vinnie Sperrazza, Nasheet Waits, Lenny White, & Jeff Williams*

Kush Abadey

My father and Billy are close friends, so I've known Billy for practically my whole life. He's been a profound influence. When he plays, I hear the full lineage in every single beat. One moment is every moment.

Billy is the most enthusiastic student, someone who absorbs everything. When Billy was with Stan Getz, João Gilberto taught Billy the real version of the bossa nova, not the sugar-coated version. When Billy plays that sort of beat, it comes from an authentic place.

Herbie Hancock's most exciting and exploratory band was Mwandishi, and Jabali had everything to do with how that band developed. I still listen to the Mwandishi records all the time.

Washington, D.C. is not a state, it's almost not a city. It's the seat of government and was never planned to have much of a cultural identity. There's a lot of push and pull: Are we Southern or Northern? Are we conservative or revolutionary?

D.C. drummers are relaxed and malleable. Our beat sits back but never drags.

Nasar Abadey

I grew up in Buffalo, and that's where I heard Billy Hart at the Bon Ton with Jimmy Smith and Quentin Warren. At that time, there was an organ in every club in the black neighborhoods. The organ was king, and the drummers were into supporting a certain kind of popular organ sound. For example, Joe Dukes was playing with Jack McDuff, and Dukes had a real direct and basic approach.

But Billy Hart didn't sound like anybody else playing that organ circuit. Billy had a whole other level of finesse and creativity. Jimmy Smith was strait-laced, even stiff, so I'm sure Billy couldn't open up and do everything he wanted to do that night. Still, Billy Hart with Jimmy Smith was a supreme example of a drummer with an organ trio.

A few years later, Herbie Hancock's sextet played at the Revilot, and that's when I figured out who Billy Hart really was. He was playing textures. Sure, there were beats, and he'd ride on the cymbal, but he was also treating his cymbals like orchestral percussion. The cymbals could just be a surface to play gestures on. At the same time, the drum set had the African approach, with beautiful melodies between the tom-toms.

I struck up a conversation at the Revilot, and Billy and I started to become friends.

He's so humble. He never really projected himself as a star drummer. I had my little posse with me at the Revilot, and he wanted to know what we were listening to, as if he was going to learn from us instead of the other way around. A year later, when I moved to New York and started trying to break into the scene, he realized I was there, so he called me and said, "We are on the same level now."

Eventually I moved to Washington, D.C. When my wife, Baiyina, and I went to see him with Stan Getz at Blues Alley in 1977, Billy saw us, leapt up, and said, "What are you doing *here*?"

We've been pretty tight since then. One of our bonds is the topic of spirituality, often with an esoteric tilt. John Coltrane plays an important role in these conversations. Billy and I have both read *The Urantia Book* and have endlessly discussed the meaning of life and the role music plays in the development of a higher consciousness.

Barry Altschul

I met Billy Hart in 1965 in Copenhagen. There were three American drummers there, we played a big concert together. Rudy Collins was with Dizzy Gillespie, Billy Hart was with Jimmy Smith, and I was with Paul Bley. After the gig we all went to the Montmartre jazz club. It was late, and we all wanted to sit in, even though it was the last tune. We decided that each one of us would play with a different soloist, and eventually we also did a round robin on the drums, trading 8 bar phrases with the band, taking turns on the same drum set.

Appendix 1. Other Drummers Discuss Billy Hart

Later, when he was with Herbie Hancock and I was with Chick Corea, we were in a lot of the same places and hung out. It was always a pleasure to hear Billy. He's such a flexible and creative player, with a beautiful touch and a great feel.

Jeff Ballard

As a kid I was really into big bands, especially Count Basie, and my favorite drummer was Sonny Payne. But at a jazz camp I was at, I found this Jim McNeely LP, *The Plot Thickens*. Billy was on drums. I had never heard playing like that. It was a totally different animal. I didn't realize it at the time but within a few beats, Billy Hart had pushed me into modernity. (I had never heard brushes played like that before. Revelatory!) Among my next purchases were Billy's own great albums *Enchance* and *Oshumare*.

He shares something with Donald Bailey—a kind of homemade cooking. Nobody can change either of them. They are what they are, and they do what they do because they believe in it. Because they hear it. They are confidently unorthodox and humbly in the service of what they hear. I listened to them both very carefully and deeply. I guess they both gave me permission to break the rules.

One night we were both at a European festival. I was playing with Chick Corea, and we hung out afterward in my hotel room. He talked for some time, breaking down Roy Haynes, Elvin Jones, and Billy Higgins, emphasizing their similarities in such an insightful intelligent way—made connections with such understanding. I could hear how much Billy was a student of the music; such a thoughtful cat. It was a wonderful and revelatory lesson.

On another occasion, I went to the Village Vanguard and Billy was there talking to someone from the band that was playing. I walked up to say hi to Billy and hopefully meet this other person, but Billy held up his hand, warning me off with a look. I felt snubbed and left the club soon after, bent out of shape about it. Then Billy called me up the next morning! I didn't even know he had my number. I couldn't believe it. He explained that he was deep in a private conversation last night and now wanted to make sure he hadn't insulted me, and said he hoped my feelings weren't hurt. What a gentleman! A real classy guy. That whole generation of his—a class act.

Just last year, Billy came to the Vanguard where I was playing with Kurt Rosenwinkel. He sat behind me on that famous "drummer's row." I was electrified—really happy and a little nervous, I have to admit. When I had this open intro to "Xmas Song," right as I started, I realized that every single phrase I played was from Billy. Now understand me, I was not at all trying to play for him some of *his* stuff. Not at all. I was trying to play *my* stuff. But no matter what I played, it sounded like it was his—like something he would do. I knew and saw so clearly that it was coming directly from him. Maybe it was because he was sitting behind me. I was happy and shocked at the same time.

Johnathan Blake

I call him "Uncle Billy." My dad, the violinist John Blake, played in one of Billy's bands around the time that they were both making records for Gramavision. When I was just a little boy, my dad would take me to New York to see gigs where Uncle Billy was playing.

He's a forever student of this music, and he's always telling me and other people, "I need to study with *you*." (By the way—no, he actually *doesn't* need to study with anybody.)

In a particular twist of fate, one time he subbed for me, when I was with Tom Harrell's band. It was a week at the Village Vanguard, and I got back in time to hear the last night. Since I knew the repertoire so well, it put me in a position where I could really see how his approach was so *unique*, and so *him*, and just so *deep*! I didn't want to hear anyone else play Tom's book after that.

Another time at the Vanguard, with his own quartet, he played a drum solo that featured the snare drum. It shook me, because I hadn't heard that level of snare drum intensity since I had the opportunity to study with the Maestro Max Roach in Amherst during the Jazz In July summer camp when I was 15 and 16. I thought I knew all my Billyisms and my Hartisms, but he came with something else and took it to another tier. It was simply dumbfounding. I said to myself, "How does this man *continue* to grow?"

Obed Calvaire

I was driving Billy Hart home one night, and he told me something I will never forget: "Most musicians aren't happy unless they sound like someone else." I love everyone from Papa Jo Jones to Vinnie Colaiuta, and I take from them all. But it was a good reminder from Billy to always keep your voice in whatever you do.

He's always going out to see everybody and support the younger drummers. He must have been to twenty of my gigs, stopping by just to listen and offer some words of support. There's nobody else of his era who has participated quite like that.

From his discography, I'll mention the brushwork on "Jitterbug Waltz" with Clark Terry and Oscar Peterson, where he's dancing on the drums. With Miles Davis on *On the Corner*, his funky beat puts the listener in a trance. With Yelena Eckemoff on *Leaving Everything Behind*, he paints pictures of the elements in a landscape: wind, storm, calm.

Terri Lyne Carrington

I was maybe 12 years old when my father arranged for me to get together with Billy Hart. It was at the club Lulu White's in Boston and Billy met me there in the afternoon before he played the gig that night. Now that I know the perils of touring, I can understand the effort it took Billy to show up for me that day. He was enthusiastic and supportive; I demonstrated some triplet exercises I was learning from my teacher Alan Dawson, which Billy associated with the style of Elvin Jones. It is such a great memory for me to have been with Billy Hart at the drum kit that day when I was just a kid.

After moving to New York when I was 18, I saw Billy play a lot. For me he was a natural extension of Roy Haynes, but with his own voice. Like Roy Haynes, Billy Hart has an approach that never grows old, it's perpetually hip and in the moment.

Alan Dawson taught me balance and control with a certain fluidity, but Roy and Billy have another kind of push and pull with the time. That approach to time is still something I strive for. When I ask myself, "How do I get out of these more even distributions of the beat?" I think of Billy Hart for the answers.

He's not the kind of player who draws from an arsenal of licks; instead, one idea organically leads to the next, which makes for a lot of surprises at a Billy Hart gig! Often when I play, for inspiration I'll think of my influences, and try to imagine what they might do. For jazz, it is usually Roy Haynes, Jack DeJohnette, and Billy Hart. Even though I don't *really* know what they would do, it's a way to fight being habitual and find fresh ideas in the moment.

Billy Drummond

I wrote two letters: one to Max Roach when I was quite young, and one to Billy Hart several years later.

Billy's first record, *Enchance*, was a happy surprise, with the lineup of Dewey Redman and Oliver Lake. But then, several years later, I was shocked again by *Oshumare*, which was right up my alley. I just loved the personnel, the repertoire, and the way it was recorded. So I wrote Billy a letter, thanking him for the music and saying that *Oshumare* was the best album I'd heard all year.

At the time I was playing five nights a week with a Top 40 band in Virginia, but I'd get away on my nights off to go to New York. I saw Billy at The West End Cafe, and afterwards we sat in his car and talked a bit. I was so excited to be talking with Billy Hart! He was so friendly and open, the way he always is with younger musicians. Towards the end of our talk, he asked me, "You're going to go see Philly Joe Jones tomorrow, right?"

I couldn't go, because I needed to fly out the next morning and get back to my gig. That didn't seem to make much of a difference to Billy, who asked me again, "You're going to go see Philly Joe tomorrow, right?"

I would have preferred to stay and see him — and Billy was adamant about my doing so — but my gig back in VA was something I couldn't miss. It was more like a job, not something to sub out (unfortunately). It was just very, very serious as to how Billy saw it. How Dare You Go Home when Philly Joe Jones Will Be Playing Tomorrow Night!

Peter Erskine

When I joined the Stan Kenton Orchestra in 1972, I was listening to a lot of Billy Hart, specifically his playing on the Herbie Hancock album *Crossings*. Everything he played (especially the drum solo that opens "Sleeping Giant") made so much sense to me ... like a Beethoven string quartet—perfect in every way.

I finally got to meet him during my next road gig with Maynard Ferguson, when Maynard and Stan Getz's bands played opposite one another at a couple of different theater-in-the-round venues, one in Valley Forge, PA, and one on Long Island. It was during the Valley Forge double bill that Billy asked me to sub for him with Stan Getz for one set because he would be recording in New York City and would most likely not get back to the theatre in time. I was more than happy to agree. So,

I'm playing with Stan (the rest of the band included Mike Richmond and Andy Laverne) and really having fun. The stage is turning while we play ... and all of a sudden, as we come 'round one of the revolutions, there's Billy sitting in the audience with his eyes locked on me, smiling.

This made me feel really good, of course. But the more valuable part of the experience was yet to come. He offered in-between shows, "Yeah, Peter. Sounded great. But, you know ... you don't need to keep playing your hi-hat on beats 2 & 4 *all* of the time. You can loosen up that left foot," or something to that effect.

This was such a revelation. Buddy Rich's tenor player back in the mid-60's, Jay Corre, was a high school friend of my dad's, and Jay spent one high school summer mentoring me, emphasizing over and over that I must *never* stop playing the hi-hat on beats 2 & 4!

Billy Hart turned the key for me.

Bill Goodwin

Billy and I are only a year apart, he's the slightly older brother I never had, and it was a joy to record with him just recently, two drummers in the same room with George Garzone and Ben Street.

He can play with literally anybody, and he never ceases to please. He's assertive but also a team player. For a time, I was producing quite a lot of records, and he was the first guy I would call. The Tom Harrell date *Stories* came out especially well.

We first met in about 1966, when he was on tour with the Montgomery Brothers at Shelly's Manne-Hole in Los Angeles. I was living there and playing the Manne-Hole often. Most nights, if I wasn't working somewhere else, I would go there anyway. We ended up hanging out quite a bit during the day, going to record shops and the drum stores. He said that the three Montgomery Brothers didn't like to hang out, so he was especially grateful for someone to show him around L.A.

Hyland Harris

Billy Hart is a member of an increasingly shrinking fraternity: musicians who ensure the band is going to swing. Obviously, this is a result of his years playing with Jimmy Smith, Wes Montgomery, and Shirley Horn. You can visibly see the music embodied in his movement when the band locks in. This unshakable feeling is within his bone marrow, but Jabali has a wildcard in his back pocket. At any moment, the music can take a wide rhythmic twist; there's even the possibility of him communicating in a contrapuntal manner. The twinkle in his eye is not one of mischief, but one of curiosity.

I was working in a record store when Billy asked me for a copy of Andrew Hill's *Smokestack*. He was preparing for a gig with Hill and Richard Davis. The record had not yet been reissued so I told him to come back the next day and I would give him a tape of the record I had at home. He invited me to the gig and his playing was nothing like Roy's on the original recording. It was a huge lesson in "Having an Opinion."

Jabali's series of duets at the Knitting Factory with Andrew Cyrille and Rashied Ali were eye opening. Everything your ear gravitates to in more traditional kinds of music was present: Listening, Supporting, Creating Space, Dynamics, Form, Phrasing, Texture, Subtlety and Brashness, Call and Response, Forward Motion, Strong Musical Narratives, Multiple Layers of Time, and the sense of being a representative of a lineage but not bearing the weight of history on one's shoulders.

I went home afterwards and listened to Shirley Horn's *A Lazy Afternoon* with a new set of ears. "Yup, that's the same guy. How come I never heard this before?"

The precious few musicians such as Billy Hart are treasures. Their contribution is greater than any award could acknowledge.

Eric McPherson

Billy Hart! Born in 1940! Definitely a major part of the evolution of the multi-percussion vocabulary. It was a natural progression.

I first saw him in about 1983, when I went to a performance of my godfather, Richard Davis. Those Richard Davis gigs were essentially my introduction to this music. Usually the drummer was Freddie Waits, but this time it was Billy Hart.

Freddie Waits, Michael Carvin, and Billy Hart were my first teachers and mentors. I feel grateful that these three helped me, for they were all connected to the history and the long thread of true information. Getting encouragement from those three has meant the world to me.

Since he's still here, I can ask Billy about the older people who were gone by the time I arrived. Billy Hart is not just the past, though, and certainly never a generic makeover of what came before. He is always contemporary—right now!

Appendix 1. Other Drummers Discuss Billy Hart

Allison Miller

I fell in love with Billy's playing on two specific recordings. Pat Martino's *Exit* with Gil Goldstein and Richard Davis, and Joe Lovano's *Live at the Village Vanguard Quartets* with Tom Harrell and Anthony Cox. His timing on both albums is masterful. Specifically on Lovano's *Quartets* album, Billy's performance is a masterclass on how to approach music with openness while maintaining an underlying current of deep swing and fire.

Shortly after moving to NYC, folks would tell me I needed to pick a scene and that I shouldn't play bebop one night and head down to Tonic the next night to play avant-garde. Someone told me bandleaders would be confused by that and not call me to work. But then I heard Billy live, and his musical approach quickly disqualified their remarks. Billy was doing exactly what they said couldn't be done…even within one gig. He was playing *freedom*, and I felt his pulse no matter what context.

Last year I witnessed Billy swing his band so deeply just by playing quarter notes on the ride for the entire piece…no hi-hat, and his left hand was moving silently in a swirling motion for every quarter note. Damn, it was brilliant! He took every audience member to the stars and back. I had shivers and teared up listening.

The way he plays brushes on Shirley Horn's *A Lazy Afternoon* is a perfect example of his beat. During the head of "I'm Old Fashioned" he's swinging that quarter note so hard and accenting Shirley's piano hits with so much conviction…and when he picks up the sticks and rolls into the second chorus! WHOA!

Also central to Billy's playing is his playful curiosity and commitment to the music. It's as if the bandstand is his sandbox and he is inviting the other musicians to jump in and get dirty. This is so evident on a recent recording I can't get enough of—Angelica Sanchez's *Sparkle Beings*! Just incredible!

Last year I was performing with Artemis at Oberlin Conservatory, where Billy teaches. I didn't know he was in town but near the end of the performance I noticed him hanging in the back of the room. Afterwards, he came up to me and seemed perplexed about something. I asked him if he was OK, and he told me he was blown away because he'd never heard another drummer respond to the musical conversation in the same way he would. I was reacting with the same rhythmic responses that he was simultaneously hearing in his head, and he didn't understand how this was possible. I had a simple answer for him. "Billy, it makes perfect sense to me. You are one of my biggest inspirations and I've listened to you continually for the past 30 years! It's no wonder!"

Lewis Nash

Enchance was a favorite record of mine, I remember buying it when it was new, and I still have that very copy. Billy can inhabit all these different worlds and sound like himself, whether it is swinging or more exploratory. The bands around him change, but he doesn't change.

In 1979 I made my first trip from Phoenix to New York City to study with Freddie Waits. I went to a drum shop near Times Square, and when I came out, a big old American car pulled up next to me. Billy Hart was driving, he rolled down the car window and called, "Hey, *drums*! Get in!"

I had never met Billy, but I recognized him, and I guess he had noticed my drumsticks and cymbal bag. I got in his car and he drove me around, asking me questions and telling me stories. The whole experience was so unexpected, it really caught me off guard. I had an ear-to-ear smile the whole time!

Later on that same summer, I went to see Frank Foster at the Village Vanguard with his Non Electric Company, which included Ted Dunbar, Earl May, and Mickey Tucker. (I loved Mickey Tucker, he was really playing great, what a bad dude.) Billy was on the gig, but he was a bit late. Frank Foster saw me sitting in the front row with my stick bag—I had sort of nudged the bag up with my feet so it was visible—and asked, "Hey, I know you, right?"

I had never met Frank Foster in my life, but I was hungry, so I nodded my head. Frank told me to play one, and fortunately they started with something medium, something easy to get a good feeling on, and soon everyone in the band was smiling. Halfway through the tune Billy arrived, so I stood up for him to take my place, but he emphatically gestured for me to sit back down and keep going. As I kept playing, he sat down near me and beamed, and then he applauded when the tune was done.

Billy Hart has always been so encouraging, not just to me, but to so many people.

Appendix 1. Other Drummers Discuss Billy Hart

Adam Nussbaum

I try to call whoever's left on Father's Day. That used to include people like Elvin Jones, Mel Lewis, Roy Haynes, Jimmy Cobb, and Al Foster; this year I'll certainly call Jack DeJohnette and Billy Hart. They showed the way and showed us in person. The records are great, and some of the books are okay, but it *is* an oral tradition. The fathers learned it in the community and on the bandstand.

Billy Hart actually shares a birthday with me, November 29, I'm exactly 15 years younger than him. Hard to believe he's turning 85 this year and I'm turning 70! This means I've been inspired by Billy for over 50 years. He's a seeker, someone who comes out of the tradition but has never been handcuffed by that. As a teenager I saw Billy with Herbie Hancock, McCoy Tyner, and Stan Getz. A little later there was that great Hal Galper band with Michael Brecker, Randy Brecker, Wayne Dockery, and Billy Hart. My parents lived in Norwalk, Connecticut, and not too far from that in the adjoining town of Westport was a venue called Players Tavern. Tim Smith ran that club, and he booked the Hal Galper band on several occasions. One night Stan Getz was in the audience because Billy had told Stan about this hip new band.

When I moved to New York in 1975, Billy was all over town. He was everywhere with everybody, but on every gig he brought total commitment. One night at Boomer's he was playing with the trumpeter Charles Sullivan, and I felt the room start to levitate. An unforgettable moment.

Billy Hart and Buster Williams were often in the rhythm section in the NYC jazz clubs during the '70s and '80s. They were just *dangerous* together. I hear the bass lineage as Paul Chambers to Ron Carter to Buster Williams. The walk, and the bump, and the hump in Buster's beat is just unreal. Oh, baby! Put Buster with Jabali and that's a whole other level.

Bobby Previte

In 1979 I was fresh in New York on an NEA grant to study with Billy—essentially three weeks of him driving me around everywhere, taking me to all his gigs, meeting people like Pharoah Sanders (!) backstage at places like the Vanguard.

One day, as we were cruising around upper Manhattan somewhere near Minton's, Billy was trying to explain the socio-economic-political implications of bebop. We were stopped at a light, and apparently I wasn't quite getting it. Without warning, Billy punched the accelerator to the floor, went through the red, pulled the wheel hard, did a 360, and went BACK through the same red the OTHER way, all at like 60 mph. As we roared ahead, I turned to him in surprise. He just looked at me and said, "That's bop."

Thank you Maestro. Message received.

Jorge Rossy

I had seen Billy Hart play in a quintet with Freddie Hubbard, Joe Henderson, Michel Petrucciani, and Buster Williams—which was incredible—but when I met him in person in Sevilla at a workshop, it really changed my life. He went to the drum class and wrote on the blackboard, "Vernel Fournier." I had no idea who that was. He then said, "What about Ahmad Jamal?" I didn't know Ahmad yet either, but I never forgot those names after Billy presented them so strongly. Then at the concerts with the other clinicians—Jack Walrath, Dave Schnitter, Steve Brown, Bill Dobbins, and Todd Coolman—I stood one meter away from him and drank in his sound and dynamics. It was so intense—"banzai!" It wasn't just drums or music; it was his whole life, his awareness of history. Billy Hart is an *event*.

After he heard me play, he was so supportive and talked to me at length. Years later in New York, when I was first with the Brad Mehldau trio alongside Larry Grenadier, Chris Potter hired Brad, Larry, and Billy for a record date. After I attended rehearsal, Billy asked me how it was playing with Brad. I told him I was just trying to make sure that everything that I played was connected with what was going on and that I was responding appropriately, and that the band interaction was cool. Billy looked at me like I was crazy, and replied, "Connected? Interaction? Just play the music. Fuck interplay. Play the music."

Years later, I got it. You can't depend on the other musicians. You've got to have your opinion and your own connection with the music. What is your point of view? You interpret the music and the story, and then you embody it. Of course, you are still listening, but you're listening from a very different perspective. You're not depending on the others. You have your own story to tell. And then it's a really good conversation.

Appendix 1. Other Drummers Discuss Billy Hart

Damion Reid

The timbre of Billy Hart's kit is unique. It has one of the most modern and progressive tunings in the acoustic world, where the drums are muffled perfectly but still have great attack and resonance, all supported by one of the best bass drum sounds I've ever heard.

During a jam session at the Blue Note in the early aughts, I was playing this Paiste cymbal that my mentor Billy Higgins gave me. After the set, Billy Hart walked up to me and said, "That cymbal sounds like Higgins." Since then, we have been friends, and I have trusted him to give me his honest and candid assessment about whatever I'm bringing to the table.

One night I was watching him at the Village Vanguard, where he was driving his quartet with a kind of whipping motion with his right arm, getting a different kind of articulation out of the cymbal, with even more urgency out of the beat, maybe a little on top of the beat, but not rushing. It did something to me that night, I can tell you. It's all part of his mastery, his touch, his outlook on the music. Billy Hart has some of the best ears and is very astute. No matter who he is playing with, he can find a way to make it groove.

Vinnie Sperrazza

As a teenager, I was aware of Billy Hart as a revered presence in the music. Then I purchased his album *Oceans of Time*. What *was* this? Blues, modern, and free, with rock guitar (Dave Fiuczynski) and classical violin (Mark Feldman)? I filed the record for further consideration.

A few years later in New York, I started going to hear Hart in person and fell in love. When he formed the Quartet in 2004 with Mark Turner, Ben Street, and Ethan Iverson, we had a chance to hear the master like never before. The quartet played several times a year and it became one of the essential gigs for the younger cohort of students and fans. Billy swung the blues, navigated complex modern jazz, and opened up multidirectional rhythms, all while invoking his family and the jazz pantheon.

When I returned to *Oceans of Time* decades after first listening, what had been previously perplexing was now perfectly clear. The dizzying array of styles Billy showcased were just aspects of a single beam of light.

Nasheet Waits

Billy Hart attended the wedding of my parents, Hakimah and Freddie Waits. I was born two years after they tied the knot, so Billy has joked to me, "I knew you when you were a twinkle in your father's eye." My father, Billy, and Horacee Arnold had a group together for a time called Colloquium III.

When I started to play the drums in professional situations, Billy would often pop up and listen. He has always been vested in the scene. Instead of going home from the airport, he'd stop by the club and hear what was happening. At the Village Vanguard, there is a row of embankment seating that is where other drummers can closely observe the drummer on the gig. The first few times I worked there, I looked down that aisle and would see Joe Chambers, Arthur Taylor, Max Roach, and Mr. Hart. They were all there looking at my hands and feet. It was a harrowing experience. Pure pressure.

After hearing me on various gigs Billy would always be very kind and positive, but he'd also offer cryptic comments that I'd need to think about and try to decode later. (When I spent time with Max Roach, Max also offered the same type of cryptic advice.) I was working with Mark Turner—also at the Vanguard—and I was doing some things with three against four which prompted Billy to say, "You do things that I think are instinctual to you. I'm not sure if you know what or why you're doing what you're doing."

This was gentle encouragement to go investigate the history. It wasn't exactly a clear direction to go check out a specific record or a certain drummer, but as you apprise yourself of the history, you learn that the way the music was transferred and transformed was through cultural experience. The greats weren't just great musicians by themselves, they were a part of a network of communities. When Billy plays, he is playing all these homages to everyone he has heard from all those communities. It's always so fresh! There is great presence of mind and he never coasts. Distinctive ideas appear in unexpected places and in unexpected ways. It's a surprising adventure, but Billy always knows where he is coming from. He has repeatedly told me that he plays something from my father on every one of his gigs.

Recently Billy and I did a listening session at the Jazz Gallery together. He brought in *Bird with Strings*, and he sang Charlie Parker's alto solo on "Just Friends." Then he sang the bass line, and then some of the inner moving parts. The drummers of that era really knew the music. They would sing the solos—not the drum solos, but the horn solos. When I was in the car with Charli Persip and my father, they would put on Horace Silver records and sing along with the horn solos.

Billy's dedication to the music is absolute and unyielding. It's not solely informed by economics but also by the culture from which the music is spawned.

Lenny White

I call him William S. Hart, after the famous silent movie star who made Westerns.

One day, as a young kid in Jamaica, Queens, I went to my nearby friend George Cables's house to play a jam session. Billy Hart was there, playing great and looking like Roy Haynes. Not long after that, Billy recommended me to Buddy Montgomery, so—thanks to Billy—I did my first road tour ever as part of the Buddy Montgomery quartet. (The rest of that band was also part of the Jamaica contingent, George Cables and Clint Houston.)

Billy Hart knows how to translate knowledge and musical language from one scene to another; he can co-exist with whoever he is working with.

If you want to work, especially as a drummer, you need to do a lot of translation. If you can't translate, you won't get many gigs. But if you can speak many languages, your phone can ring a lot of different ways.

Jabali Billy Hart *always* works. He gets *all* the gigs, and he's been getting *all* the gigs for such a long time! It's because he can translate any language and make anybody else sound great. He puts that little Jabali thing in there and the music comes together.

Jeff Williams

In 1970 I drove from Oberlin, Ohio to Detroit's Strata Gallery to see Herbie Hancock's new band, not knowing what to expect. I remember it being one of the most exciting nights of music I had ever seen, largely because of Billy Hart. I hadn't been aware of him before. He seemed to have encapsulated all that had been accomplished in jazz drumming along with having his own spin on modern innovations. Mind blown, I got in my car and made the return journey, too shy to have spoken to him.

We would meet later in New York, one common thread being our mutual experiences playing with Stan Getz and Dave Liebman. Billy's typical comment to me when I would compliment him was, "I'm just trying to sound like you." He treated me like a peer, although I wasn't entirely fooled. He once said, "If I'm playing somewhere and you feel like sitting in, come on up." I never took him up on it.

Mastery combined with humility is something of a rarity, but all the great ones have it. To have been able to see Billy play in so many different groups over the years is a blessing. No one can copy him of course, but something in the spirit of his playing has been passed on to all who have heard him.

Appendix 2. Partial Discography as a Sideman

Billy Hart's albums as a leader are discussed in Chapter 10, "Striking Up the Band." Depending on how you count it, there are something like 600 additional records with Hart's name in the credits. When videos, private tapes, and bootlegs are added, the number swells even further.

The following list is not everything, but they are all albums either intended for commercial release or notably significant. Scott Douglass and Ethan Iverson made the joint decision to leave off records where Billy only plays on one tune or occasions where the release was probably a low-stakes unauthorized bootleg.

In 2025, Billy is still in the studios, which means this list will be outdated the moment the book goes to press. Still, one can make a pretty interesting chart of jazz history from this selection running from 1961 to the present day.

Albums with an asterisk* are referenced in the text; taken as a group, the albums with an asterisk also give a reasonably complete picture of Hart's breadth and depth, especially when collected next to Hart's albums as a leader.

Buck Clarke *The Buck Clarke Sound* (1961)
Jimmy Smith *Christmas '64* (1964)
Jimmy Smith *Live in Concert - The Incredible Jimmy Smith* (1965)
Jimmy Smith *In Hamburg Live* (1965)
Buddy Montgomery *The Two-Sided Album* (1968)
Paul Jeffrey *The Electrifying Sounds of Paul Jeffrey* (1968)
Eddie Harris *Silver Cycles* (1968)
*Pharoah Sanders *Karma* (1969) **"The Creator Has a Master Plan" with Leon Thomas was a big hit**
Pharoah Sanders *Izipho Zam* (1969)
*Eddie Harris *High Voltage* (1969) **Varitone sax and groove music**
*Melvin Jackson *Funky Skull* (1969) **Hart's most commercial drumming on record**
Eddie Harris *Pourquoi L'Amérique* (1969)
Eddie Harris *Free Speech* (1969)

*Joe Zawinul *Zawinul* (1970) **First record with Herbie Hancock**
*Herbie Hancock *Mwandishi* (1970) **Hancock band, now known as Mwandishi**
Marian McPartland *Ambiance* (1970)
Wayne Shorter *Odyssey of Iska* (1970)
*McCoy Tyner *Asante* (1970) **First record with McCoy Tyner**
Hal Galper *Wild Bird* (1971)
*Harold Land *A New Shade of Blue* (1971) **Good modernist swinging action with Buster Williams and Hart together**
Mtume *Alkebu-Lan (Land of the Blacks)* (1971)
Pharoah Sanders *Black Unity* (1971)
*Herbie Hancock *Crossings* (1971) **Hancock band, now known as Mwandishi**
Pharoah Sanders *Village of the Pharoahs* (1971)
Pharoah Sanders *Live at The East* (1971)
*Herbie Hancock *Sextant* (1972) **Hancock band, now known as Mwandishi**
Buddy Terry *Pure Dynamite* (1972)
Marc Levin *Songs, Dances & Prayers* (1972)
Pete Yellin *Dance of Allegra* (1972)
*Miles Davis *On the Corner* (1972) **Perhaps the most famous record in this discography**
Miles Davis *Big Fun* (1972)
Norman Connors *Dance of Magic* (1972)
Wilbur Little *Natural* (1972)
Catalyst *Perception* (1972)
Hannibal Marvin Peterson *The Sunrise Orchestra* (1973 and 1974)
Eddie Henderson *Realization* (1973)
Eddie Henderson *Inside Out* (1973)
Charles Earland *The Dynamite Brothers* (1973)
Stan Getz *Live at Sir Morgan's Cove* (1973)
Catalyst *Unity* (1974)
Carlos Garnett *Black Love* (1974)
Mtume *Rebirth Cycle* (1974)
*Bennie Maupin *The Jewel in the Lotus* (1974) **Herbie Hancock's only ECM record**
*McCoy Tyner *Sama Layuca* (1974) **The better of the two Tyner albums with Hart**
Cecil McBee *Mutima* (1974)
*Charles Sullivan *Genesis* (1974) **After being fired by McCoy, this nice record date picked up Hart's spirits**
Azar Lawrence *Bridge into the New Age* (1974)
Harold Vick *Don't Look Back* (1974)

Appendix 2. Partial Discography as a Sideman

Walter Bishop Jr. *Valley Land* (1974)
Bob Moses *Bittersuite in the Ozone* (1975)
Michel Sardaby *Gail* (1975)
Eddie Henderson *Sunburst* (1975)
Joanne Brackeen *Snooze* (1975)
Kenny Barron *Lucifer* (1975)
Azar Lawrence *Summer Solstice* (1975)
*Stan Getz/João Gilberto *The Best of Two Worlds* (1975) **Gilberto taught Hart about Brazilian music**
*Buster Williams *Pinnacle* (1975) **"The Hump" was sampled by several hip-hop artists**
Joe Bonner *Triangle* (1975)
*Sonny Fortune *Awakening* (1975) **First recording of a famous Kenny Barron tune, "Sunshower"**
*Stan Getz *The Master* (1975) **Perhaps the best Getz studio album with Hart, plus great Albert Dailey**
Harry Whitaker *Black Renaissance - Body, Mind and Spirit* (1976)
Pat Martino *Exit* (1976)
Jimmy Rowles *Paws That Refresh* (1976)
Eddie Henderson *Heritage* (1976)
Stan Getz *Moments in Time* (1976)
*Stan Getz/João Gilberto *Getz/Gilberto '76* (1976) **Live at the Keystone Korner, even better than the studio Getz/Gilberto record with Hart**
*Herbie Hancock *V.S.O.P.* (1976) **Hancock sextet plays "Toys" at reunion gig**
Joanne Brackeen *Invitation* (1976)
Charles Sullivan *Re-entry* (1976)
Buster Williams *Crystal Reflections* (1976)
*Zbigniew Seifert *Man of the Light* (1976) **Hart plays the contemporary busy binary style to his own satisfaction**
Lee Konitz *The Lee Konitz Nonet* (1976)
*Hal Galper *Reach Out* (1976) **Quintet with Michael and Randy Brecker**
Stan Getz *Live at Montmartre* (1976)
Joanne Brackeen *Tring-a-ling* (1977)
Richard Davis *Harvest* (1977)
David Amram *Havana/New York* (1977)
John "Spider" Martin *Absolutely* (1977)
Ben Aronov *Suavity* (1977)
*Philly Joe Jones *Drums Night* (1977) **A traumatic experience for Hart and Al Foster**
Bobby Watson *Estimated Time of Arrival* (1977)
John Stowell *Golden Delicious* (1977)

*Stan Getz *Gold* (1977) **Getz's 50th birthday concert**
Mike Richmond *Dream Waves* (1977)
Andy LaVerne *Another World* (1977)
Stan Getz *Another World* (1977)
Doug Raney *Introducing Doug Raney* (1977)
Niels-Henning Orsted Pedersen *Live at Montmartre* (1977)
*Eddie Jefferson *The Main Man* (1977) **Arguably Jefferson's best record**
Stan Getz *Mort D'Un Pourri: Stan Getz with the London Symphony Orchestra* (1977)
Hamiet Bluiett *Resolution* (1977)
Billy Harper *Soran-Bushi, B.H.* (1977)
Jamey Aebersold *Herbie Hancock: Volume 11* (1978)
Jimmy Rowles *Grandpaws* (1978)
*Buck Hill *This Is Buck Hill* (1978) **Hart gets his mentor a record date**
Don Friedman *The Progressive Don Friedman* (1978)
John McNeil *Embarkation* (1978)
Buster Williams *Heartbeat* (1978)
Derek Smith *New Soil* (1978)
Pepper Adams *Reflectory* (1978)
Walter Bishop Jr. *Cubicle* (1978)
Don Friedman *Hot Knepper and Pepper* (1978)
Arnett Cobb *Arnett Cobb Is Back!* (1978)
Hannibal Marvin Peterson *Naima* (1978)
*Shirley Horn *A Lazy Afternoon* (1978) **Hart gets another mentor a record date—the start of Horn's ascent in the jazz industry**
Albert Dailey *That Old Feeling* (1978)
Stan Getz *Poetry in Jazz* (1978)
Derek Smith *My Favorite Things* (1978)
Doug Raney *Cuttin' Loose* (1978)
Mack Goldsbury *Anthropo-logic* (1978)
Buster Williams *Dreams Come True* (1978)
Don Friedman *Love Music* (1978)
David Schnitter *Thundering* (1978)
Cam Newton *The Motive Behind the Smile* (1978)
Benny Bailey *Grand Slam* (1978)
Jimmy Knepper *Just Friends* (1978)
Nancy Harrow *Anything Goes* (1978)
Multiphonic Tribe *Now Is the Time* (1979)
Andy LaVerne *Metropolis* (1979)
Frank Foster *The Frank Foster Non Electric Company* (1979)
Yoshio "Chin" Suzuki *Matsuri* (1979)
Charles Davis *Dedicated to Tadd* (1979)

Appendix 2. Partial Discography as a Sideman

*Clark Terry with Oscar Peterson *Ain't Misbehavin'* (1979) **One of the few times Hart was part of a Norman Granz production**
James Williams *Everything I Love* (1979)
Louis Smith *Prancin'* (1979)
John McNeil *Faun* (1979)
Lee Konitz *Yes Yes Nonet* (1979)
Jimmy Raney *Stolen Moments* (1979)
John McNeil *Look to the Sky* (1979)
Glen Hall *The Book of the Heart* (1979)
Jim McNeely *The Plot Thickens* (1979)
*Mickey Tucker *The Crawl* (1979) **Good document of straight-ahead mastery with Marcus Belgrave, Junior Cook, Slide Hampton, and Earl May**
Steve Giordano *Daybreak* (1979)
John Scofield *Who's Who?* (1979)
Niels-Henning Orsted Pedersen *Dancing on the Tables* (1979)
Buck Hill *Scope* (1979)
Lee Konitz *Live at Laren* (1979)
Chico Freeman *Spirit Sensitive* (1979)
Pierre Dorge *Ballad Round the Left Corner* (1979)
Duke Jordan *Change a Pace* (1979)
Bob James *All Around the Town* (1979)
Chico Freeman *Peaceful Heart, Gentle Spirit* (1980)
Armen Donelian *Stargazer* (1980)
Chico Freeman *The Search* (1980)
Mingus Dynasty *Live at Montreux* (1980)
Ralph Simon *Time Being* (1980)
Tom Varner *Tom Varner Quartet* (1980)
Doug Raney *Listen* (1980)
Teddy Edwards *Out of This World* (1980)
Jesper Thilo *Swingin' Friends* (1980)
Harry Whitaker *One Who Sees All Things* (1981 and 1982)
Jim Shannon *Street Talk* (1981)
Terumasa Hino *Double Rainbow* (1981)
Franco Ambrosetti *Heartbop* (1981)
Joachim Kuhn *Nightline New York* (1981)
Hamiet Bluiett *Dangerously Suite* (1981)
Jay Hoggard *Mystic Winds, Tropic Breezes* (1981)
Ralph Simon *As* (1981)
John McNeil *Clean Sweep* (1981)
Tom McKinley *Life Cycle* (1981)
Buck Hill *Easy to Love* (1981)

*Shirley Horn *All Night Long* (1981) **Slow ballads with delayed beats**
Buck Hill *Impressions* (1981)
Shirley Horn *Violets for Your Furs* (1981)
Arnie Lawrence *Renewal* (1981)
Art Farmer *A Work of Art* (1981)
Bruce Forman *20/20* (1981)
Pepper Adams *Urban Dreams* (1981)
Cecil McBee *Flying Out* (1982)
Stan Getz *Blue Skies* (1982)
Chico Freeman *Tradition in Transition* (1982)
Stan Getz *Pure Getz* (1982)
Jimmy Knepper *1st Place* (1982)
Tom Harrell *Play of Light* (1982)
Pat Peterson *Introducing Pat Peterson* (1982)
Tom Varner *Motion/Stillness* (1982)
Eri Ohno *Eri, My Dear* (1982)
Mark Morganelli *Live on Broadway* (1982)
Nathan Page *Page-ing Nathan* (1982)
James Newton *Daydream* (1982)
Masaru Imada *Songs on my Mind* (1982)
Johnny Coles *New Morning* (1982)
*James Newton *Luella* (1983) **Lush production with John Blake and Kenny Kirkland leads into Hart's own Gramavision albums as a leader**
Jill McManus *Symbols of Hopi* (1983)
*Conjure *Music for the Texts of Ishmael Reed* (1983) **Taj Mahal offers advice**
Art Farmer *Nostalgia* (1983)
Chico Freeman *Tangents* (1984)
Sonny Fortune *Laying It Down* (1984)
Jim Snidero *On Time* (1984)
Larry Coryell *Comin' Home* (1984)
Jimmy Knepper *I Dream Too Much* (1984)
Charlie Shoemake *Incandescent* (1984)
Van Morrison *I Can't Go On...But I'll Go On* (1984)
Anita Gravine *I Always Knew* (1984)
Peter Leitch *Exhilaration* (1984)
Rick Stone *Blues for Nobody* (1984)
Big Nick Nicholas *Big Nick* (1985)
Dick Griffin *A Dream for Rahsaan* (1985)
Larry Coryell *Equipoise* (1985)
Didier Lockwood *Out of the Blue* (1985)
James Newton *The African Flower* (1985)
Pepper Adams *The Adams Effect* (1985)

Appendix 2. Partial Discography as a Sideman

Johnny Mbizo Dyani *Angolian Cry* (1985)
Doug Raney *Guitar, Guitar, Guitar* (1985)
Duke Jordan *Time on my Hands* (1985)
Duke Jordan *As Time Goes By* (1985)
Idrees Sulieman *Groovin'* (1985)
Paul Bley *My Standard* (1985)
Helen Merrill *Helen Merrill Sings Jerome Kern* (1986)
Larry Coryell *Welcome My Darling* (1986)
*Quest *Quest II* (1986) **The first (and one of the best) of many albums Hart recorded with Quest, an important band**
Great Friends *Great Friends* (1986)
Steve Brown *Child's Play* (1986)
Khan Jamal *Thinking of You* (1986)
John Scofield *Strings Attached* (1986)
*Ralph Moore *623 C Street* (1987) **Hart meets David Kikoski on a good record that also features Buster Williams**
Rena Rama *The Lost Tapes* (1987)
Quest *Midpoint: Live in the Montmartre* (1987)
Jed Levy *Good People* (1987)
Santi Debriano *Obeah* (1987)
Laurent de Wilde *Off the Boat* (1987)
Chico Freeman *Lord Riff and Me* (1987)
Quest *Live* (1988 and 1991)
Tom Harrell *Stories* (1988)
Doug Raney *Something's Up* (1988)
Gust William Tsilis *Possibilities* (1988)
Quest *N.Y. Nites - Standards* (1988)
*Horace Silver *Music to Ease Your Disease* (1988) **Only Silver record with Hart**
Gary Bartz *Monsoon* (1988)
*Hank Jones *Great Standards* (1988) **All of Hank Jones's trio albums are good, including the many with Hart**
Quest *Natural Selection* (1988)
Larry Coryell *Air Dancing* (1988)
Mingus Big Band *Live at Theatre Boulogne-Billancourt, Paris* (1988)
John Handy *Excursion in Blue* (1988)
Nick Brignola *Raincheck* (1988)
Paul Bley *The Nearness of You* (1988)
Gary Bartz *Reflections of Monk - The Final Frontier* (1988)
Jeff Gardner *Continuum* (1988)
Jamey Aebersold *Autumn Leaves* (1989)
Hal Galper *Portrait* (1989)

James Newton *If Love* (1989)
Lars Moller *Pyramid* (1989)
Hank Jones *Great Standards Vol. 3 and Vol. 4* (1989)
Christian Escoude *Gipsy Waltz* (1989)
Klaus Ignatzek *Take It Easy* (1989)
Joey DeFrancesco *Where Were You?* (1989)
Dave Stryker *First Strike* (1989)
Jerome Barde *Feliz* (1989)
Eddie Henderson *Think On Me* (1989)
Jane Bunnett *Live at Sweet Basil* (1990)
Ed Sarath *Voice of the Wind* (1990)
Lou Volpe *Where Were You* (1990)
Hank Jones *Great Standards Vol. 5* (1990)
Kenny Drew and the Great Jazz Trio *New York Stories* (1990)
Shirley Horn *You Won't Forget Me* (1990)
Nancy Harrow *Anything Goes* (1990)
Quest *Of One Mind* (1990)
Judy Niemack *Long As You're Living* (1990)
The Reunion Legacy Band *The Legacy* (1990)
Amani A.W.-Murray *Amani A.W.-Murray* (1990)
Antonio Farao *Viaggio Ignoto* (1991)
Gust William Tsilis *Sequestered Days* (1991)
Fabio Morgera *The Pursuit* (1991)
George Cables *Night and Day* (1991)
Jarmo Savolainen *First Sight* (1991)
Bob Kenmotsu *The Spark* (1991 and 1992)
Marc Copland *At Night* (1991 and 1992)
Miyuki Koga *But I Love You Still* (1991)
Joanne Brackeen *Is It Really True* (1991)
David Janeway *Inside Out* (1991)
David Murray *David Murray-James Newton Quintet* (1991)
David Kikoski *Persistent Dreams* (1991)
Sonny Fortune *It Ain't What It Was* (1991)
Tom McKinley *Jazz Alive at Pittsburgh* (1992)
Western Jazz Quartet *Firebird* (1992)
David Stoler *Urban Legends* (1992)
Hank Jones *Standard Jazz for Lovers* (1992)
David Liebman *The Seasons* (1992)
Niels Lan Doky *Manhattan Project* (1993)
Santi Debriano *3-Ology* (1993)
Mina Aoe *The Shadow of Love* (1993)
Denise Jannah *A Heart Full of Music* (1993)

Appendix 2. Partial Discography as a Sideman

Charles Lloyd *The Call* (1993)
Peter Hertmans *Waiting* (1993)
Jane Bunnett *The Water Is Wide* (1993)
Warren Vache *Horn of Plenty* (1993)
Stanley Cowell *Setup* (1993)
Mitch Hampton *Mitch Plays* (1994)
*Reuben Brown *Ice Scape* (1994) **Hart gets his childhood friend (and major Washington D.C. pianist) a record date**
Ivo Perelman *Man of the Forest* (1994)
Ulf Wakenius *New York Meeting* (1994)
Sonny Fortune *Four In One* (1994)
Jerry Bergonzi *Vertical Reality* (1994)
Ed Schuller *To Know Where One Is* (1994)
Grover Washington Jr. *All My Tomorrows* (1994)
Jarmo Savolainen *True Image* (1994)
*Joe Lovano *Live at the Village Vanguard* (1994) **One of Lovano's best records, with Tom Harrell and Anthony Cox**
Jon Ballantyne *The Loose* (1994)
Ron McClure *Never Always* (1994)
Rick Margitza *Work It* (1994)
George Cables *Quiet Fire* (1994)
Tim Ries *Imaginary Time* (1994)
Eddie Harris *Freedom Jazz Dance* (1994)
Charles Lloyd *All My Relations* (1994)
Caecilie Norby *Caecilie* (1994)
Jim Snidero *San Juan* (1994)
Dick de Graaf *New York Straight Ahead* (1994)
Western Jazz Quartet *Blue Harts* (1995)
Kevin Hays *Go Round* (1995)
Sonny Fortune *A Better Understanding* (1995)
Marc Copland *Paradiso* (1995)
Shirley Horn *The Main Ingredient* (1995)
Frederick Washington Jr. *Lilac, Vol. 1* (1995)
George Mraz *My Foolish Heart* (1995)
Ray Drummond *Vignettes* (1995)
George Mraz *Jazz* (1995)
Eddie Henderson *Dark Shadows* (1995)
Michael Hornstein *Innocent Green* (1995)
Tim Armacost *Fire!* (1995)
*David Liebman *John Coltrane's Meditations* (1995) **A new way of playing multidirectional for Hart**

*Don Byron *Bug Music* (1996) **Hart plays 4/4 quarter notes on the bass drum for a repertory project featuring music from the 1930s**
Tom Harrell *Labyrinth* (1996)
Andy Goodrich *Motherless Child* (1996)
Chris Potter *Moving In* (1996)
Chip Jackson *Is There a Jackson in the House?* (1996)
Lee Konitz *It's You* (1996)
Ron McClure *Concrete Canyon* (1996)
Steve Smith *Chantal's Way* (1996)
Andy LaVerne *Bud's Beautiful* (1996)
Marc Copland *Second Look* (1996)
Don Braden *The Open Road* (1996)
Richie Beirach *The Snow Leopard* (1996)
Horace Tapscott *Thoughts of Dar Es Salaam* (1996)
Judy Niemack *Night and the Music* (1996)
Ron McClure *Closer to Your Tears* (1996)
Boulou Ferre *New York, NY* (1996)
Dave Stryker *Big Room* (1996)
George Cables *Dark Side, Light Side* (1996)
Charles Lloyd *Canto* (1996)
Julian Coryell *Duality* (1997)
Mack Goldsbury *Songs I Love to Play* (1997)
Michael J. Rossi *Beauty and the Blues* (1997)
David Liebman *The Elements: Water* (1997)
Simon Spang-Hanssen *Instant Blue* (1997)
Lutz Hafner *Lutz Hafner* (1997)
Valery Ponomarev *A Star for You* (1997)
Nick Brignola *Poinciana* (1997)
Bob Dorough *Right On My Way Home* (1997)
Rob Schneiderman *Dancing in the Dark* (1997)
Jerry Tilitz *The New York Tapes* (1997)
Ray Drummond *1-2-3-4* (1997)
George Colligan *Stomping Ground* (1997)
Ron McClure *Dream Team* (1997)
Cecil Bridgewater *Mean What You Say* (1997)
Doug Raney *The Backbeat* (1997)
David Murray *Creole* (1997)
Bruno De Filippi *You My Love* (1997)
Dave Douglas *Moving Portrait* (1997)
Mitch Hampton *Mitch Swings* (1998)
Tom Knific *Home Bass* (1998)
Ethel Ennis *If Women Ruled the World* (1998)

Appendix 2. Partial Discography as a Sideman

Ari Ambrose *Introducing Ari Ambrose* (1998)
Andy LaVerne *Another World Another Time* (1998)
Marc Bernstein *Blue Walls* (1998)
Joey DeFrancesco *The Champ* (1998)
Rich Perry *Doxy* (1998)
Dave Stryker *Shades of Miles* (1998)
Doug Raney *You Go to My Head* (1998)
Tim Armacost *The Wishing Well* (1998)
Tommy Cecil *Samba for Felix* (1999)
David Fiuczynski *JazzPunk* (1999)
Yuko Yasunaga *Yuko's Piano* (1999)
Debora Seffer *Standards* (1999)
Niels Vincentz *Early Reflections* (1999)
Janet Lawson *The Janet Lawson Quintet* (Late 1990s)
Simon Spang-Hanssen *Identified* (1999)
Nick Brignola *All Business* (1999)
Caecilie Norby *Queen of Bad Excuses* (1999)
Kenny Werner *Beauty Secrets* (1999)
Joe Beck *Strangers in the Night* (1999)
Bob Dorough *Too Much Coffee Man* (1999)
Christophe Schweizer Normal Garden *Physique* (1999)
Kenny Barron *Spirit Song* (1999)
*Ethan Iverson *The Minor Passions* (1999) **Iverson hires Hart—the book in your hands comes out 26 years later**
Ron McClure *Double Triangle* (1999)
Peter Leitch *Blues on the Corner* (1999)
Sarah Jane Cion *Moon Song* (1999)
Richie Beirach *What Is This Thing Called Love?* (1999)
Gary Keller *Blues for an Old New Age* (1999)
Andrew Chesire *Magic* (1999)
Ben Besiakov *Aviation* (1999)
Christine Tobin *Deep Song* (1999)
Mel Martin and Bebop & Beyond *Friends and Mentors* (1999 and 2000)
Western Jazz Quartet *Sabine's Dance* (2000)
Christophe Schweizer *Full Circle Rainbow* (2000 and 2002)
Bruce Barth *Somehow It's True* (2000)
Billy Childs *Bedtime Stories* (2000)
Andy LaVerne *Know More* (2000)
LeeAnn Ledgerwood *Paradox* (2000)
George Mraz *Morava* (2000)
Gordon Brisker *My Son John* (2000)
John Nugent *Live at the Blue Note* (2000)

Sarah Jane Cion *Summer Night* (2000)
Johannes Enders *Sandsee* (2000)
*The Mary Lou Williams Collective *Zodiac Suite: Revisited* (2001) **Geri Allen's repertory project**
Richie Beirach *Romantic Rhapsody* (2000)
Karlheinz Miklin *From Here to There* (2000)
Marco Tamburini *Two Days in New York* (2000)
Pat Martino *Live at Yoshi's* (2000)
Mark O'Leary *Levitation* (2000)
Renata Artman Knific *West of Everywhere* (2001)
SteepleChase *Jam Session, Vol. 1* (2001)
Adam Kolker *Sultanic Verses* (2001)
Tim Armacost *Brightly Dark* (2001)
Barry Wedgle *Paradise* (2001)
Curtis Lundy *Purpose* (2001)
George Garzone *Hey! Why Don't We Play* (2001)
Roberta Piket *September of Tears* (2001)
Will Lee *BirdHouse* (2002)
Charles Lloyd *Lift Every Voice* (2002)
Greg Abate *Evolution* (2002)
Eddie Henderson *So What* (2002)
Richie Beirach *No Borders* (2002)
Heather Bennett *Suite Talk* (2002)
Ezra Weiss *The Five A.M. Strut* (2002)
Peter Hertmans *Stone Sculpture* (2002)
Karlheinz Miklin *In Between* (2002)
Tetsuro Kawashima *True Eyes* (2003)
Dave Stryker *Strike Up the Band* (2003)
Lars Moller *Jazzpar Concerts* (2003)
Craig Harris *Souls Within the Veil* (2003)
James Scholfield *All Stations* (2003)
Frank Morgan *City Nights: Live at the Jazz Standard, Vol. 1* (2003)
Frank Morgan *Raising the Standard* (2003)
Frank Morgan *A Night in the Life - Live at the Jazz Standard Vol. 3* (2003)
George Robert *Soul Searching* (2003)
Saxophone Summit *Gathering of Spirits* (2004)
Joshua Douglas Smith *Unstuck in Time* (2004)
Ezra Weiss *Persephone* (2004)
Chris McNulty *Dance Delicioso* (2004)
Gary Versace *Time and Again* (2004)
Marco Tamburini *Frenico* (2005)
Eddie Henderson *Precious Moment* (2005)

Appendix 2. Partial Discography as a Sideman

Mimi Fox *Perpetually Hip* (2005)
Piotr Wojtasik *We Want to Give Thanks* (2005)
Quest *Redemption: Quest Live in Europe* (2005)
Frank Morgan *Reflections* (2005)
Oberlin Conservatory Jazz Faculty *Beauty Surrounds Us* (2006)
Billy Robinson *Swift* (2006)
Ezra Weiss *Get Happy* (2006)
Richie Beirach *Manhattan Reverie* (2006)
Vladimir Shafranov *New York Revisited* (2006)
Vladimir Shafranov *Easy to Love* (2006)
Dave Stryker *Latest Outlook* (2006)
The Leaders *Spirits Alike* (2006)
Tim Armacost *Rhythm and Transformation* (2007)
Betty Liste *Pensive Moments* (2007)
Benny Powell *Nextep* (2007)
John Tchicai *Tribal Ghost* (2007)
Shea Breaux Wells *A Blind Date* (2007)
David Liebman *Compassion: The Music of John Coltrane* (2007)
Marc Copland *Another Place* (2007)
Vinnie Cutro *Sakura* (2007)
Richie Beirach *Summer Night* (2007)
Saxophone Summit *Seraphic Light* (2007)
Quest *Re-Dial* (2007)
Pete Yellin *How Long Has This Been Going On?* (2007)
Andrew Rathbun *Where We Are Now* (2007)
Peter Dominguez *How About This* (2008)
Olivier Temime *The Intruder* (2009)
Betty Liste *Jazz Ventures - Pure Communications* (2009)
Jean-Michel Pilc *True Story* (2009)
Emilio Solla & The Tango Jazz Conspiracy *Bien Sur* (2009)
Johannes Enders *Zen Tauri* (2009)
Inaki Sandoval *Miracielos* (2009)
Mike Fahie *Anima* (2010)
Contact *Five On One* (2010)
*The Cookers *Warriors* (2010) **The first album from an important band of veterans, overseen by David Weiss**
Johannes Enders *Billy Rubin* (2010)
Quest *Live in Paris* (2010)
The Cookers *Cast the First Stone* (2010)
Karlheinz Miklin *Cymbal Symbols* (2010)
Brian Landrus *Traverse* (2010)
Stephane Belmondo *The Same As It Never Was Before* (2010)

Mads Vinding *Open Minds* (2010)
Olegario Diaz *Having Fun* (2010)
Dave Stryker *Blue Strike* (2011)
Stephen Riley *Hart-Beat* (2011)
Quest *Circular Dreaming* (2011)
Esperanza Spalding *Radio Music Society* (2011)
Andy LaVerne *Three's Not A Crowd* (2011)
Odean Pope *Odean's Three* (2011)
Michael Feinberg *The Elvin Jones Project* (2012)
Stacie McGregor *Rhythm, Heart & Soul* (2012)
Kirk Knuffke *Chorale* (2012)
The Cookers *Believe* (2012)
Niels Vincentz *Gravity* (2012)
Enrico Granafei *Alone (And) Together* (2012)
Christian Escoude *Saint German Des Pres: The Music of John Lewis* (2012)
Richie Beirach *Live at Birdland New York* (2012)
Brian Lynch *Questioned Answer* (2012)
Marcos Varela *San Ygnacio* (2012)
Karlheinz Miklin *Encore* (2012)
Rene Bottlang *Autumn in New York* (2012)
Fareed Haque *Out of Nowhere* (2013)
Yelena Eckemoff *Lions* (2013)
Yelena Eckemoff *Lions Live in New York* (2013)
Niels Vincentz *Is That So* (2013)
Riccardo Del Fra *My Chet My Song* (2013 and 2014)
*Bobby Hutcherson *Enjoy the View* (2014) **Bobby Hutcherson's final record**
Michael Cain *Sola* (2014)
Jukkis Uotila *The Herbie Hancock Legacy - Featuring Billy Hart* (2014)
John Raymond *Foreign Territory* (2014)
The Cookers *Time and Time Again* (2014)
Yelena Eckemoff *A Touch of Radiance* (2014)
Johannes Enders *Mellowtonin* (2014)
Brian Landrus *The Deep Below* (2014)
Thomas Clausen *Blue Rain* (2014)
Sally Night *Night Time* (2015)
John McNeil *Plainsong* (2015)
Noah Preminger *Some Other Time* (2015)
Bob Gluck *Infinite Spirit (Revisiting Music of the Mwandishi Band)* (2015)
Yelena Eckemoff *Leaving Everything Behind* (2015)
Aaron Parks *Find the Way* (2015)
Luis Perdomo *Spirits and Warriors* (2016)
Massimo Farao *Swingin'* (2016)

Appendix 2. Partial Discography as a Sideman

The Cookers *The Call of the Wild and Peaceful Heart* (2016)
The Cookers *Look Out!* (2016)
LeeAnn Ledgerwood *Renewal* (2016)
Will Vinson *Four Forty One* (2017 and 2018)
Brian Landrus Orchestra *Generations* (2017)
Gene Segal *Transformation* (2017)
Enji *Mongolian Song* (2017)
Saxophone Summit *Street Talk* (2017)
Joey DeFrancesco *In the Key of the Universe* (2018)
Jared Gold *Reemergence* (2018)
Noah Haidu *Doctone* (2019)
Brian Landrus *For Now* (2019)
Adam Kolker *Lost* (2019)
Joris Teepe *The Brooklyn Sessions* (2019)
Christophe Schweizer *Stream feat. Billy Hart* (2020)
David Janeway *Distant Voices* (2020)
Noah Haidu *Slowly: Song for Keith Jarrett* (2020)
Kevin Hays *All Things Are* (2020)
Bill O'Connell *Live in Montauk* (2021)
Joe Melnicove *You Is You* (2021)
Angelica Sanchez *Sparkle Beings* (2021)
Mamiko Watanabe *Being Guided by the Light* (2022)
Jeremy Pelt *The Art of Intimacy, Vol. 2: His Muse* (2022)
Noah Haidu *Standards II* (2023)
Yotam Silberstein *Standards* (2023)
Jacky Terrasson *Moving On* (2023)
Brian Landrus *Plays Ellington & Strayhorn* (2023)
Kevin Hays *Bridges* (2023)
David Janeway *Forward Motion* (2023)
Randy Ingram *Aries Dance* (2024)
Bill O'Connell *Touch* (2024)

*Hart in 2017 with his distinctive cymbal setup clearly visible.
(Photo by Alan Nahigian.)*

Appendix 3. Jabali's Drum Set

I endorse Pearl drums. They are good drums, but I especially like Pearl's hardware, which is easy to use. In the end, the name on the drums is less important than the sizes of the drums.

Going up in pitch, the bass drum and three toms are tuned low A, C, F, high A:
- 18" bass drum with no hole in the front head, pitched at low "A."
- 14" x 14" floor tom, pitched at "C."
- 12" x 10" rack tom pitched at "F."
- 10" x 10" rack tom, pitched at high "A."

The toms are an F major triad in first inversion and can sound like a bugle call. Buster Williams advised me on these pitches.

Rack toms with 10-inch depth are sometimes called "power toms" or "concert toms." Jazz drum kits often have rack toms with 8-inch depth, which is also fine.

The snare is tuned a little higher than the high tom, B-flat or B. If it is difficult to match the pitch to the onstage piano exactly, and I prefer the drums to be a shade sharp rather than being flat.

The bass drum is prepared further with a small square of paper towel neatly folded and taped at the point where the pedal strikes the drum.

For the hi-hat, I frequently use two bottom hats (rather than top and bottom hats).

There are four larger cymbals:
- 20-inch ride without rivets
- 20-inch ride with rivets
- 18-inch ride
- large China cymbal

and three mini China cymbals to be mounted on top of the other cymbals.

Acknowledgments

Most of the Billy Hart source interviews conducted by Ethan Iverson were done over Zoom during the COVID pandemic. Both Hart and Iverson teach at the New England Conservatory of Music; a NEC Personal Development Grant supplied the funds to hire Scott Douglass and Shuja Haider.

Scott Douglass transcribed the interviews, did historical research, provided footnotes, and assembled a first draft of the discography. *Oceans of Time* would not have been possible without Douglass's contribution. Douglass plays bass, has led youth orchestras, and is currently a Lecturer at Columbia University. He has produced the academic papers "The Influence of D. Antoinette Handy," "Lonnie Liston Smith: An Oral History," and "Lionel Hampton and the Black Press" and writes the Substack *Commonwealth of Jazz*.

Shuja Haider edited *Oceans of Time*; he is a rare literary technician who also understands music, having written about Bennie Maupin's *The Jewel in the Lotus* for Pitchfork, and published music criticism at *The New York Times*, *The Believer*, *Bookforum*, and *Jacobin*. Haider has also edited several Iverson essays for the magazine *The Nation*.

Thanks also to the many drummers for their contributions in the first appendix.

About the Authors

Drummer Billy Hart spans it all, comfortable in diverse contexts ranging from straight-ahead to avant-garde to pop. In the '60s and '70s Hart bore witness to many major changes in the music while working in the bands of Shirley Horn, Jimmy Smith, Wes Montgomery, Pharaoh Sanders, Herbie Hancock, McCoy Tyner, and Stan Getz. In time he was the drummer of choice for many others, appearing as a sideman on more than 600 recordings; he has also released a dozen albums as a leader. In 2022 Hart was named a NEA Jazz Master, in 2023 he received the Living Legacy Jazz Award from Mid Atlantic Arts, and in 2025 was part of the first group of musicians awarded the Jazz Legacies Fellowship from the Mellon Foundation and the Jazz Foundation of America. *The Detroit Free Press* explained: "Freedom, discipline, daring, passion, swing, broken rhythm, orchestral textures, interactive sparring, shocking dynamics, astounding creativity and authority. Want to know what jazz is really about? Listen to Billy Hart."

Pianist Ethan Iverson has known Billy Hart three decades, and has been part of the Billy Hart quartet since 2003. Iverson was a founding member of The Bad Plus; since leaving that group, Iverson has released critically-acclaimed albums on ECM and Blue Note. Iverson also has a long-standing relationship with modern dance choreographer Mark Morris. As a writer, Iverson has published significant criticism in *The Nation*, *JazzTimes*, *The New York Times*, and the Culture Desk of *The New Yorker*, in addition to posting frequently on his Substack, *Transitional Technology*.

Ethan Iverson and Billy Hart at the ECM session for All Our Reasons, *2012. (Photo by John Rogers.)*

Also from Cymbal Press

cymbalpress.com

Life in E Flat – The Autobiography of Phil Woods
Book of the Year - Jazz Journalists Association
Life in E Flat – The Autobiography of Phil Woods is the life story of the legendary saxophonist, composer, band leader, and National Endowment for the Arts Jazz Master. Look for it in paperback, hardcover, and e-book at cymbalpress.com.

Praise for Life in E Flat
"*Life in E-Flat* is a gift, a compelling and entertaining memoir by one of the leading alto saxophonists in jazz for 60 years. Phil Woods was a star soloist, influential lead alto player, savvy bandleader, underrated composer-arranger, and consummate studio musician. He was also a charismatic storyteller with a typewriter—literate, funny, insightful, self-aware, with a keen eye and ear for details that reveal character, including his own personal failings. Heroes and colleagues like Charlie Parker, Dizzy Gillespie, Quincy Jones, Benny Carter, and Ben Webster are drawn in quick, astute sketches. Observations about the music business, jazz education, and the vagaries of the jazz life are laced with wisdom and sardonic wit. The book is also an invaluable portrait of world that has vanished: Juilliard at midcentury, the band bus, the bustling post-war bebop academy of the streets, the New York studios of the '60s, the European jazz scene of the early '70s, and the energy and excitement of a remarkable life lived among some of the greatest giants in jazz history." —Mark Stryker, author of *Jazz From Detroit*

"Phil Woods's voice on the page is as raw and lyrical and unmistakable as the sound of his alto. If you want to really know about The Life—the true day-to-day of a working jazz musician, with all its agonies and ecstasies and tedium and the ever-exciting challenge of getting paid something like what you're worth for playing your heart out—look no further. *Life in E Flat* pulls no punches and tells no lies."
—James Kaplan, author of *Sinatra: The Chairman, Frank: The Voice* and *Irving Berlin: New York Genius*

Also from Cymbal Press

The Jazz Omnibus: 21st-Century Photos and Writings by Members of the Jazz Journalists Association

The Jazz Omnibus is a spectacular anthology of works by 90 international experts in jazz and related music. Both the paperback and the deluxe dust-jacketed hardcover edition is an essential collectible for any music library.

90 contributors represent the finest music writers and photographers alive today. Their skill, wisdom, insight, and generosity converge to produce a timeless contribution to music criticism, history, and scholarship. The Jazz Omnibus captures the expansive breadth of jazz-its past present, and future-through the ears of its great artists and the pens and cameras of its most admired journalists.

As jazz embarks on its second century, this book stands alone as a compendium of reportage and analysis of an art form offering pleasure and insights while building communities that celebrate creative individuality and ensemble play.

A few examples of what readers will find in The Jazz Omnibus:
- Ted Panken on Sonny Rollins
- Michael Jackson interviews Keith Jarrett
- Jordannah Elizabeth on Amina Claudine Myers
- David R. Adler on Meshell Nedegeocello
- Nate Chinen on Sun Ra
- Debbie Burke on Jewish women songwriters
- Willard Jenkins on becoming a jazz journalist
- Rob Shepherd speaks with Mary Halvorson
- Deanna Witkoswki on Mary Lou Williams
- Ashley Kahn surveys the new American expatriates
- Ted Gioia on Amy Winehouse, jazz singer
- Howard Mandel at Ornette Coleman's birthday party
- Larry Blumenfeld on Arturo O'Farrill in Cuba
- Suzanne Lorge on Carla Bley

The Jazz Omnibus is an indispensable resource for curious newcomers to jazz, casual listeners, aficionados, educators, students and researchers.

Also from Cymbal Press

Pity the Genius: A Journey Through American Guitar Music in 33 Tracks by Joel Harrison

Pity the Genius is a deep dive into the often-tumultuous lives of 33 extraordinary guitarists, their brilliance, triumphs, and struggles. From Arthur Rhames' volcanic performances to the introspective elegance of Pat Martino, Joel Harrison captures the essence of these musicians in a way that is both intimate and illuminating. The tracks he selects tell the story of American music, across time and genre. Jazz, rock, blues, country, folk, roots music, and more are all represented.

This book goes beyond the music, delving into the personal challenges and societal obstacles these artists faced. Whether it's the tragic early deaths of guitar prodigies like Danny Gatton and Jimi Hendrix, or the enduring influence of genre-defining musicians like Prince and Joni Mitchell, *Pity the Genius* presents a vivid tapestry of musical stories that have shaped the sound of America. Ultimately, it is a celebration of guitarists and the extraordinary music they gifted the world.

Praise for Pity the Genius
"This is really profound, evocative stuff—Joel is not only a great player, he's a great writer. Everyone should read this book."
—Mike Stern: Jazz Guitarist

"What a wonderful series of essays. While Harrison is writing about guitarists, his subject really is how people deal with the need to make art, what happens at the intersection of creativity and personality. And Harrison was there: Allan Holdsworth, Danny Gatton, you're finding out what it was like to be in their presence, what the world was like then, what was expected, what happened. Deep, deep stuff, sometimes profoundly sad, sometime ecstatic, but always illuminating."
—Peter Watrous: NY Times jazz critic 1986-2000

Also from Cymbal Press

The Landfill Chronicles: Unearthing Legends of Modern Music by Dan Ouellette

Discover the untold stories and intimate moments of music's greatest legends in Dan Ouellette's groundbreaking collection, *The Landfill Chronicles: Unearthing Legends of Modern Music*.

Peek behind the music scene with Dan's personal recollections and never-before-published anecdotes.

For over four decades, Dan Ouellette has been at the forefront of music journalism, chronicling the lives and careers of the legends who shape modern music. His interviews and writing about giants of jazz, blues, rock, and pop have graced the pages of magazines like *DownBeat* and *Billboard*, and newspapers from coast-to-coast.

Part memoir, part archive, and wholly entertaining, these articles shed light on musicians' innermost thoughts at crucial points in their storied careers.

- Relive the last-ever interview with Frank Zappa before his untimely death from cancer. This is a poignant and unusually personal long-form interview, previously lost in the pages of a now-defunct magazine.
- Go behind the scenes with Joni Mitchell during the creation of her album Shine and hear her exclusive track-by-track insights.
- Join Regina Carter on a journey to Genoa, Italy to play the famous Paganini Violin.
- Follow Dee Dee Bridgewater as she explores her African roots in Mali.
- And many more...

Experience the magic of musical storytelling like never before. Pick up your copy of The Landfill Chronicles today and embark on a journey through the extraordinary lives of music's most enduring icons.

Also from Cymbal Press

Jazz Dialogues with Jon Gordon

Backstage, on the bus, or in the studio, saxophonist Jon Gordon, winner of the prestigious Thelonious Monk International Jazz Saxophone competition, chats with several generations of great musicians. From Jay McShann to Renee Rosnes, *Jazz Dialogues* lets the reader hang out with dozens of jazz artists to learn about their careers, influences, and the dues they've paid. These candid, poignant, and often hilarious conversations paint a first-person portrait of jazz history.

Artists include: Jay McShann, Eddie Locke, Cab Calloway, Maria Schneider, Jan Garbarek, Ken Peplowski, Tim Hagans, Mark Turner, Hank Mobley, Bill Easley, Doc Cheatham, Scott Robinson, Eddie Bert, Phil Woods, Danny Bank, Billy Drummond, Ben Monder, Charles McPherson, Milt Hinton, Ben Riley, Bill Stewart, Art Blakey, Jon-Erik Kellso, Eddie Chamblee, Jimmy Lewis, Chuck Redd, Bill Charlap, McCoy Tyner, Melissa Aldana, Ronnie Mathews, Kevin Hays, Jim McNeely, Steve Wilson, Red Holloway, Barney Kessel, Joe Williams, Quincy Davis, Bob Mintzer, Dick Hyman, Lee Konitz, Leroy Jones, Renee Rosnes, David Sanborn, Gil Evans, Don Sickler, Sean Smith, Sarah Vaughn, Derrick Gardner, Sylvia Cuenca, Harold Mabern, Gene Bertoncini, Mike LeDonne, Essiet Okon Essiet, Bill Mays, and Joe Magnarelli.

Praise for Jazz Dialogues
"Jazz Dialogues is a rarity among books about jazz: It's a book about people—the individual creators who devote their lives to the making of this profoundly individualistic art. It took a writer who's a first-call musician himself to capture the way jazz artists think and feel, on the bandstand and off. From Cab Calloway and Doc Cheatham to Maria Schneider and Steve Wilson, Jon Gordon brings us face to face, mind to mind, heart to heart, with dozens of fascinating musicians. Like a great player in a jazz band, Gordon knows not only how to play, but how to listen."
—David Hajdu, author of *Lush Life: A Biography of Billy Strayhorn*

Also from Cymbal Press

Ruminations & Reflections: The Musical Journey of Dave Liebman & Richie Beirach

The Jazz Book of Two Lifetimes
NEA Jazz Master saxophonist Dave Liebman and pianist Richie Beirach have enjoyed a fifty-year friendship on and off the bandstand. They've performed with Miles Davis, Elvin Jones, Stan Getz, Chet Baker, Freddie Hubbard, and their own bands. Ruminations and Reflections takes readers on a rollicking journey through their musical lives. Along the way, they share their views on jazz education, prominent musicians, and musical preparation. Liebman and Beirach pay tribute to their musical mentors, tour their discography, and suggest essential recordings to study. The book's conversational style will engage students, professionals, and music lovers alike.

For Fans of Jazz Masters and Legends
Ruminations and Reflections showcases never before told anecdotes and opinions about musical legends including John Coltrane, Bill Evans, McCoy Tyner, Jack DeJohnette, Wayne Shorter, Michael Brecker, Randy Brecker, Chick Corea, Lee Konitz, Sonny Rollins, Herbie Hancock, and Wynton Marsalis. Jazz fans will delight in the in-depth analysis of over twenty of this duo's best recordings, providing insight and history to this important discography.

Praise for Ruminations & Reflections
"We really don't have an exact name for musicians like Dave and Richie. Across decades of recordings and concerts, their aspirations obliterate the definitions of any single genre. This volume reveals the deep insight and wisdom required to resolve their shared quest for meaning in music. Both are master players who continue to strive for what goes beyond and what lies beneath. Reading their words and following their stories in this wonderful book affirms the feeling that they share on the bandstand as one of the great long-term partnerships in this music." – Pat Metheny

www.ingramcontent.com/pod-product-compliance
Lightning Source LLC
Chambersburg PA
CBHW070534170426
43200CB00011B/2420